William E. Prendergast, PhD

Treating Sex Offenders
A Guide to Clinical Practice with Adults, Clerics, Children, and Adolescents

Second Edition

*Pre-publication
REVIEWS,
COMMENTARIES,
EVALUATIONS . . .*

"This book points the way forward in understanding, treating, and reducing reoffending sex abusers. A particularly important new chapter researches current attitudes within different creeds and religions, rebalancing that perspective, and offering practical, intelligent means to assess the likelihood of possible offenses before 'triple damage' can occur. There is so much practical knowledge in this book that I feel it should be implemented in all cultures to halt the rise of abuse in future generations."

Vera Diamond, Dip APsych, MBAS
Psychotherapist,
British Autogenic Society

"Dr. Prendergast remains the preeminent authority on the subject of treating sex offenders. *Treating Sex Offenders* is timely, important, and an absolute must-read for therapists in today's social context. In the book, Dr. Prendergast illustrates the principles he learned during his forty years treating sex offenders by interspersing actual case studies with analysis and ideas for practical application. He is candid in describing both his successes and his mistakes, allowing the reader to truly understand the nature of the treatment process, and to anticipate, avoid, or overcome obstacles. The result is a book that is comprehensive, insightful, functional, and readable."

Bill Taverner, MA
Director, The Center
for Family Life Education,
Planned Parenthood
of Greater Northern New Jersey;
Co-author, *Streetwise to Sex-Wise:
Sexuality Education for High-Risk Youth,
Second Edition*

Treating Sex Offenders
A Guide to Clinical Practice with Adults, Clerics, Children, and Adolescents

Second Edition

HAWORTH Criminal Justice, Forensic Behavioral Sciences, & Offender Rehabilitation
Nathanial J. Pallone, PhD
Senior Editor

New, Recent, and Forthcoming Titles:

The Merry-Go-Round of Sexual Abuse: Identifying and Treating Survivors by William E. Prendergast

Chaplains to the Imprisoned: Sharing Life with the Incarcerated by Richard Denis Shaw

Forensic Neuropsychology: Conceptual Foundations and Clinical Practice by José A. Valciukas

Inaccuracies in Children's Testimony: Memory, Suggestibility, or Obedience to Authority? by Jon'a F. Meyer

Kids Who Commit Adult Crimes: Serious Criminality by Juvenile Offenders by R. Barri Flowers

Family Empowerment Intervention: An Innovative Service for High-Risk Youths and Their Families by Richard Dembo and James Schmeidler

Treating Sex Offenders: A Guide to Clinical Practice with Adults, Clerics, Children, and Adolescents, Second Edition by William E. Prendergast

Treating Sex Offenders
A Guide to Clinical Practice with Adults, Clerics, Children, and Adolescents

Second Edition

William E. Prendergast, PhD

The Haworth Press®
New York • London • Oxford

The Haworth Press, Inc., 10 Alice Street, Binghamton, NY 13904-1580.

Second edition of *Treating Sex Offenders in Correctional Institutions and Outpatient Clinics: A Guide to Clinical Practice* (The Haworth Press, Inc., 1991).

Cover design by Jennifer M. Gaska.

Library of Congress Cataloging-in-Publication Data

Prendergast, William E.
   Treating sex offenders : a guide to clinical practice with adults, clerics, children, and adolescents / William E. Prendergast—2nd ed.
      p. ; cm.
   Rev. ed. of: Treating sex offenders in correctional institutions and outpatient clinics. c1991.
   Includes bibliographical references and index.
   ISBN 0-7890-0930-7 (hard cover : alk. paper)—ISBN 0-7890-0931-5 (soft cover : alk. paper)
   1. Sex offenders—Rehabilitation. 2. Psychosexual disorders—Treatment.
   [DNLM: 1. Pedophilia—rehabilitation. 2. Sex Offenses—prevention & control. 3. Psychotherapy—methods. 4. Sexual Dysfunctions, Psychological—rehabilitation. WM 610 P926t 2003] I. Prendergast, William E. Treating sex offenders in correctional institutions and outpatient clinics. II. Title.
   RC560.S47 P74 2003
   616.85'83—dc21

                                       2002153152

CONTENTS

ABOUT THE AUTHOR

William E. Prendergast, PhD, is certified as a sex therapist by the American Association of Sex Educators, Counselors, and Therapists (AASECT) and holds the Diplomate as a certified sex therapist and clinical supervisor of the American Board of Sexology. In 1991, he was presented with the Distinguished Service Award of the New Jersey Child Assault Prevention Project for his contributions to treatment and the training of other professionals in the specialized techniques of treating sex offenders in correctional institutions and outpatient clinics. Dr. Prendergast is the author of *The Merry-Go-Round of Sexual Abuse: Identifying and Treating Survivors* (Haworth) and *Sexual Abuse of Children and Adolescents: A Preventative Guide for Parents, Teachers, and Counselors.*

BOXED ILLUSTRATIONS

Preface

In the twelve years since the publication of my first work on sex offenders, *Treating Sex Offenders in Correctional Institutions and Outpatient Clinics: A Guide to Clinical Practice* (The Haworth Press, Inc., 1991), there continues to be an *increase* in the number of survivor (victim) referrals made to my office. A striking factor resulting from these referrals is that these individuals display ever-increasing postabuse damage lasting into adulthood. Although many new and important findings and advances in both diagnosis and treatment have occurred, there are still professionals and programs that dabble in treating sex offenders and have little or no training in this highly complicated skill. In addition, society and the professional community are finally beginning to realize the importance and extent of the adolescent sex offender problem and its relationship to a majority of adult sex offenses.

My earliest experiences in this field were with child and adolescent sex offenders and their victims, and I have always believed that *sex offender pathology is progressive and can begin as early as seven years old* (see Skippy, Chapter 13) but rarely forms later than early adolescence.

This second edition of my early work will integrate adolescent and adult sex offenders and emphasize similarities as well as differences in their personalities, their behaviors, and, most important, their treatment. As in the first edition, case studies will be found throughout this work and hopefully will add clarity and emphasis to each type.

I begin each section of every chapter of this book with adult sex offender factors, traits, treatments, and cases and at the end of each section discuss the child/adolescent sex offender in relation to and comparison with what has just been discussed.

In addition, in the past twelve years, I have made additions and changes to some of the treatment techniques I use with sex offenders (and survivors) based on changes in their personalities and character that I have observed during this period of time. These will be integrated where applicable.

In addition, due to the 2002 witch-hunt for Catholic priests who molested children and teens, it was necessary to include discussions of this problem in a special Chapter 19 dedicated to this subject.

Finally, wherever the first edition was used, in university classes, professional presentations, staff-training sessions, etc., feedback and suggestions from those exposed to the work have been insightful and helpful. Many of these observations will be covered in the new edition with examples to illustrate.

Where case studies are repeated in this revision, wherever possible, at the end of each case, there will be an update as to the progress or failure of each individual.

How It All Began

During my forty years of working with both sex offenders and their victims, it has become all too apparent that traditional treatment concepts, methodologies, and frameworks do not always work and that many new, experimental techniques in use today fail as well. There is an element of déjà vu in all of this, reminiscent of my first attempts at treating sex offenders at the Rahway Treatment Unit (RTU).*

We opened the first sex offender treatment facility (RTU) in New Jersey on May 15, 1967, with only myself and a secretary as staff. One hundred sex offenders were then transferred from the three state mental hospitals and other correctional facilities where they had been housed since the New Jersey State Sex Offender Statute was initially enacted in 1949. For the first year or more, per diem consulting psychologists, psychiatric social workers, and psychiatrists fumbled around, attempting to treat this first group of offenders by employing traditional methods. None of these therapists had had any special training in treating sex offenders and all were looking to see what would work. All forms of then-known therapy modalities, including traditional, individual, and group techniques, were tried with little success. *Nothing seemed to work!* The literature of the time offered little help. It became apparent that if the program were to succeed, new methods were needed to meet the needs of this very distinct group of individuals.

---

*Originally within the walls of Rahway State Prison, it is now renamed East Jersey State Prison in New Jersey.

At the end of that first calendar year, a meeting was held with the then five or six per diem consultants (clinical psychologists and psychiatric social workers). There was an immediate consensus that what we were trying to do was not working. It was obvious that all of the treatment staff, including its director and the consultants, as well as the offenders themselves, were frustrated.

During this period, several schools of psychotherapy were represented: Freudians, behaviorists, Gestalt psychologists, Rogerians, and eclectics. However, none of the staff felt that the methods they were using were meeting the needs of this unique population.

Following the philosophy of "Anna" in the King of Siam story—"By your pupils you'll be taught"—a meeting was held in the one-room dormitory with the director (with no other staff present) and the 100 convicted repetitive-compulsive sex offenders. In a totally open manner, the frustrations of the staff were discussed, and the resident population was told that since they were the offenders who had the psychological and sexual problems, we needed their help.

As radical as this approach appeared, it was necessary because few other states were treating sex offenders at the time, which left us little room for recourse or other assistance. Most of the other programs were contained in mental hospital settings; none were in a correctional setting. The available literature was void of any help except for a few works that were primarily theoretical and did not apply.

A resident committee was formed to act as liaison and advisor to the staff. Almost immediately, suggestions and criticisms came pouring into the director's office, both critical and positive. As suspected, the offenders knew what their deficits were. They clearly listed needs that they felt were paramount in their treatment and gave the staff a totally new perspective. This feedback from the offenders worked so well that, from that day forward, a resident committee became an integral part of the treatment program.

The second attempt at a solution consisted of a staff meeting at the director's home. I had always suspected that *all the sex offenders had certain traits in common, regardless of the offense they had committed.* At this time, we had a full variety of offenders in the unit: rapists, child molesters (both pedophiles and hebophiles), incestuous fathers, and exhibitionists ("flashers"). Regardless of professional background, the entire staff agreed that they had felt the same frustration during their contacts with the sex offenders in the previous year or more preceding the meeting.

As a result of both attempts, the following principles and concepts for treatment emerged.

The first factor that became apparent was that *passive, nondirective, or Rogerian techniques would not work with this group of offenders.* With a completely supportive environment, these individuals not only became comfortable but also remained totally blocked by defense mechanisms. This was due to their overwhelming need for acceptance and concomitant fear of rejection by the therapists (now perceived as parental substitutes). A combination of confrontation and supportive techniques became the norm and worked. Each technique will be discussed later.

The second factor that became apparent, from meetings and discussions with the resident committee, was that *homogenizing groups was a fatal error.* A group of all rapists, for example, became supportive of one another and teamed against the therapist. The agreement between group members was, "You protect me and I'll protect you." Challenge and/or confrontation thus became neutralized in a ten-to-one battle, in which the therapist always lost. In a group of all child molesters, boredom and lack of participation or involvement became the major problem. The inherent passivity and paralyzing fears of this group made therapeutic interaction almost impossible. Thus, the second principle of treating this specific population became to mix all of the groups together—rapists, child molesters, incestuous fathers, and flashers (the four main groups in the facility).

The third and next important factor we quickly learned was *not to believe anything that these individuals verbalized unless it was proven by behavior.* As director, a challenge to the staff was made to name a single therapeutic change that could not be observed in the daily behavior of our residents. To this day, no one has been able to name one specific example to dispute this maxim. This does not mean that the behavioral change must be seen in the therapeutic process alone. Evidence of any meaningful change will also occur in the individual's work, recreation, leisure time activities, and in all of his* interpersonal interactions. Therefore, work supervisors, teachers, correction officers, and families were all solicited for changes that they either

---

*Although both men and women commit sex crimes, the pronouns "he" and "him" will be used throughout this book to refer to sex offenders.

did or did not observe in their connected offender. No clues as to what we were looking for were ever given, only a generic inquiry as to how an individual was doing at the time.

The fourth factor was understanding that *individual therapy, as the primary or exclusive treatment modality, did not work.* Since we considered the sex offender pathology a peer or adolescent crisis reaction phenomena (see Chapter 2), it was important that each offender expose himself and his problems to his peer group. It appeared that these individuals could easily confess their pathology, deviant thinking, and behavior to a therapist since they saw the therapist as more of a "father confessor" (at this time in the program, there were no female therapists permitted in the treatment unit per Department of Correction mandates) who would accept anything they said, would not be punitive, and would not criticize or reject them. Since they had a strong adolescent need for peer acceptance, group therapy was considered the appropriate treatment milieu.

Also, the groups were needed to confirm/deny what the elusive, defensive, and denying offender was saying. Living with one another, they knew things that it was impossible for the therapist to know which were essential to both the treatment process and the evaluation process for potential release. Thus, the therapists were trained to use their groups to be sure that what was being portrayed by the "man on the floor" was real and not a manipulation or defensive response. This process became known as *confirmation*. Group therapy, then, became the treatment modality of choice for this population.

The fifth principle that became quickly apparent was that *psychotherapy by itself would not work.* The pathology of the compulsive sex offender appeared to involve his entire being: body, mind, spiritual process, social nature, and emotions. Thus, a *holistic* or *wholeperson* approach was adopted that will be discussed in some detail in Chapter 15.

We now had a beginning, and all of the therapists felt more comfortable treating this very individualistic and unique group of individuals. Utilizing these protocols, we continued to learn, step by step, and after a period of a year or two began to feel that we were finally reaching this population and seeing proof of therapeutic change.

By the opening of the Adult Diagnostic and Treatment Center (ADTC) in Avenel, New Jersey in 1976, from an original population of 100 offenders, the population increased to more than 465 in treatment (as of my retirement from ADTC), with thirteen psychologists conducting two to three groups each, seeing individuals in individual contacts, conducting ancillary therapy programs, and evaluating each individual's progress every six months. Each therapist was responsible for twenty-five to thirty-five offenders. Only dedicated individuals would accept the pressures and stresses of this type of program.

For the past forty years of treating both the sex offender and the victim, I have also tried to share what I have learned and the mistakes I have made through presentations, seminars, and training programs with many groups in New Jersey, in many other states around the country, and in the United Kingdom as well. Participants have ranged from the general public, to parents of either offenders or survivors, to professionals of all types; I have spoken to medical doctors, registered nurses, psychiatrists and psychologists, social workers, correctional personnel including administrators, survivors, and even to sex offenders themselves.

This second edition parallels workshops and courses that I continue to conduct and, as in the first edition, may not be as scholarly as some would prefer. The language level is set for all of the audiences listed, as much as possible. A parallel work on the *survivor* of sexual abuse, titled *The Merry-Go-Round of Sexual Abuse: Identifying and Treating Survivors* was published in 1993, also by The Haworth Press, Inc., and a third volume titled *Sexual Abuse of Children and Adolescents: A Preventive Guide for Parents, Teachers, and Counselors* was published in 1996 by The Continuum Publishing Company.

In the following chapters, as in the first edition, each individual aspect of the makeup and treatment of the compulsive adult sex offender as well as the adolescent sex offender (as I have experienced them), whether in a residential setting or in my private practice, is explored. For each of the many treatment techniques, its inception, the principles behind the technique, its evolution as the population changed, and its success and/or failures will be discussed.

It is the author's hope that sharing the fumbling and errors that were made early in our experience (and continue at times to be made), will prevent other therapists from making the same errors. This applies especially in using techniques or principles that were tried in our years of immersion in this field and failed.

An additional hope is that this book will be read by adolescents and adults who may already be on the road to becoming sex offenders, or by their parents, families, or relatives, and that they will be motivated to seek treatment and prevent further victimization of innocent children, adolescents, and adults.

It should be noted that, in keeping with the human subjects regulations of the federal government, although all of the case histories cited are based on real individuals, sufficient changes have been made in age, race, nationality, employment, family makeup, etc., to protect their identity. I have personally worked with each of the individuals discussed in some therapeutic modality or as their primary therapist.

Acknowledgments

This book is dedicated to my beloved wife Mildred, who continues to support and tolerate me—through all of these thirty-seven years of marriage and through five surgeries that have left me disabled—not only as spouse and partner but also as a friend, a nurse (her profession), and a patient reader-editor for all of my writings, providing direct and invaluable aid and advice in the preparation of this manuscript; to Dr. Nathaniel J. Pallone, Rutgers University, who motivated me to write the original book and who has remained a mentor and friend through the pangs of producing three books in the field of sex offenders and treating the survivors of sexual abuse; to my friends and co-workers over the course of the years at the Rahway Treatment Unit and at the Adult Diagnostic and Treatment Center, Avenel, New Jersey; to Kinnerett Nubel who graciously offered to be my library researcher and who became a motivator as well; and to the thousands of sex offenders and survivors of sexual abuse who continue to teach me everything I know today.

Finally, a special word about a wonderful and courageous young man in England. When a baby-sitting pedophile attempted to seduce him by fondling him, the boy hit the abuser's hand away, grabbed a portable telephone, locked himself in the bathroom, and called his mother at school. He later insisted that they go the police where he gave a full videotaped statement to them. Although only nine years old, this young lad, brought up superbly by his single mother, had the morality and courage to do what was right. Our kudos to them both. If we had more young people like him, pedophilia would be on the way out.

SECTION I:
IDENTIFYING SEX OFFENDERS

Chapter 1

Distinguishing Characteristics of Sex Offenders: The *Who* of Treatment

INTRODUCTION

It may be self-evident that before treatment of a sex offender or any patient can begin, the therapist must know something of the *who* (that is, the characteristics that make up the patient plus the characteristics of the disorder he or she is suffering) and the *why* of the patient who is seeking help (that is, the motives the patient has in seeking treatment, whether treatment has been imposed or mandated by external bodies such as the courts or the criminal justice system, etc.).

Unfortunately, it has been my experience that members of diverse professional groups (whether psychologists, social workers, counselors, mental health center workers, or probation or parole officers) often know little about the *who* of the sex offender. In contrast, they may know much more about the *what* (that is, that the disorder to be treated is either a psychiatric disorder in sexual functioning or an illegal behavior, or both) and the *why* (usually because of court proceedings or, less often, because the client has recognized unwanted thoughts or feelings that he or she fears may lead to illegal behavior).

As a result, the client may become a guinea pig for the therapist who is just beginning to work with sex offenders or who has been assigned by an administrator to take the case. The inevitable result is frustration for both the patient and the therapist at best—or, in a worst-case scenario, that more sex crimes and more victims will follow. This remains as true today as when I first began treating sex offenders more than forty years ago. Each time I conduct a training workshop on the subject of sex offender pathology and treatment, when the session is finished, several participants ask to talk to me and "confess" that when assigned sex offenders to their caseloads, they had no prior training or knowledge regarding these individuals and felt uncomfortable, scared, and inadequate in working with them. Many supervisors and administrators insist that since an individual has a professional degree (bachelor's, master's, or doctorate) this qualifies him or her to treat all types of individuals with problems. This is a faulty assumption.

To gauge the extent to which beliefs, especially those of beginning mental health workers, rest on myth or on fact, I often give a brief, unannounced self-scoring test at the beginning of a training workshop. Rarely is a hand raised indicating a score above 70 percent. That test is reproduced in Box 1.1. Take it yourself, then try to find the answers to the questions throughout the rest of the book or turn to Appendix A for the answers.

A CLINICALLY DERIVED TABLE OF TRAITS

When we began this work in May 1967, as detailed in the preface, little was known empirically about the population we had been assigned to treat. The entire staff agreed we desperately needed some form of schematic picture of the characteristics of personality and behavior that have been found to clinically and empirically differentiate the sex offender from all other types of criminals or mental-health patients.

Consider the importance of such a list. Our hypothesis was that *if* such a list could be constructed and could identify at least the principal characteristics of those offenders who have been convicted of criminal sexual behavior, then we would have the outline for an effective and comprehensive treatment program for this population. The list would enable us to choose treatment modalities to address traits, counteract deficits, and engender appropriate values and skills—or substitute effective skills for those which have proven ineffective or harmful. Optimally, such a list should extend to all sex offenders, regardless of their individual form of deviant behavior or their choice of victim by sex or age. As stated in the preface's chronology for the opening of the first treatment program in the state of New Jersey, after a year of fumbling around and trying all then-known treatment techniques, the entire staff felt quite strongly that regardless of the deviant behavior or offense, most of the offenders sent by the courts for treat-

1.1

Beliefs About Sex Offenders: Myth or Reality?

Respond *true* (T) or *false* (F). Find the answers as you read the following chapters—or, if you cannot wait, skip ahead to Appendix A. Give yourself 5 points for each correct response.

T/F 1. All adult sex offenders, regardless of offense, have major personality traits in common.

T/F 2. All adult sex offenders were themselves sexually victimized as children and this explains their behavior.

T/F 3. Sex offender pathology can be genetically linked.

T/F 4. Pedophiles and hebophiles have the same characteristics and prognoses for treatment success.

T/F 5. Fixated pedophiles may appear normal in their social, work, and interpersonal functions.

T/F 6. Hebophiles and incestuous fathers have many traits in common and a similar (and more positive) prognosis for treatment success.

T/F 7. The *King-of-the-Castle* syndrome is a major distinguishing characteristic of incestuous fathers.

T/F 8. Supportive and nonconfrontational treatment techniques work better with adult sex offenders than do other treatment modalities.

T/F 9. Psychotherapy itself will produce positive results with both adult and adolescent sex offenders.

T/F 10. Following their victimization, victims of sexual abuse have many traits in common with sex offenders.

T/F 11. Adolescent sex offenders have the same traits as adult sex offenders.

T/F 12. Adolescent sex offenders have no visible (i.e., detectable) signs of their problems.

T/F 13. Peer relationship problems are a major factor in the development of adolescent sex offenders.

T/F 14. Adolescent sex offenders always come from a home where there are problems.

T/F 15. Of all problems in the adolescent sex offender's life, lack of or poor communication is a major one.

T/F 16. Treatment issues and techniques for the adolescent sex offender are identical to those for the adult sex offender.

T/F 17. Parent(s) or guardian(s) must be an integral part of the adolescent sex offender's treatment.

T/F 18. Supportive and nonconfrontational treatment techniques work better with adolescent sex offenders.

T/F 19. A combination of individual and group therapy plus ancillary treatment modalities is the best complete treatment program for the adolescent sex offender.

T/F 20. Both the adult and the adolescent sex offender can be cured with an intensive treatment program.

ment had certain identifiable traits in common. Each staff member, independently and without discussion, was asked to submit a list of the major personality traits that he (female therapists were not permitted to be employed in the prison at that time) felt characterized the personality of the sex offender. Once the lists were tabulated, a meeting was held, and the final list was developed. Next, using the list, the director and the staff reformulated the entire treatment program and developed modalities to deal with each of the delineated traits.

The list fulfilled our expectations beyond our anticipations or hopes, and, for the first time, the staff (as well as the patients) saw therapeutic progress begin. Changes in behavior, attitude, and motivation were all observed both in and outside of the treatment unit (by officers, supervisors, families), and over the next year or two more and more treatment modalities were included in the program in accordance with the table, which became a basis for the treatment program. Although it was constructed in 1969, it is still is use and effective today.

In Box 1.2, each of these traits has been found in differing degrees, and in differing combinations, in several thousands of cases that I

1.2

Distinctive Characteristics of Sex Offenders

- Basic inadequate personality
- Negative self-image (exaggerated)
- Exaggerated need for acceptance
- Selective perception
- Exaggerated control needs
- Pervasive guilt with persistent need for forgiveness
- Subjective judgment memories
- Nonassertive
- Poor to no interpersonal relations
- No peer interaction
- Emotions suppressed/displaced
- Strong sexual performance needs
- Small penis complex (unreal)
- Distorted sexual values
- Deviant arousal patterns
- Defective goal-setting system
- Identity confusion
- Cleverness in dealing with others
- Highly manipulative and controlling
- Fear of but desire for being exposed

have treated and/or examined diagnostically. Although it is my personal belief, based on my own clinical experience and the insights my colleagues have shared with me, that each of these traits can be found in each sex offender, each trait may not always be immediately visible. Sex offenders are often clever, highly manipulative individuals with the strongest defense mechanisms that a clinician may ever encounter (except, perhaps, for the true multiple personality). Therefore, a thorough understanding of interviewing techniques, specialized treatment techniques, and many, many other caveats are necessary to work with this population.

In addition, an understanding of the origin of each of these characteristics and the degree to which they control and determine the lifestyles and behavioral repertoire of the offender is essential before treatment is possible. Each characteristic, along with its source and its importance and implications in treatment, will be discussed in detail in succeeding chapters.

THE OBSESSIVE-COMPULSIVE PATTERN

It is not uncommon that, by the time he is apprehended and enters the criminal justice system, the sex offender has been committing deviate sexual acts for many years. In fact, a significant percentage of sex offenders began their deviant fantasies and behaviors in their late childhood or early adolescent years. What occurs strongly resembles an obsessive-compulsive disorder (OCD). In this disorder, compulsive and repetitive acts are preceded or accompanied by obsessive thoughts.

The distinguished encyclopedist of mental health, Benjamin Wolman (1989, p. 236), defines *obsession* as

> An idea or impulse which persistently preoccupies an individual even though the individual prefers to be rid of it. Obsessions are usually associated with anxiety or fear and may constitute a minimal or a major disturbance of or interference with normal functioning and thinking.

Similarly, Wolman (1989, p. 68) defines *compulsion* as "The state in which the person feels forced to behave against his or her own conscious wishes and judgment."

To clarify these definitions, it may be easier to understand the process in the following manner:

- First, the idea occurs, usually triggered by some traumatic event. A fantasy quickly follows.
- The idea/fantasy persists, regardless of all attempts to eradicate or extinguish it. Obsession now exists.
- The obsession results in a masturbation fantasy to the deviant idea and becomes habitual, then compulsive. Here again, all attempts to eradicate or extinguish the fantasy fail.
- Over a period of time, or physical development in the case of preadolescents, masturbation no longer satisfies the obsession, and the fantasy is then acted out in some form.
- In young to preadolescent children, the first form the obsession may take is either voyeurism or exhibitionism with the primary obsession in the fantasy during the act. Although a ten-to-twelve-year-old may not have the strength or courage to commit an overt sexual act with someone, he can peep through a window to watch a person undress or to watch a couple engage in intercourse. He masturbates as he imagines being in the room and being an actor in the event.
- As both his physical strength and body development increase, the behavior becomes more and more in tune with the *need* generated to complete the obsessive fantasy. At this point, the sex offender is the most dangerous and, if not detected, will victimize someone.

THE QUESTION OF CHOICE

Although a disturbed childhood, poor parental relationships, and sexual trauma help to *explain* the development of the sex offender and his choice of pathological behavior, it neither justifies nor exculpates that behavior. However unpopular such a concept may be among those of my colleagues (and perhaps particularly among my academic colleagues) who hew to a deterministic explanation of behavior, I believe strongly that free will still exists in these individuals, although it may be dimmed (but not eliminated) by the dynamics which lead to compulsive behavior. Shorn of the niceties that surround what the courts and the legislature have defined as the acceptable grounds for exculpation on the basis of psychological factors (that is, for a successful plea of not guilty by reason of insanity), this position essentially comports with the state of the law as well.

In the thousands of cases we have treated over the past four decades, each has demonstrated this principle. If offenders are asked to describe in minute detail the events immediately preceding the offense, there are always many, many points at which they could have altered their course of action. Some general examples may clarify the point.

Sexually assaultive persons (rapists, assaultive child molesters, forceful incestuous fathers) usually describe several points, from the inception of the urge to the completed act, at which they became afraid, had doubts, or considered stopping the scenarios. Many sexually assaultive persons admit to instances of a rape in progress where once the victim was subdued, on the ground, and exposed, their need was satisfied and they left. Many seductive child molesters describe getting the child into the location of the act (a closet in the school, their apartment, etc.), undressing the child, and then panicking and ending the intended molestation.

It is not difficult, during intensive confrontive therapy, to elicit these conscious mental interruptions of an intended sex crime scenario. The overwhelming evidence of all therapists we have dealt with supports the fact of the sex offender's ability to stop himself during the offense at several distinct points in the chronology of the crime, especially during the early phases of the compulsion.

This same free will/choice exists in their masturbation fantasies, with a majority of them reporting that they have interrupted a deviant fantasy and either changed the fantasy to something positive or stopped the masturbatory behavior completely. Unless we are dealing with overt psychosis, this appears to be a valid observation. (*Note:* This factor will be used in Masturbatory Reconditioning [see Chapter 14] and will be explained in depth in the treatment chapters of this work.) Why doesn't this prevent sex crime? Considering the depressed, quitting quality of the offender's personality, the answer appears simple and obvious. At the juncture of the event, when the doubt or *choice* occurs, their thought processes include:

- Well, you've gone this far, you may as well finish it.
- It's no worse to finish than to stop. The punishment will be the same.

- I've already committed the sin, so I may as well get the pleasure.
- If I finish it and make them feel good, maybe they won't report me.
- You know you're a pervert (rapist, child molester, etc.), so you may as well act like one.

The variety of justifications to continue the deviant fantasy/behavior is as strong as the variety of the reasons to interrupt or stop the behavior.

As will be seen in the chapters on treatment, as treatment progresses and the offender becomes stronger and more positive toward himself, these interruptions become more frequent and more successful with the goal of extinction or, at least, substitution of normal behavior for the deviant behavior. It is not uncommon for sex offenders to report promises, desperate attempts that fail, and many other means of attempting to extinguish the compulsion, but it never works unless therapeutic intervention and sometimes removal from society (where the trigger stimuli are) is accomplished. This is most true of the child molester groups. At this point an example is needed for clarification.

EDWARD, at age twenty-nine, is an obscene phone caller to older women who sound motherly. He asks them if they would allow him to perform sexual intercourse on them (using street slang). From his earliest memories, Edward had problems with interpersonal relationships, especially with females. Edward had been a fat little boy and not particularly good looking, which did not help his relational problems. His mother was overprotective and seductive and had a strong to violent temper. Arguments and fights were frequent in his home. When Edward was fifteen, his parents separated, and he moved to California with his mother. Within a month of their moving into their new home, Edward's mother moved him into her bedroom and into her bed, telling him that now he was the man in her life. She then proceeded to undress, fondle, and fellate him, his first sexual experience outside of masturbation. These sexual encounters continued for several years, even when Edward finally found a girlfriend, whom the mother despised. Edward's mother never permitted him to have penetrating intercourse with her, stating "You're not man enough or big enough to satisfy me that way. When you grow, I'll think about it!" The more Edward persisted, the more vehement were her refusals and rejections.

Edward finally ran away and returned to live with his father in the East and to work at his father's business where he was maltreated and verbally abused. No matter what he did, nothing satisfied his father, a demanding old-world type and a craftsman. Within a month, during which he compulsively masturbated to the fantasy of having intercourse with his mother, the obscene phone calls began. Fewer than twenty calls were made before he was apprehended when he phoned a senator's wife by accident, whose line was tapped due to threats against the senator's life. Edward was arrested and sent to my practice for treatment as a mandated condition of probation.

Although his treatment will be discussed later, some of his statements are relevant to this discussion:

- No matter how hard I tried, I couldn't get having sex with my mother out of my mind.
- Even if I masturbated to pornography or to the fantasy of my girlfriend with whom I am having sex, eventually my mother replaces all images in the act. If she doesn't, I am unable to reach a climax.
- I was always afraid my friends would find out about me and my mother. I knew it was abnormal, but no matter how hard I tried the thoughts and fantasies as well as the masturbation became more frequent and more demanding. I even masturbated in the bathroom after just having an hour or more of sex with my mother, especially when she wouldn't let me fuck her.
- At times, I thought that the only way to stop these things from happening was to kill myself, and I even tried once but chickened out.

Guilt, sin, and fear of exposure, arrest, and imprisonment are all tried by compulsive sex offenders to control or eliminate their deviant fantasies and/or behaviors to no avail. It is my belief, based on my clinical experience and that of many of my colleagues, that until the early sexual traumas are relived, ventilated and all the emotions and distorted values dealt with through therapy, no lasting or meaningful change will occur. In addition, *the harder the sex offender tries to stop his deviant thoughts, fantasies, or behaviors, the stronger the compulsion becomes and the more frequently it occurs.* Throughout this work, compulsion will always be understood as a characteristic of all sex offenders, and especially of the fixated pedophile group.

Other experts in the treatment of sex offenders feel, to the contrary, quite strongly that aversive behavior therapy produces significantly more positive results. The reader is referred to the instructive volume *Rehabilitating Criminal Sexual Psychopaths: Legislative Mandates, Clinical Quandaries* by Nathaniel J. Pallone (Transaction Books, 1990). Pallone presents an excellent survey of both standard and ag-

gressive methods of treatment for sex offenders and their legal con-
straints that includes such aggressive treatment modalities as bio-
impedance measures, including surgical and chemical castration, and
aversive modalities, including aversive behavior therapy, revulsion,
electroshock, and pharmacologically induced aversion (nausea). Examples and studies are included for each type of therapy.

THE CHILD/ADOLESCENT SEX OFFENDER

Right from the beginning of this discussion, it must be understood
and accepted that the child/adolescent sex offender displays a more
complicated picture. Most children who commit sex offenses are repeating what was done to them as an "undoing" mechanism. Some, if
what was done to them was pleasant and exciting, find it hard to believe that other children would not find the same positive enjoyment
in these sexual behaviors, while others care little or nothing about
their victim and are concerned only with their own pleasure or needs.
Their immaturity and lack of moral development contribute highly to
their acting-out behaviors.

Adolescent sex offenders, on the other hand, are much more complicated due to the very nature of adolescence. This is a period of confusion, change, hormone-driven urges, and a powerful need to be accepted and like their peers. In fact, at PTAs and other parent training
workshops, I often begin with the question "How can you tell that
your offspring has entered adolescence without a physical examination?" Most respond with size, rebellion, physical or sexual development, and so forth. I have never found a parent, guardian, teacher, or
child care worker who answered this question correctly. The main,
highly noticeable change that occurs is that the emerging adolescent
is no longer concerned about *adult approval* whether from parents,
teachers, or any other adults with whom he or she has contact and
from whom this approval in the past was extremely important. Now,
the need is for approval and acceptance from their peers, and this demands (in their thinking) conformity to peer values, behaviors, and
beliefs. This is the age at which clothes become a major issue in the
home. Hairstyles, body piercing, tattoos—all become issues between
adolescents and parents. This is also an age where conflicts over
home rules and customs become issues. Curfew, going to the mall
with friends and not adults, music, TV shows, and so on, all become

disputed areas. Probably the paramount need is for privacy. Thus, communication between adolescents and their parents or other adults becomes a serious issue.

Although all of the traits and characteristics in Box 1.2 apply equally to the adolescent sex offender, as can be seen in Box 1.3, the therapist must be much more careful and thorough in checking for all or a majority of these traits as well.

A case that is ongoing as of this writing will help illustrate.

DOM is an eighteen-year-old who lives with his parents, two brothers, and a sister. Throughout his childhood, Dom had many physical problems and was a special education student. He is totally open, honest to a fault, pleasant and polite, with a friendly and accessible personality.

This is Dom's second referral for therapy. He was originally referred when he was twelve years old for touching a boy's penis in the boy's lavatory (see Chapter 11 for full story of incident). Therapy continued for almost a year when Dom told me and then his mother that he no longer wanted to come and would not be open or cooperative. A conference with the mother resulted in a "temporary termination" of therapy. This lasted until the incident when he was eighteen.

Recently, a disturbing behavior emerged that greatly upset and shocked his parents. Dom began sliding notes under his sister's bedroom door asking her to please come to his room and give him a "blow job." He also sent a similar note to his sister's friend who was visiting for the weekend. His siblings hid the notes and did not inform their parents until the mother found one of the notes on the sister's bed. They then exposed the extent of the problem, and he was brought in for treatment.

Dom was open and honest about the behavior and related that a girl he knew at his community college had fellated him on one of the school's science hikes, and from that point on he could not get it out of his mind. He compulsively masturbated to a fantasy memory of the event but did not know how to get her to do it again.

Within a few sessions, it became apparent that sex was not the problem, only the symptom. Slowly, Dom admitted that he had concealed a great deal of anger, jealousy, and thoughts of revenge about his siblings since they all had many friends, were popular everywhere they went, and appeared happy and content, while he was a loner with one male friend (also a "weirdo" [his phrase]) and did not know how to relate to peers, only to adults who were usually protective of him.

When the oral sex event was more fully explored, Dom admitted that while he watched the girl fellating him, his thoughts were that she was a slut, dirty, shameful, etc. Thus, he wanted his sister to repeat this action, so he could feel superior and demean and degrade her.

1.3

Distinctive Additional Traits of Adolescent Sex Offenders

- An intense need to be accepted by peers at any price
- Uses negative means to attract attention
- Difficulty in postponing pleasure needs (impulse problems)
- Serious empathy deficits
- Little or no religious/moral value system
- Incredible sexual naïveté
- Feelings of being unloved, unwanted, alone
- Very strong belonging needs
- Self-worth and self-image are damaged
- Unrealistic negative body image
- Fear of being compared to peers in any manner
- Attention deficit disorder often present
- Little, if any, communication with parents and/or other adult figures
- Emotionally immature
- Utilizes all defense mechanisms, especially denial, rationalization, and projection
- Self-defeating/self-punishing behaviors due to guilt and anger at self
- Trust a major problem in all areas due to multiple betrayals (real or perceived)
- Uses manipulation and pity mechanisms to avoid punishment and to be accepted
- Sexual acting out power driven, anger/retaliation driven, and/or seduction driven
- As in adult offenders, control a major factor, regardless of expression
- Successful therapy a long and difficult process

Therapy will take time and must involve the whole family. Though eighteen years old, Dom is more like a twelve-year-old emerging adolescent, and this must be taken into consideration throughout his treatment.

IMPULSIVE VERSUS COMPULSIVE

A major difference between the adult sex offender and the adolescent sex offender is that a majority of adolescent offenders act out on impulse (a characteristic of adolescence) rather than in a preplanned manner as adult sex offenders do. This is an extremely important factor since it becomes a predictor of future behavior, as well as a positive predictor for treatment outcome.

JEFFY is a sixteen-year-old male from a broken home who was accused of putting his penis in a two-year-old neighbor boy's mouth. Jeffy never knew his father, who abandoned the family when he was one year old. Jeffy is a handsome, well-developed teen who is outgoing and open. He went to juvenile court, pled guilty, and received three years probation with a stipulation of intense therapy.

In many ways, Jeffy was a typical high school student who liked girls and lost his virginity at age twelve. Sex was sex, and there were no emotions attached. The one thing missing in his sexual life was oral sex, and he masturbated compulsively to fantasies of "the world's greatest BJ." He constantly heard stories from his teen male friends of how great a BJ (blow job) was and how often they talked girls into doing it, although he could never get one to do it to him.

On the day of the incident, Jeffy had just come home from school and was in his darkened bedroom, naked, and masturbating on his bed. The two-year-old, who lived in the apartment below and who often was baby-sat by Jeffy's mother, walked into the bedroom and up to the side of the bed. Without a second's thought, Jeffy, erect and horny, stood up and told the boy to open his mouth. The boy did, and Jeffy inserted his penis. He felt revulsion and panicked at what he was doing. He stopped and sent the boy out of the room. Within minutes, Jeffy thought little about the incident and continued his masturbation. A week or so later, Jeffy was arrested.

In therapy, his new openness and interest in bettering himself made progress swift and positive. He has not had a recurrence in the past seven years and calls frequently with updates about his life. More information on Jeffy appears in the chapters ahead.

I have experienced twenty to thirty cases of this type in preteens and teens accused of a single sexual incident. All consisted of a nonplanned, impulsive act when a set of circumstances occurred while they were sexually stimulated/excited and while there was an unfulfilled need that they were and had been obsessing about. More on these instances appears in later chapters.

The Danger

Although a significant number of both child and adolescent sex offenders fall into the impulse category, there is a serious danger even in this group. *If* the deviant behavior is pleasurable and satisfies the intended need and *if* the behavior goes unnoticed, unreported, unpunished, or is seen as "just a phase," "all boys do these things and he will grow out of it," "nothing serious to be concerned about since no one was *really* injured," the serious danger is that the behavior will be repeated and eventually become compulsive instead of impulsive, and a new sex offender will be born.

There is a second and more insidious danger. An example will clarify.

Quite recently, I received a phone call from a panicking mother who related that a nine-year-old boy had sexually molested her eight-year-old son in the boy's rest room of his grammar school. I had them come into the office immediately and interviewed each separately.

The mother was in a near panic state. She was also quite angry that the school officials would do nothing about the incident. In fact, when the eight-year-old returned to his classroom, quite upset, the teacher allegedly told him, "I don't want to hear anything about that sort of thing." She then told him to see the principal who actually avoided him for the rest of the day. The mother is seeking legal recourse.

The little boy, on the other hand, was quite calm and levelheaded about the incident. He was standing at the urinal, and the other boy came up behind him and tried to touch his penis. He pushed him away and ran out of the boy's room and back to class. He confirmed the mother's story about the teacher and the principal.

The mother's panic, anger, and litigious reactions can and will determine the eight-year-old's emotional health and long-term effects from this incident. With his positive and mature present attitude, there need be no long-term effects. However, if the mother keeps the incident focused in his mind and keeps insisting that he has been "permanently damaged" by the incident, he will be affected for many years. Fortunately, she came in and was counseled regarding this danger.

On further checking with a school authority, I discovered that the nine-year-old was from a broken minority home and had been in all sorts of trouble both in the neighborhood and in the school. It was obvious that the school authorities were "afraid" of the family and potential legal problems that could reach the media. Six months have passed, and nothing has been done.

Left on his own and not confronted or treated, this nine-year-old is headed for serious trouble in the future, most likely of a sexual nature since the majority of complaints about him have been sexual touching, peeping, and exposing incidents. *None* of these incidents have been followed through, and he has received no counseling or other help.

This "danger theory" of mine is based on treating and dealing with more than 1,000 convicted sex offenders and learning from them that their deviant behavior began as early as nine years old and that they were never caught, never involved in therapy, or, if they were, how easy it was to *get over* on untrained therapists with smiles, tears, or feigned naïveté. Over 90 percent of the compulsive sex offenders I have had contact with began their deviant career in late childhood or early adolescence. The older and more physically developed they became, the more serious and more frequent the acting out occurred.

Early identification and detection of these individuals is essential if we seriously want to lower the incidence of sexual victimization. This issue will continue to be discussed in later chapters under different topics.

Chapter 2

The Inadequate Personality

INTRODUCTION

Of all the traits that sex offenders have in common, none is as dominant and recurrent as that of the *inadequate personality,* a characteristic seen in each and every one of them.

Traditionally, inadequate personality has referred to "That class of personality disturbances in which the individuals are characterized by inadaptability, social incompatibility, and inadequate response to intellectual, emotional, social, and physical demands without being grossly physically or mentally deficient upon examination" (Wolman, 1989, p. 250).

As used here, this term applies to those individuals who do not feel equal to their peers, constantly measure themselves *upward* against others (focusing on peers who are better in all ways), and, therefore, come up failing or below them in all areas. Regardless of how well they do, they feel they "should have done better." *Perfectionism* is part of their syndrome, yet they never achieve perfection. They are passive, compliant, and willing to pay any price for acceptance and love (even though they realize it is not real). They are constantly out to please others and attempt to *buy* their friendships, beginning as preschool children (parents describe them as shy, timid, afraid to compete or be compared, and always looking for attention and acceptance) and continuing into adulthood. Regardless of the methods parents, siblings, friends, and other adults employ, they never feel equal to others, almost as if they fear equality, because then others will expect more (too much) of them.

The main characteristic of this group of individuals is their compulsive need to measure and compare themselves to everyone else and always come up failing. This need is so consistent and so pervasive that they will go to any lengths to assure their coming up short; in other words, *they set themselves up to fail.* Their negative self-image and defunct self-esteem have been present since early childhood and are so ingrained that it is often next to impossible to change either.

As children, for example, these individuals may be able to name all the pupils in their class who scored higher than they did on a test but are unconcerned about those who scored lower. *They only measure upward.* If, by some happenstance, they score a 98 percent on a test, it should have been 100 percent; if they score 100 percent, the test was too easy. They never give themselves positive feedback or praise, nor will they accept it from anyone else.

This compulsive need to compare and fail applies to all areas of their lives. They practice this degrading behavior in school, sports, and employment, as well as in friendships and other relationships. The overall effect is a pervasive unhappy and depressed state. This eventually leads to social avoidance in all areas as a safety measure. They also start using the rationalization that *"if I don't try, I can't fail."* An example, at this point, may be helpful.

Billy: Defective Self-Image Inviting Molestation

BILLY comes home from school one day with his report card, containing seven A's and one C. With a great deal of anxiety, Billy hands the report card to his father, who immediately responds "What's that C doing there?" just as Billy knew he would and had done many times before. Billy does not respond but, with guilt and a deep sense of failure, goes to his room with one more confirmation that no matter what he does, he will never be able to satisfy his father. Billy's father has taught him to see only the negative and to ignore the positive. The seven A's don't count; only the one C is important. Without any conscious standard of measurement or effort, this ruler is now firmly established and will remain there for some twenty years, applied to everything he does, as will be seen.

The unfortunate, all-encompassing effect is that Billy will now see himself as below his peers in everything he does. Although enjoying compliments at the moment they are given, he never internalizes them and remains, for all intent and purposes, incapable of seeing himself in any positive manner.

Billy also concludes that, somehow, all of this *must be his fault,* since the fathers of his friends and classmates do not treat their sons in the same negative way. (These individuals are constantly comparing and observing the behaviors of others in all areas of their lives.)

Eventually *adopting his father's ruler,* Billy becomes his own worst enemy. No matter how hard he tries, he never gives himself credit or praise, but through a distorted process that I call "subjective judgment" (further discussed in Chapter 5) he admires, respects, and praises the accomplishments of his friends and peers on a regular basis.

This need also makes children with this syndrome much more vulnerable to being victimized and used by both peers and adults due to their intense needs for acceptance and approval. For this reason, they often become victims of all forms of abuse, including sexual abuse early in their lives.

This syndrome, when applied to sex offenders of all ages, results in the following finding from my years of experience: *sex offenders handle criticism and insults far better than compliments or praise,* although their need for acceptance and approval simply gets stronger and stronger.

BILLY, as has been seen, cannot please his father, feels rejected and unloved, and desperately needs a father's care and concern. His mother, also a very inadequate and frightened woman, cannot help Billy with his father's negative attitude. In an attempt to compensate for Billy's lost fatherly love, she enrolls Billy in the Big Brother program at the church she attends. She confides Billy's problems with his father to the intake interviewer and asks him for help. He readily agrees.

Billy reluctantly awaits his first contact with his new big brother, Tom, predicting failure and ultimate rejection from this man, just as he received from his father. From the first week, Tom, to Billy, was a dream come true. Each week they went to movies, to parks, on trips, or for long walks. Tom took a personal and positive interest in Billy and was always touching him in one way or another. He put his arms around his shoulders, gave him hugs at their meeting and leaving, tousled his hair, etc. Billy had never received so much attention.

After about a month, Tom suggested they take a weekend camping trip. Billy was thrilled, and his mother happily and readily gave her permission. On Friday afternoon, Billy and his new father substitute left for a state park.

During the trip, Tom rubbed Billy's leg and constantly found reasons for touching Billy. After setting up a tent in a secluded area of the park near the lake, Tom suggested a swim "in their birthday suits," and Billy agreed. At this point, Billy would do anything to please Tom. In the waters of the lake, Tom again found reasons for touching and tickling and explored Billy's body.

When they finished with the swim, Tom suggested they sunbathe nude to dry off and take a nap. Happy and tired, Billy fell asleep quite quickly and later awoke to Tom fellating him. Surprised, frightened, and confused, Billy asked what Tom was doing, and Tom's reply was "Showing you how much I love you!" The sex act itself felt good, and Billy simply lay back, eventually having his first orgasm. Tom asked nothing in return, and the rest of the trip was fun and games.

However, from that trip on, each time Tom took Billy anywhere, they ended up at his apartment and, if it was a Friday, Billy slept over. The "love games," as the sexual molestations became known, not only continued but also increased. Tom now wanted proof of Billy's love through reciprocal sex. The relationship continued for three years until Tom suddenly moved out of town. (Another boy had been molested and the big brother leadership asked Tom to resign or be reported to the police. In a panic, Tom left town that weekend, without contacting Billy. The big brother leadership, embarrassed and fearing a potential lawsuit, never contacted Billy or his mother.) The results were devastating. Billy felt rejected and betrayed but, as always, put the blame on himself. "I must have done something to upset/anger Tom and he is punishing me." Some twelve years later Billy, in the same manner, molested another young boy much like himself and is now serving time for this offense.

THE EFFECT OF ADOLESCENT SEXUAL CRISIS

In childhood or adolescence, the sex offender personality typically behaves differently from the normal childhood personality. Although both groups may experience similar behaviors due to their inadequate personalities, those who eventually become sex offenders also appear to experience *some form of sexual trauma,* active or passive, conscious or repressed, that, if unresolved, too often leads to sexual dysfunction and/or deviation in later life. As a result of lengthy experience with these individuals and with victims of sexual abuse who did not become sex offenders, some theories have been derived of how the two groups develop on different paths.

A schematic representation of this trait clearly shows how the early development of a negative, never-to-be-satisfied *mental ruler* separates the sex offender from the normal and natural progression of other children, who also experience this type of inadequate personality phase. The normals somehow adjust, get help, or are helped through this state by parents, teachers, counselors, or other interested adults and tend to blossom at adolescence; the sex offender does not (see Box 2.1).

For both groups of children, a crisis occurs, *usually* at adolescence, precipitated by the beginnings of self-evaluation, comparison to peers, and a dramatic change in the *source for their social and accep-*

2.1

A Representation of the Relationship Between Childhood Personality, Sexual Crisis in Adolescence, and Normal or Pathological Sexual Adjustment in Adulthood

THE BASIC FORMULA

Inadequate personality in childhood
+ Sexual trauma in childhood or adolescence
(conscious or repressed, active or passive)
+ Crisis, usually at puberty
= Adult outcomes

ADULT OUTCOMES

Deny-ers, Who Control and Overcompensate

Nonsexually

- Noncriminally, through sports, power, money
- Criminally, as wife beaters, muggers, assaultive personalities

Sexually

- Noncriminally, as playboys, ladies' men, macho personalities
- Criminally, through sexually assaultive behavior against children or adults

Adjust-ers, Who Get Help Through Counseling or Therapy or Positive Life Experiences and Thus Mature

Accept-ers

Nonsexually

- Noncriminally, by becoming mama's boys, happy henpecked husbands, or generally passive persons (e.g., the last clerk in the office syndrome)
- Criminally, through embezzling, arson, fraud, and other noncontact offenses

Sexually

- Noncriminally, as passive homosexuals, perennial bachelors, voluntary celibates
- Criminally, as seductive pedophiles or hebophiles, flashers who control in this manner

tance needs. Although as children they wanted and needed to *please adults* for approval, security, and acceptance, they now change to wanting to *please peers* in order to gain acceptance, security, and approval from this group.

"Identity," instead of being linked to the father-ideal figure (for boys) and to the mother-ideal figure (for girls), now shifts to admiration for the peer model who is accepted, popular, and assertive, as well as successful in the eyes of the newcomer. A new need emerges: to be like his or her peers.

The "normal adolescents" simply enter a new stage of life and smoothly adjust with little visible trauma (except possibly for their parents). They join their peer group and quickly establish a new identity, different from childhood, and continue to grow and mature as they encounter new and challenging experiences, sexual awakening, and plans for the future. However, for the inadequate personality types, this transition is not easily made or accepted. A different, *pathological* path is taken.

MODES OF PATHOLOGICAL ADJUSTMENT IN ADULTHOOD

For the potential sex offender, the previously established negative ruler determines the course he will take. He responds to the adolescent crisis in a totally different manner and comes to a crossroad where he can go in only one of two directions and become either a "deny-er" or an "accept-er."

The deny-er, by definition, cannot face the perceived inadequacy. Through reaction-formation and denial, he overcompensates for the inadequacy either: (1) *legally* through excelling in sports, power, wealth, "macho" behaviors, and persistent proofs of his physical and sexual prowess. In all of these attempted solutions to his problem he fails, and each failure triggers an even stronger need for more and more proof until the behaviors become compulsive. Alternatively, he may act out (2) *illegally* through rape, wife abuse, breaking and entering, daring and risky robberies, etc., again to prove his masculinity and, now, his superiority over his peers. However, the overcompensation never works and never ends, increasing in intensity, violence, and daring.

An example of the legal deny-er might easily be the playboy who has to have a different conquest each night; consistently needs a high rating of his sexual performance; brags continuously to fellow workers of his latest sexual success; and simultaneously is overcompetitive in the workplace, throwing ethics out of the window in order to advance and to win out over everyone, including his supervisor. He also has to act at being happy since he never really is.

An example of the illegal deny-er is the rapist who is never satisfied with his sexual performance or having a willing and cooperative partner but must take what he wants and cause pain while doing it. In therapy, the rapist will frequently allude to the partial motivation that he wanted someone else to feel the pain he felt all of his life.

Another pertinent example would be the incestuous father who must rule the lives of his family as a dictator to prove his control, power, and worth. Regardless of how the family tries to please this individual, they cannot succeed, and he steadily graduates from physical and financial control to sexual control over his wife and his children.

On the other hand, he may choose the second road, that of the accept-er who accepts his situation and comes to the conclusion quite early in life that he will never change and never meet his or anyone else's expectations. As a result, he does nothing to alleviate his state. He then may, *legally* and sexually, become the passive homosexual who does anything to please his partner (usually a dominant figure similar to his father) and is never secure in his relationship. He usually destroys the relationship with his insecurity, jealousy, and suspicions of betrayal, literally pushing his partner away, in order to confirm the predicted rejection.

Nonsexually, he becomes the happily henpecked husband or remains the mama's boy; quits easily at everything he attempts (one strike and he quits the team; one bad grade or recitation in school and he quits the class); or becomes the clerk in the fiftieth desk of an office where the fiftieth desk is the lowest. Although his true goal there is to work for twenty years, possibly getting to the forty-ninth desk and retiring with his gold watch, he continually complains when someone else in the office is given, or earns, a promotion. These individuals will be relatively happy with their lot, since it poses no risk of failure that any change, promotion, or advancement would, so he never asks or applies for one. Were his supervisor to select him for training for a higher-level position, he would perceive it akin to being asked to jump off the Empire State Building and fly. He would probably find a way to sabotage this chance or quit and run away since *escape* is his main protective defense and coping mechanism.

On the other hand, *illegally* and sexually he becomes the child molester (either pedophile or hebophile, depending on the degree of inadequacy or the age bracket of his own sexual molestation) or the exhibitionist. In these cases, his need is to please the child, not himself, and quite often he performs on the child hoping to pleasure him or her and be accepted for it. He rarely expects or asks for reciprocal pleasure. *Illegally* and nonsexually he becomes the arsonist, embezzler, or the bookie, or he may choose many other noncontact forms of criminal behavior.

Howie: The Ultimate Inadequate Personality

An example of this type of individual is Howie, one of the most difficult cases that I have ever encountered.

HOWIE was a mama's boy who lived in a totally matriarchal household with a passive, almost nonexistent older father. All of his life, his need was to please mother. During college, Howie was incapable of making a decision, and never had a true friend, was never involved in an equal relationship.

Howie chose teaching as a career and grammar school as the level he would teach. He felt safe in this environment, as he did not see the young children as a threat. From the beginning of his teaching career, he felt strangely attracted to young boys. His primary attractions were all to what he termed "Adonises," who were the most popular boys in the class and the school (the opposite of what he had been).

Howie, being a loner most of his life, chose photography as a substitute social life and slowly but surely talked several of the young boys into posing nude for him on field trips and camping weekends (which he supervised for the nature club). He never touched any of the boys, although he did get erections from seeing them naked. Only after years of therapy could he even admit to himself that there was a sexual attraction or component to his behavior. Howie also never masturbated until he was thirty-one years old, when he saw one boy do it in the woods and then imitated the behavior. Were it not for a nosy relative who went into his darkroom and rifled through his photos, discovering the pictures of the nude boys, Howie would never have been caught. The boys never told anyone about the nudity or the photographs for two reasons, the first being their own embarrassment and fears of being labeled "queer," "weird," and so forth by their peers; the second reason was that Howie made it clear that if they wanted to go on more camping trips and remain in his favor they had to remain secret and loyal to him. This is a typical ploy of the majority of child molesters. It is doubtful that he would have progressed to actual physical contact or overt sexual behavior since his fears of both physical contact and sex were so paralyzing and since he was so content with what he had—the photos.

Howie will be further discussed in Chapter 7.

The Inadequacy May Be Hidden

It must be noted here that the pervasive and omnipresent inadequacy may not always easily be seen, especially in the deny-ers. Their social and work images are carefully rehearsed and orchestrated to prevent their true nature (their inadequate personality) from being seen or discovered. They work very hard to create the image of normalcy, aptitude, and expertise in their vocation. This applies especially to the professional groups (teachers, ministers of all denominations, scoutmasters, big brothers, policemen, doctors, lawyers, psychiatrists/psychologists, etc.).

One key to their diagnosis and detection, if one looks for it, is that although they always seem to know a great deal about their colleagues and fellow workers, no one interviewed knows anything really personal about their private lives outside the workplace. They rarely, if ever, have a real friendship or relationship on an intimate level. The examples of two such offenders might help to clarify this phenomenon.

Frank: Overcompensation for Sexual Victimization

FRANK was a very popular child, good athlete, and honor student, both in grammar school and in high school. His parents had no complaints about his behavior at home, and in every way, Frank was considered a normal boy. Frank successfully hid both his feelings of inadequacy and the compensatory need to excel, as well as his anger and hatred for all women.

Early in Frank's life (when he was around eight years old), a teenage female baby-sitter who sexually molested him and undressed him and herself, had him lick her vagina (which was not too clean), and then laughed and ridiculed him about his then small penis. Frank could not perform to her satisfaction and could not please her, although he desperately wanted to. She concluded the molestation with the traumatizing statement "Kid, you'll never be a real man, and you'll never be able to please a woman!"

Frank never forgot the experience or the baby-sitter's words but was too frightened and embarrassed to tell anyone about it. Concurrently, he had problems with his two older sisters, who picked on him and resented the fact that they had to baby-sit for him when their parents went out. The two sisters physically abused him: pinching him, tickling him until he cried, spanking him naked with a hairbrush, and also *laughing at his small penis,* which they went out of their way to focus on and ridicule.

When he entered adolescence, Frank's attitude was "love them and leave them," and his intercourse with any woman was brutal and aimed to cause pain. Threats were used to keep all of his secrets. In the sports locker rooms he always had an excuse not to shower with the other players but still was sure to check them out and compare himself, especially genitally. Naturally, he always came out lacking.

In his first and all subsequent employments, Frank was an excellent and diligent worker, always exceeding what was asked of him and always competing with the other workers. Although he was socially friendly on the surface, no one really knew much about Frank's private life, but that was okay with his friends.

Frank was known as a ladies' man and was always seen with a different date. He had grown into a good-looking, muscular hunk on the outside, but inside he was still a small, weak, and frightened little boy. After a particularly important date during which he experienced impotence and was ridiculed for it, all of the "old tapes" began to play. After brooding for hours, he went out in the middle of the night and committed his first brutal rape. The victim was a young college woman, hitchhiking home from studying with a friend. She was subsequently hospitalized for her injuries and required plastic surgery on her face. She never again returned to college and is still in psychotherapy.

Frank's rapes continued for more than three years before he was caught. During that time, he associated with many policemen and discussed the unsolved rapes with them and also with his friends at work. His attitude was always one of horror and disgust toward the rapist, and he adamantly insisted that the animal should be castrated or killed when caught. Never was Frank suspected, and when he was finally apprehended and identified by one victim, no one, including his policemen friends, believed the story. The whole community came to his defense. Only after he finally confessed, out of guilt and to experience some relief, did his true personality become known, even to his own family.

Update: Frank successfully completed the treatment program at the Adult Diagnostic and Treatment Center, in Avenel, New Jersey, and was paroled. Today, he lives in another state, is married, has two children, and is very successful in his business operating an automobile body shop. He continues to make contact with me on at least an annual basis, usually at Christmas.

HOWIE (discussed earlier in this chapter) was a certified grammar school teacher. He was well liked by the students and also by the teachers who elected him their union representative. Although he attended all school social functions and even dated one of the teachers (a frightening and unpleasant experience as he was later to relate), he had no real, intimate friends, and as with Frank, no one really knew anything about his personal life except that he was dedicated to teaching and to his students. He was labeled by one of his administrators as "almost too good to be true," and this certainly proved to be the case. Upon hearing of his arrest, all who knew him were shocked. His parents (especially his mother), to this day, refuse to believe the extent of his pathology or the number of children he was involved with (more than 100 over four years). Howie chose the perfect place to hide his truly inadequate personality: a grammar school. There was no competition for him to be concerned with, and he certainly physically could handle sixth graders.

Both Howie and Frank are typical sex offenders, and their cases are in no way unique. Due to the ability of the sex offender to hide and compensate for his pathology, sex offenders are *invisible threats* and not easily screened out of the situations that both feed and satisfy their illness. In subsequent chapters, I will discuss many other cases of this kind.

THE CHILD/ADOLESCENT SEX OFFENDER

The inadequate personality is developed during childhood and then carried over into adolescence *if there is no intervention*. It necessarily follows that, were these individuals identified early enough and subsequently treated by properly trained therapists, not just whoever is available (e.g., the counselor at the individual's school, a parish priest/minister, rabbi, a family friend in the field, etc.), this inevitable progression could be stopped. There are times and cases that I have seen where inept, untrained professionals have done more damage than good to children and adolescents. Unfortunately, there presently is no certification for treating sex offenders or the survivors of sexual abuse. As I will repeat elsewhere in this work (especially in Chapters 9 and 20), too many practicing professionals accept new patients for economic reasons rather than because they are skilled in treating a particular problem.

At the original Diagnostic Center at Menlo Park, New Jersey, (presently demolished and replaced with a Target store), patients were assigned to a treatment staff composed of a psychiatric social worker, a clinical psychologist, and a psychiatrist, who all had training in dealing with a particular type of problem or disturbance in a child or adolescent, male or female. Economics and ego were not involved, since all of the staff were salaried state employees with equivalent caseloads. All of us learned from one another and held regular training sessions and staff interactions sessions discussing individual cases. All staff members, equally, had input and feedback at the end of a presentation and learned from these interactions. Not only did the staff benefit from this type of milieu, but the patients also did as well if not better than patients treated with other models.

Although some mental institutions still hold staffing sessions, the child/adolescent that we are discussing would not normally be sent to one of these facilities, especially when the first, minimal symptoms occurred. For example, if a boy in grammar school or even high school exposed himself to another student, he first would be sent to the school counselor and, most of the time, out of fear of parental reaction, the incident would be minimized and considered "a normal phase of growing up." Although it could have been just that, it also could have been an indication of far more serious problems.

At the junior high school where I was a consultant (again referred to in Chapter 3), the suggestion that a student should have a psychological workup or needed therapy produced an instant panic reaction from the principal who rejected the suggestions "out of fear of powerful or influential parents and their anticipated reaction to suggesting that there was something wrong with their offspring."

In my own private practice, I have had many children and adolescents referred to me that were already inadequate personalities and were already overcompensating or withdrawing into a private world filled with sexual fantasies that, if acted out, would have victimized innocent people. Others were so full of rage that their fantasies were violent and often sadistic in nature. It was usually only their small size and lack of physical strength that prevented these fantasies from becoming reality.

Several warning signs should be taught to all parents, teachers, physical education instructors, and any other individual involved in the lives of children and adolescents. (*Note:* In the following list, each traits will have an opposite listed. The first trait, in such a pair, belongs to the *accept-ers,* and the second trait belongs to the *deny-ers,* which have already been discussed in this chapter.

Warning Signs of Impending Problems in Children and Adolescents

Accept-ers	**Deny-ers**
School grades drop	Excels in sports
Loner, few friends, if any	Popular but a bully

Answers questions with one word or is evasive	Justifies, projects, denies
Secrets abound	Brags to friends about all anti-social behaviors
Avoids family activities	Conforms at home to con parents and get what he wants
Emotionally flat, easily depressed	Emotionally high, appears stable, hides anger
Acceptance needs dominate, will do anything for it	Independence dominates
Compulsively masturbates with fantasies that are normal but age inappropriate	Acts out sexually, uses partners to satisfy his need to conquer
Follower in all things	Leader, has his own followers
Fears adults/authority	Manipulates authority as proof of his superiority

In the following chapters, the distinctive traits of the "inadequate" sex offenders will be individually discussed along with treatment considerations.

Chapter 3

The Never-Satisfied Parent: Negative Self-Image and Selective Perception

INTRODUCTION

Add to the already basic inadequate personality a "never-satisfied parent" and the overall effect can be and usually is devastating. In every aspect of the developing sex offender personality, the results are the same: negative. Whether in school performance, sports, social events, family behavior, or physical development (size, strength, appearance, body image) the subject perceives himself to be at the bottom of the totem pole and erroneously concludes that he will never measure up.

Then, through an identification with the never-satisfied parent, the sex offender becomes his own worst enemy. From childhood on, no matter what he does, it is never good enough to satisfy either his perfectionistic parent(s) or his own perfectionistic self.

Kevin: Progression from Exhibition to Violent Rape

KEVIN is a very bright and creative adult (WAIS Full Scale IQ = 157) who is a compulsive rapist. After some time in his first treatment experience (he is presently a parole violator from another state and again is incarcerated), Kevin unexpectedly joined the art therapy program at the institution where he was being treated. He displayed a truly remarkable talent in both painting and sculpture. His works were originals (many others in the program copied from books, great artists, etc.) and showed a warmth and sensitivity not seen in his daily behavior or in any of his therapy modalities. Both staff and patients admired his works and often came to him for advice, suggestions, and help when their projects were not going well. He gladly helped and seemed to enjoy doing so.

One day, during a therapy session, Kevin asked his therapist to keep one of his works in his office, and the therapist agreed. The therapist also commented enthusiastically on the rich quality, the creative flair, and the originality of the painting. Kevin immediately went on a tirade about the flaws in the picture: proportional problems, poor color choices, etc. It was obvious that he was extremely uncomfortable with the praise he had received and needed to negate it as quickly as possible. Although he could identify his own reaction as coming from what he expected from his father as a child, this insight did not alter his critical opinion of the painting. He withdrew his request to hang the picture in the therapist's office and left with the painting. It was never seen again.

This was typical behavior for Kevin, as it is for the majority of sex offenders. They receive some instant gratification from praise and support, then a form of panic sets in and their perfectionism takes over. It is almost as if they fear any positive comment, although underneath they yearn for it.

PERFECTIONISM AND THE FEAR OF FAILURE SYNDROME

Perfectionism, then, becomes a paramount therapeutic concern and barrier to be surmounted. The patient's perfectionism needs to be replaced with a more realistic appraisal of his life and ultimately of himself.

A "fear of failure syndrome" develops as a natural consequence of the perfectionism and becomes exaggerated to the point where fear of trying becomes phobically entrenched. Cognitions attached to this syndrome include the following:

- If I try, I'll fail, and then I'll feel even worse about myself than I do now, so it is better not even to try.
- I'll take a risk, but as soon as I get scared or start to fail, I'll quit and run for the safety of not ever trying again.

Thus, if such a patient is talked into going back to school (as an adult), he may quit at the first sign of an unacceptable teacher (parent/authority substitute) response and never return. Similarly, if he joins a softball team and, when up to bat, hears "Strike one!" he throws down the bat, turns in his uniform, and quits the team.

Although these two examples may seem exaggerated, I have seen them both occur hundreds of times in sex offenders. Whether encouraged to become involved in school, a sports program, art programs, new groups, volunteer activities; to approach an authority figure; or to join in any other activity that is perceived as a risk, the sex offender will avoid these situations at all costs.

Fear of failure, more than any other factor, makes motivating the sex offender very difficult, especially when it involves taking risks by exposing himself in his group. It can take as long as seven to ten years of passive silence and high levels of resistance before any really meaningful therapy takes place. Thus, there is an essential need for patience on the part of therapists choosing to work with this population.

The more inadequate and the more pathological the offender, the more he resists and the more time will be needed to see even the most simple changes and/or gains. For some offenders, fear of failure is so encompassing and so paralyzing that they never participate in therapy to a meaningful degree, nor do they ever expose what is really going on in their thoughts and fantasies. In addition, they never discuss the childhood traumas or experiences that led to their deviation. Effective therapy under these circumstances does not exist. The real danger here is that *confinement increases their illness, whether their pervasive inadequacy or their suppressed rage, and they eventually return to society more dangerous than when they were first confined.*

There appears also to be a direct correlation between the degree of resistance and the degree of abuse they incurred as children or adolescents.

During his first sentence to the treatment program, KEVIN denied any real pathology or problems and projected all blame onto his parents, especially his demanding and unsatisfied father. In treatment, although willing to participate and to help others, he was unwilling to expose his own personal and deep-seated problems. At the end of three years, he was released, now more dangerous than when he arrived as a flasher. Exposure to therapy had brought many old memories and traumas to consciousness, and his already deep sense of inadequacy had increased.

Shortly following release, he began flashing again with fantasies of rape. Within the first several months of his return to the community he met a woman (with whom he was not compatible), and after a brief courtship married her against the advice of his family and his outpatient therapist. Within a year of the marriage, Kevin began raping and had assaulted over sixty victims before he was eventually discovered.

A different example will help to further clarify the concept.

Todd: A Victim of Incest Who Becomes a Serial Rapist

TODD spent most of his adolescence and young adult years in trouble with the law and either on probation or in an institution of one type or another. When I first met him, he was sentenced to thirty years for rape. Todd was likable, a good inmate, and popular with both the staff and his peers. He had a great deal of talent in the electronics area and was assigned to work in the maintenance department of the video studio complex.

In therapy, he was passive and rarely participated in group, either for himself or others. In individual therapy, he was a bit more involved but participated only by answering direct questions. After more than a year, he began to open up more and one day related that he had been sexually molested at age twelve by an older brother. Their sexual behavior began with Todd being talked into masturbating his brother (with no reciprocation). In return, the brother allowed Todd to drive his car, join him on camping or hunting trips, and to hang out with the brother's older friends. Todd felt accepted and was willing to pay for this acceptance and involvement.

Not too long after their sexual involvement began, Todd's brother changed the format of the sexual behavior and painfully sodomized Todd. Both during and after the sodomy, his brother compared Todd favorably to the girls he had been with. This increased the degree of trauma for Todd, but once hooked on the benefits of submitting, he could not refuse and was at the mercy of his brother's frustrated sex life. Almost concurrently, Todd's school grades and behavior deteriorated. He became quiet and withdrawn, was socially isolated from his peers, and spent all of his time either with his older brother or doing favors and chores for him.

The only reason Todd brought this trauma up in individual therapy was that he was bleeding rectally from inserting objects into his anus for pleasure. He was at a point where he could not masturbate to orgasm without something inserted into his rectum. Shame, disgust, and fear also motivated him to expose this secret in group. I referred him to the hospital for treatment, and although the physician warned him of the dangers of continuing this practice, Todd ignored the warning, saying that he could not stop.

TREATMENT CONSIDERATIONS

For the particular problem of fear of failure that the sex offender invariably brings into therapy (as do many survivors of sexual abuse), one early and very important treatment goal should be to encourage risk-taking activities and behaviors that are likely to result in success. To begin this process, *goals are set that ensure success with little or no chance of failure.* Building on some base of an already familiar behavior, improvement goals are set extremely low to prevent failure. Two examples will clarify.

1. One of the offenders in a therapist's caseload is interested in improving his physical condition and wants to run laps on the gymnasium's track. He tells the therapist that yesterday he ran two laps and will run again today. The natural tendency would be to either repeat the goal of two laps or to increase the goal to at least three laps. With this type of individual, both of these goals are dangerous and could produce a failure that surely would result in his ending this activity. Therefore, he is taught to set his next goal at one lap. Thus, if he runs two laps again, he has exceeded his goal and that becomes a bonus that he must accept as both positive and a success. It is all the better if he runs three or even four laps.

2. If the goal for the offender is to reduce his isolation and fear of talking to others on his housing wing or place of employment in the community, the initial goal would be to come out of his room or work space at least one time during the morning, afternoon, and evening and say "Hi!" to one other person. If he speaks to two or more individuals or becomes involved in either a short or lengthy conversation, this is a bonus that must be seen as positive and a success.

This *minimal goal setting below the client's true ability,* technique, works with all offenders who are willing to try it, whether in an institution or in the community. The technique applies to all phases of the offender's life. As self-confidence increases, the therapist may then suggest attempts at behaviors that are more related to the offender's specific problems or fears. However, again, each new behavior demands the same "setting himself up to succeed" technique as opposed to his old "setting himself up to fail" behaviors. (*Caveat:* In using this technique it is extremely important to begin these new behaviors with choices that the offender has some knowledge of and some former experience with. Beginning new and unfamiliar behaviors *before self-confidence is firmly established* can confirm his old perception of being a failure and worthless and must be avoided.)

As with all techniques, there will be times when even this minimal goal-setting system fails. These situations afford the therapist the opportunity to alter an old perception of failure. Replace the idea that

"Failure is painful, embarrassing, depressing and to be avoided at all costs" with "Failure is positive!" The offender may respond with confusion, but the therapist should simply ask him to explain the statement. Eventually, they all come to realize that the reason failure is positive is twofold: you can learn from your mistakes, but more important, in order to fail you had to try or you had to take a risk, and that is always a positive. Sex offenders are able to identify with this second factor quite easily since trying has been one of their greatest deficits.

From "performance behaviors," the next progression in the process is to "interpersonal behaviors," where the offender perceives the greatest risk taking to exist. Depending on the case and the individual, these might include the following:

- Making a new friend or associate
- Beginning to share more personal information about himself with one person
- "Taking the floor" more frequently in group
- Beginning to share frightening or embarrassing secrets with the therapist and eventually the group
- Sharing feelings with just one person
- Saying "No," possibly for the first time in his life, to someone he fears losing as a friend or parent-substitute (such as the therapist)
- Asking for advice and then following his own decision anyway, a very important step in his progress
- Admitting the offense with full responsibility rather than rationalizing, projecting, or denying
- Increasing socialization behaviors and expanding his circle of friends and associates
- Where appropriate, confronting individuals in his life who have negatively affected him, hurt him, or possibly abused him, either physically or sexually

Personal growth and self-confidence will result, slowly but definitely, as these exercises continue and become more daring. The reward is the formation of a new and stronger ego (self) and self-image that are decidedly necessary if the offender is to succeed.

At this level of progress, a major caveat is necessary: The overall and ultimate goal of these treatment techniques is the formation of a new and functional personality structure. Since the choice of what will embody this new personality is the offender's decision, the therapist must be cautious about how this choice is made.

NEW IMAGE DANGERS

Becoming What Others Want

For most of their lives, especially as children, sex offenders were total conformists to others' wishes in order to gain the acceptance and love they so desperately craved. This survival behavior pattern will not be extinguished overnight. In fact, residual elements of this behavior will unconsciously recur on a regular basis, and the offender must consistently be made aware of each occurrence.

Not only does this danger apply to his new image, but it also is extremely important in any new career choice(s). Many (if not the majority of) offenders have chosen to follow the occupation or trade of their fathers, brothers, uncles, grandfathers, or some other significant influence in their lives. Often the result is disastrous, with the offender either failing in this chosen field or hating it and living unhappily.

The same danger applies to choosing a new personality. A statement such as "My father always wanted me to be tough and strong and assertive" is indicative of this syndrome.

A physician who had attended one of my lectures called for an appointment. DR. AMBROSE (not his real name) arrived dressed casually and was quite open and friendly. He is a sixty-year-old, physically in-shape, male who was totally open from his first statement. Dr. A had been a family doctor for some thirty-five years and hated every minute of it.

When he was born, his father, a family doctor, bought him a T-shirt with the wording "Harvard Medical School, 19??." Two of his uncles were also physicians, one in urology and one a gynecologist. Throughout his youth, it had always been determined that he would follow the family line and become a physician. He did. Now, Dr. A was miserable, depressed, and feeling unable to continue in a life that he so despised.

Therapy was quite simple. I asked him what he would really like to do, and he instantly answered: "Be the publisher of a small newspaper in a small, out of the way, western town." My response was simply "What's stopping you?"

In less than a month, after gathering his immediate family and telling them the news, he sold his practice, began searching, and found the exact paper of his dreams for sale. His family remained (his two sons were also doctors), and he left on his new and great adventure.

The next Christmas, I received one of the first issues of his five-page newspaper plus a letter informing me that he had never been as happy in his entire life.

Imitating an Idol

In a similar manner, when there is no one in the family that the offender wants to imitate, the next choice they tend to make is to become like someone they idolize, respect, or admire. It could be the therapist, a close friend they have known for years, someone they met in their group, or simply someone who symbolizes all that they have always wanted to be and could not be. Examples of this syndrome might include statements such as "I'd like to be like my father or my brother," "If only I could be as tough and assertive as my Uncle John," or "I want to be like John Glenn, become an astronaut, and become famous."

Becoming the Opposite of "Their Old Selves"

This is probably the second-worst choice that the offender could make. Being someone whose thinking is all black and white (extremes) and who has problems with gray areas (moderate) is one of the offender's major problems. If this occurs, the therapist's function is to help the offender find positive facets of his personality that work well for him and that he should retain in his new personality development. In my experience, I have never met an offender who was all bad and who did not possess many positive traits, talents, skills, values, and behaviors.

For example, the majority of the offenders I have worked with have been excellently skilled either in some professional area such as teaching, the ministry, or even counseling, or in some business or technical field such as electronics, computer programming or repair, construction, and even finance. (Very few sex offenders that I have encountered were day workers or nomadic types.)

There is always a way to utilize these valuable skills in their new lives. Some (such as teachers, ministers, and priests) will be unable to return to their former profession or employment. However, there is no reason that a former grammar school teacher could not become a vocational-technical teacher with adults or even teach in a junior college, college, or business school.

Many that I have treated have done just that and were successful at it. Priests and ministers, although they may not be allowed to return to active parish level work where they have contact with children, adolescents, or young adults, can certainly teach in seminaries or theological colleges. These possibilities must be carefully pointed out to the offender with the caveat that the choice must remain his.

Staying the Same

Fear of taking risks is paramount in the offender group. They have consistently failed so often throughout their lives that they anticipate failure at every new venture. The result is that *it is easier to stay the same* because it is safe and comfortable. Moving the offender from this position is probably the greatest challenge that the therapist will meet. The old embedded value *"once a _____ always a _____"* returns over and over again, and the resistance to replacing this value with a more realistic one is tremendous.

Small, new, risk-taking behaviors with minimal danger and little or no consequence for failure become primary homework assignments that *must* be part of the offender's treatment. These assignments should begin almost from the first session. They should be consistently given at the end of each session and then evaluated at the beginning of the next session. If the outcome was positive, realistic praise and reinforcement should be given; if the offender failed, then an analysis of *why* he failed becomes the focus of the first part of the therapy session. Either way, the assignments must continue until he is able to set goals of this type on his own.

Dennis, who will be discussed in more detail first in Chapter 6, has remained rooted in this choice for over twenty years. He hates it, is constantly depressed, and even after four years of regular therapy sessions has not changed. In a recent phone call, after telling me how depressed he was, immediately stated, "I know, I know, I'm still choosing safety to happiness." This individual, and many others like him, proves that insight alone does not produce change.

"I Don't Deserve to Change"

When this barrier to a new personality is encountered, it indicates guilt is still so overpowering that any attempts at making changes at this juncture are doomed to failure. Thus, the "new personality development phase" must be suspended and the total focus of treatment aimed at resolving the degree of guilt present, its origin, the values associated with it, and the means to assuage it. Until the level of guilt is reduced to a level where the offender feels that he is deserving of positive feedback without becoming self-destructive, no further therapy goals can be set or activated.

(*Caveat:* Too often, the block to resolving the guilt is that there is still an unrevealed conscious or unconscious incident or act that has not been uncovered and resolved. This "missing secret" must be found and may take a great deal of time. Peter, discussed in Chapter 10, is a memorable case of just such a guilt.)

"I Don't Believe Change Is Possible for Me"

Here, the double standard of the sex offender is alive and well. Although he is willing to admit that change for everyone else in the world is possible, he perceives it as impossible for himself. From my personal experience, I feel strongly that this barrier is closely tied in with feeling undeserving. In fact, the two appear to be intimately linked. In most cases, resolving the degree and level of perceived guilt is sufficient to resolve this barrier and allow the new personality development to proceed.

Incidentally, these "new image dangers" are also found in the treatment of the survivors of sexual abuse, and the procedures for resolving them are practically identical.

SELECTIVE PERCEPTION

A characteristic of the offender that accounts for many of the problems just discussed is "selective perception," one of the most startling traits found in these individuals and traceable to their youths. This term refers to the ability to block out parts of reality that do not conform to the need to constantly measure upward and to compare unfavorably to the peer group.

An example may help to clarify this concept.

One late afternoon as I was about to leave a junior high school where I was employed part-time as a psychological consultant, the principal asked me to see just one more young man who had always been a polite, scholarly, and very popular individual during his grammar school years, but who suddenly had become a habitual truant. Tired after a full day, I tried to postpone the case until my next scheduled appointment day. However, the principal insisted that I see RONNY today, since if he were truant one more time he would be reported to the authorities and would possibly end up in a reformatory. I agreed.

When Ronny entered my office, I observed a well-developed, handsome young man who had knocked on the door, called me "sir" when asking to enter, and appeared to be a polite and well-mannered individual. Tired and pressed for time, I went straight to the heart of the matter and stated, "Look, Ronny, I really don't have a great deal of time to listen to a long story. Just tell me what I can do to get you back into classes, and we'll get along fine." He immediately said, "Get me out of gym classes."

After a moment I agreed and wrote him a note on my stationery, excusing him from gym classes until further notice. He immediately asked, "What's the trick, Doc?" I stated that there was no trick and that I understood how he felt since he must have the smallest penis in the class. He asked, "How did you know that?" I did not respond, and he continued: "And that's not all; guess what my nickname is? Bald eagle!" Noticing his closely cropped crew cut, I told him that I thought it looked fine, and he informed me that I was looking in the wrong place and pointed to his crotch. He then explained that he was the *only boy in his gym class* who was totally hairless, while all the others were not only larger in all ways but also had pubic hair.

At this point, I asked Ronny for a favor. I needed him to return to his gym class just one more time and, in the shower, to check out all of the other boys, in case there was another boy with a similar problem. Although he assured me that there was not anyone else like him in the class, he agreed. The next day, Ronny came knocking on the door, yelling, "Doc! Doc! you won't believe what happened!" He then related that he had done as I had asked and that there were five more "bald eagles" and that, even more startling, there were three boys with penises as small or even smaller than his. With a very serious face, I asked, "Ronny, why did you lie to me the last time we met?" With the most sincere facial and vocal expression I had seen or heard in quite a while (pay close attention to his answer) Ronny stated, "I swear, Doc, they weren't there the other times."

As one might guess, they had been there all the time. However, by selective perception, Ronny measured himself upward only and perceptually blocked out the other similar or even smaller boys until specifically directed to take notice of them. This same phenomenon occurs in all other areas of the sex offenders' lives, from home, where they measure themselves against siblings and parents, to society, to school, and to all other situations where comparison or measurement occurs.

Selective perception is another of the factors that makes treating either the sex offender or the victim of sex offenses so difficult and meticulous a task. All through the therapy process, whenever the patient becomes self-judgmental, this factor must be looked for and eliminated before moving any further. His perception of himself is continually colored and distorted by this factor, and to move past even the smallest judgmental statement without checking its validity can affect the remainder of the session and even alter the course of therapy. Selective perception must be dealt with as early as possible during therapy. Specific techniques will be discussed in later chapters.

THE CHILD/ADOLESCENT SEX OFFENDER

This entire chapter is about children and adolescents with perfectionistic, never-satisfied parents and other authority figures. This particular type of parent makes it clear, quite early in the child's life, that *no matter what he does and no matter how hard he tries, the child cannot please/satisfy his parent(s).*

Parents who want the best for their children, as well as parents who, consciously or unconsciously, want their child(ren) to achieve or become what they never were or could be, often make this mistake. Self-introspection is essential when this problem is suspected. For some of these parents or authority figures, therapy is necessary.

Sadly, the solutions that they appear unable to see are quite simple. Criticism that is constructive and then followed by love and acceptance is better medicine than is penicillin for an infection. Take the example of the seven-A, one-C report card (see Billy in Chapter 2). Had his father simply asked Billy why he got the C and how he could help him to bring this grade up to a B or an A, none of the damage described would have occurred.

Thus, parent education is essential where teachers or relatives suspect that this pattern is occurring in a child's/adolescent's home. Being able to procreate does not guarantee an individual becoming a "parent" rather than a baby maker. Children are not born with a technical manual for parents to refer to when a problem erupts. Ideally, all prospective parents should be required, by law, to take and pass a course on parenting during the nine months of gestation.

For these children/adolescents with an inadequate personality, therapy works well. The earlier this problem is discovered, the easier and shorter in duration therapy will be. When the problem has been lifelong (see the case of Dennis, Chapters 6, 12, and 14), therapy is much more difficult and prognosis for change much poorer. Some of these individuals are so immersed in their pathology that they have become comfortable and feel "safe" staying the way they are. They pay for this decision with loneliness, unhappiness, and a mediocre lifestyle, at best.

A very high percentage of sex offenders fall into this category.

Chapter 4

Exaggerated Needs for Control

Control is a constant and dominant factor in an overwhelming percentage of sex offenses, regardless of the type of act or the age of the victim. The ways in which the need to control may be expressed in antisocial sexual behavior are presented in Box 4.1, offering a picture of how such control needs may be expressed by degrees, from minimal control to total control.

CONTROL METHODS OF EXHIBITIONISTS AND VOYEURS

Even in noncontact sex offenses, such as exhibitionism, control exists. As soon as the offender gets the intended victim(s) to look at his exposed genitals, a smile appears on his face, the cognition "Gotcha!" or "Made you look!" occurs, and his satisfaction begins. If he gets no further with his behavior than to have the victim smile (if the fantasy was seductive) or scream, run, or indicate fear (if the fantasy was assaultive), the pleasure he receives satisfies his need. His ultimate fantasy (if seductive) is for the victim to approach and perform some sex act on him, from simply touching, to oral sex, to a suggestion they go somewhere and have intercourse.

In the case of voyeurism, the counterpart of exhibitionism, the control factor is found in the fantasy. If the offender is a deny-er, there will be a force and rape type fantasy; if he is an accept-er, there will be a successful seduction fantasy.

4.1

Three Avenues Through Which Sexual Deviates Express Their Needs to Control Another Person

1. Using force and violence to express anger and hatred toward the victim through
   - Sexual harassment
   - Flashing and/or obscene phone calls, with rape or assault fantasies
   - Forced acts of fellatio, cunnilingus, anal sex, urophilia, intercourse
2. Using violence and terror by denigrating the victim through
   - Sadistic injury to breasts, sexual organs
   - Sexual murder
3. Using seduction to satisfy their need for acceptance as
   - A seductive pedophile/hebophile, passive homosexual, flasher, Peeping Tom, or obscene phone caller with seduction fantasies

CONTROL METHODS OF PEDOPHILES AND HEBOPHILES

The pedophile or hebophile exerts control over victims in many ways. Although sex is the ultimate goal, they have incredible patience (if seductive, not assaultive) and first establish a relationship making the victim dependent on them for love, affection, and support. Once the victim is hooked, the offender can then become bolder and more overtly sexual in his behavior toward him or her. Quite often, the first sexual contact involves the offender trying to sexually please the victim with no reciprocation requested. Over a period of time this quickly changes, and the sex then involves total reciprocation and subjugation of the victim by the offender.

When the child/adolescent becomes older and more independent and the offender feels his control is slipping, the victim is dropped and replaced by another more inadequate and dependent one, and the cycle begins again. This "seducing/dropping" phenomenon accounts for the very large number of victims this particular group eventually accumulates. To hear from a seductive pedophile or hebophile that he has molested 100 or more victims is the norm rather than the exception.

Jon: A Longtime Seductive Pedophile

JON was the sixth grade teacher in an elementary school where the sixth grade is the last and highest grade. From there, the children go on to a junior high school across town. During the first week of each semester, Jon, a longtime pedophile, began the selection process of his victims for that school year. In his mind, he looked for a specific type of boy: one who is cute and good looking, is friendly and minimally assertive, has either no father at home or has a minimal closeness to his father, is popular with the other students, and, most important, will probably need extra help during the school year. He found five or six boys that fit these requirements each school year.

Slowly, over the next several months (no fewer than three), Jon developed a special relationship with each of the boys, independently of the others. He assigned them special jobs in the classroom, found excuses for them to stay after school, and made sure they knew that he was their friend and wanted to help them. When he felt comfortable enough with any of them, he offered them tutoring at his apartment. One of the most shocking elements of these molestations is the ease with which Jon and others like him are able to get the parents' permission for this type of activity, simply because he is a teacher—even though the parents have never met him (Jon avoided parents' nights and got away with it).

Jon's wife was a nurse and always worked the evening shift at the hospital. This gave him freedom to invite the boys over. The first session at the apartment was legitimate and very positively and supportively oriented. Jon suggested that several more sessions would be beneficial, and the boys each agreed. Jon made sure that the second or third session lasted until dinner time and then called the parents, telling them how great things were progressing and suggesting that he be allowed to take the boy to McDonald's for supper. He said that it would also be beneficial if they continued tutoring after dinner since things were going so well. If the parents sounded pleased, he then suggested that the boy be allowed to sleep over and that he would bring him to school the next day. Surprisingly, *he never had a parent refuse!*

After another half-hour or so of tutoring, Jon suggested they needed some fun and suggested card playing, which he eventually led to strip poker. He made sure to lose the first game to test the boy's reaction to nudity and, if the boy reacted with interest, laughing, etc., he made sure the boy lost the next game. Next in the well-planned scenario came Polaroid picture taking, followed by tickling when both he and the boy were nude, and mild groping. If all went well, that ended that night's adventure for Jon.

Over the next few tutoring sessions, Jon began asking questions about sex and masturbation and began to teach a sex education course, sometimes bringing his five or six chosen boys together for the first time. Jon extolled the joys and need for masturbation to become a normal, healthy man and from here on the progression was predictable: self-masturbation to mutual masturbation to contests of speed, first ejaculator, etc. All during this process, the Polaroids continued and became both security and a pressure tool to advance the deviant behavior even further to fellatio and ultimately to sodomy.

Jon's behavior went on for several years, lasting with each group of boys for only one school year. Jon felt that this practice would provide safety for him since his was the last grade in his school and the following year the boys were transferred to a junior high school across town. Each year he seduced a new group of boys (usually about five or six), and this behavior continued for ten years before he was exposed.

One day, one of his boys acted up in class and became openly defiant. Jon kept him after school and the parents then threatened to severely punish the boy for his behavior that embarrassed and shamed them. In anger and in defense, the boy related what Jon had done to him and connected it to the school punishment. Subsequently, Jon was arrested and confessed to the true number involved: between forty and sixty victims over a period of ten years.

The school authorities were shocked, as were his fellow teachers. All insisted that there "wasn't the slightest clue or hint of Jon's secret life or deviant tendencies." Part of this was due to the fact that for several years of his teaching career, Jon had been married and appeared to be the typical middle-class person in his neighborhood and at all school social functions, which he usually chaired. Jon's wife reported normal sexual behavior and a good marital relationship for the first year or so, but then his work and devotion to the school and the kids overshadowed their lives. What she did not know was that even during their sexual activities, Jon was fantasizing being with one of the young boys.

The Deception Was Almost Perfect

JON's background is quite interesting. Jon's first sexual knowledge occurred at age twelve with an older female cousin after they had been swimming. She undressed herself and Jon, had him lay on top of her, put his penis in her, and that was it. When Jon was thirteen, a male cousin, age fourteen, returned from camping and told Jon that in his cabin they had had contests to see who had the most pubic hair, and that he always won. He asked to see Jon's, and when Jon dropped his shorts, they first compared and then "he played with mine and I played with his and I liked it." Their sex play continued and progressed to mutual masturbation, then oral sex, then intercrural intercourse. Jon liked it all because "it felt good!" Jon claimed that "He showed me the attention and acceptance that I never had before from anyone." Then Jon and his family moved to a new neighborhood. "The people next door had an older boy, and my cousin and I got involved with him. They had a clubhouse, and I asked him if he had ever done anything sexual and from there we progressed to what I had done with my cousin plus mutual sodomy." This went on for a couple of years and the imprint (see Chapter 11) occurred.

During this period, Jon engaged in some petting with girls but nothing else since he "wasn't interested." He feared if he tried to go any further with a girl, she would know from his behavior (and probable failure) that he was a homosexual. In college, Jon had intercourse with a woman for the first time: "It was okay but nowhere near as enjoyable as my homosexual experiences. I felt I had to perform with girls, but with boys I never did."

Jon's masturbation continued during this time but only with homosexual fantasies. They always involved either his cousin, the boy next door, or both. In Vietnam, Jon went to the bathhouses and paid for oral sex from the prostitutes but never went any further. He wanted to have sex with many of his army friends and mates but was too afraid of exposure and rejection.

Jon married at age thirty, more out of societal pressure than desire or love. Sex was "okay" but again "never as good as the homosexual experiences."

His first molestation of a youngster occurred at the end of his first year of teaching, before he was married. At first he limited himself to fondling, but when the boy said he liked it and that he had been fellating other boys in the class (according to Jon) Jon felt this was the green light and went further. Their sexual relationship lasted from May to October and then stopped when the boy told other kids in the class and told Jon that he didn't want to do it anymore (probably due to the reaction of his peers).

Jon's marriage lasted one and a half years and ended in divorce. Six months after the divorce he returned to molesting boys, and this continued with his students for four years until he was arrested. Jon had, by then, molested over forty young male students in his charge.

Jon's inadequacy can be traced back to childhood. He never felt equal to or comfortable with peers and schoolmates until the sexual incidents. The only place he felt comfortable and accepted was when he was in a sexual situation with his male students.

Later in life, whenever he was under pressure or felt that he had failed (usually following a personal rejection), he reverted to his former inadequate self and immediately became obsessed with the sexual fantasies from the past and the need to reenact those pleasurable behaviors. He accomplished this by regressing to the age at which these experiences occurred and then looking for a playmate to have sex with. Jon vividly recalled taking some boys to an amusement park and riding all the rides with them, "feeling like I was eleven years old again—all fun, no responsibilities, someone paying the way, and free!"

This delusional regression to the child's age when everything was fun and games is quite typical of both the pedophile and the hebophile.

Update: Jon was paroled after serving three years on his total fifteen-year sentence. He readily found employment as an insurance salesmen but was unhappy with this work. Within a year, he once again returned to teaching in a two-year college where the youngest students were eighteen years old.

Jon had several homosexual liaisons while incarcerated and was now able to enjoy homosexual activity with adult males. He continued to choose males who would be known as "legal-kids" in prison. These are twenty-one-year-olds who appear much younger, often as twelve- to fourteen-year-old teens. Unfortunately, these individuals become the target of the "wolves" in prison who prey on the younger and better-looking inmates.

As of this writing, Jon is not in a long-term relationship and still lives at home with his parents.

CONTROL METHODS OF SEXUALLY ASSAULTIVE PERSONS

Where rape behavior or other forms of sexual assault are concerned, regardless of the age of the victim, the control factor is obvious. However, since in both groups sexual control is never enough and the satisfaction is so short lived, the danger is that the only ultimate and total control is murder—and this progression can and too often does take place. Many rapists I have treated confessed that as the sexually assaultive behavior progressed, the fantasies became more and more violent and eventually contained murder elements. Some sex offenders had actually reached this point prior to capture and had gotten away with one or more rape-murders that remained unsolved. These confessions become a serious moral and ethical problem for the therapist treating sex offenders and cannot be predicted by testing or any other type of screening procedure. The ways in which we have dealt with this problem will be discussed in Chapter 20.

The issue of control also becomes a serious problem in fighting therapy resistance. The sex offender is constantly in a battle with the therapist for control of the session, what is disclosed, the speed of therapy, and every other aspect of the overall treatment process. Learning to identify a particular offender's control needs and mechanisms is an important treatment consideration that needs to be addressed early in treatment.

It will be useful to look at a particular case that illustrates this type of control and its source.

BOBBY is handsome and intelligent; he was employed successfully as an engineer. His arrest for a brutal rape shocked his family, the neighborhood, his fiancée, and everyone at work and at the gym where he worked out. Everyone unanimously believed that it was a case of mistaken identity. It was not.

Bobby came from a home with a sadistically strict father and a passive, submissive mother. He had an older brother and a younger sister, with whom he got along well. For reasons never determined to this day, his father (now deceased) treated him worse than all of the other family members. Bobby's father was an alcoholic; when drunk, he became a Jekyll-and-Hyde monster. His focus always centered on Bobby, whom he beat sadistically at the slightest provocation. The extent of the sadistic treatment can be demonstrated in the following example.

Bobby had forgotten to take out the garbage before going to school. When he came home, his drunken father beat him, made him undress, put a chain on him, and tied him in one of the outdoor dog kennels (his father raised and sold pedigreed dogs). Bobby was forced to eat the same food the animals ate. He looked for help from his mother (whom he saw standing in an upstairs window looking at him with tears in her eyes), but none ever came. Out of intense fear, she did nothing to interfere with the father's sadistic treatment. His sister also watched from her bedroom window but never said a word.

This was only one of the sadistic treatments he received from his father until one day Bobby stood up to him and threatened to kill his father if he ever touched him again. From that day on, his father ignored him and never again touched Bobby.

In therapy, the focus, at first, was on his anger toward his father and anyone, including the therapist, who reminded him of his father. It took more than one and one-half years of denial before Bobby was able to even consider that his anger was more toward his mother for not protecting and defending him and that it was this anger that he projected onto his victims, nearly killing them during the rapes in uncontrollable rage.

Once this rage was thoroughly made conscious and ventilated, everyone connected to Bobby observed immediate behavioral changes. His therapeutic progress accelerated until, after another year, he was considered to be safe for return to the community.

Update: BOBBY was released on parole several years ago. He is married and has a son and another child on the way. He has returned to his former employment, having told his employer the whole story, and has been recently promoted to a supervisory position. He no longer has rape fantasies, and his wife reports that he is soft, kind, and considerate in their sexual encounters. Prognosis for Bobby remains excellent.

RAGE-TRIGGERING TECHNIQUES

For some sexually assaultive personalities, none of the standard methods of ventilating their rage are effective. Their resistance is so great that special methods must be employed to achieve this important goal.

One of the methods that we have used successfully, *Now Therapy* (discussed fully in Chapter 18), involves marathon therapy sessions and specialized badgering techniques. What occurs as a result is a regression to earlier age levels and an *actual reliving of past traumatic experiences*. This regression is frequently accompanied by hysterical conversion-reactions that result in bleeding, pain, bruises, and physical symptomology that, when examined by medical personnel, may bring a diagnoses that the trauma just occurred in the last hour or so.*

Other treatment techniques for dealing with specific aspects of the sex offender's personality will be covered fully in one of the upcoming chapters.

THE CHILD/ADOLESCENT SEX OFFENDER

Most control problems originate in childhood. It appears that trying to control their environment is a perfectly normal behavior for all children. The first problem develops when parents, out of some misguided motive, allow these control behaviors to continue and to rule their lives and the lives of other family members. Crying, screaming, temper tantrums, head banging, and breaking objects including their own toys are just a few examples of these control behaviors.

Once the child goes to school for the first time, the real problems begin. None of the enumerated behaviors will be tolerated, and the parents will constantly be sent for and clearly informed that these behaviors will not be tolerated. Now that it is too late, the parents attempt to control the child. The consequences are easily predicted.

---

*This technique is well-illustrated in an NBC TV movie (1980) titled *Rage,* based on a compilation of cases treated by this writer at the Adult Diagnostic and Treatment Center, Avenel—and strongly reminiscent of the case of Joey discussed in Chapter 13—for which I served as consultant to the writer and technical director during filming on location and in Hollywood. For other specialized techniques, the reader is referred to the chapters on treatment.

Some parents give up too quickly. I have had occasions in which a two-year-old is brought into the office and whose parents inform me, in front of the child, that "We can't handle him." This surrender is exactly what the child wants, and trying to treat these children too often requires removal from the home since that is where the real problem is.

The second problem involves adolescents. Too often, parents inform me that "he was such a good child; never gave us problems until now." In these cases, it is the transition into adolescence, when the child was never adequately prepared for it, that triggers the control-behaviors. During this stage, the child who previously wanted acceptance and approval from his parents no longer wants it, but now wants approval and acceptance from his peers. Identity is critical during this stage of development. If the child cannot handle the pressures of adolescence, development or affirmation of his inadequate personality is assured. He becomes a follower and often a slave to a more assertive, more adequate adolescent (idolized), and family-taught values are replaced with the values of the leader or idol. Drinking, smoking, drugs, sex, and other antisocial behaviors suddenly begin for this individual, and parents are shocked and bewildered when (and if) they discover what their wonderful child has become. The war between teen and parents begins. Some parents go into denial and simply do not want to know about any problems until some illegal behavior is caught or some other personal disaster (car accidents, unplanned pregnancy, drug reaction hospitalization, etc.) occurs. Other parents, when these problems emerge or are discovered, hopefully go looking for help. That is where the therapist enters the picture.

Most teenage sex offenders I have worked with fall into the first category, where parents do not want to know or are not involved enough in the lives of their teens. Exposure and/or apprehension becomes the "first time I knew about it" and the "We were so terribly shocked and unbelieving."

There is a middle road in the control problems that parents will endure with children and teenagers. Allow them sufficient autonomy and independence to develop and mature but not to the point where all parental authority is abdicated. This should apply, in particular, to demands for unlimited privacy regarding friends, after-school activities, telephone and computer e-mail or chat room contacts, smoking and drug use, and alcohol use.

Amazingly, buying a teenager a car before he has matured and proven himself responsible is a major factor in antisocial contacts and behaviors.

In summary, today's parental permissiveness and abdication of authority over their children and teenagers are major contributors to the problems we are seeing with law-breaking, alcoholic, addicted, and sexually deviant children and teenagers.

Most of the traumas uncovered in sex offender therapy occurred during the offender's childhood years. Traumas have been discovered that occurred during the teen years, but this is relatively rare.

Here again, parenting usually is the cause/problem in the trauma. If, when these traumas occurred, the child was referred to a qualified therapist and the trauma was openly discussed before it became repressed, the effect, if any, would be minimal and easily handled in treatment.

Chapter 5

Pervasive Guilt and Subjective Judgment

If one were to state that *guilt is the most destructive force in the universe,* it would be especially true when referring to the pervasive guilt of the sex offender. Differentiating between guilt and responsibility remains an important distinction in sex offender therapy that is often overlooked when dealing with resistance to change and/or "letting go" problems.

The guilt of the sex offender is not only exaggerated in degree but also is attributed to a range of actions from the immediate offense all the way back to being born. Not infrequently have we heard memories of childhood that contained hurtful parents' remarks that were never forgotten. These damaging and imprinting remarks can be placed under the most damaging statement of all: "I wish you had never been born!"

Almost equal in frequency is the memory of hearing parents discuss their problems with the child and admitting that he had not been a planned child but an "accident" that either one or both parents regretted. With his inadequate personality, a weak and defective ego structure, and his already negative self-image, either type of statement is devastating to the child. Even if the event is repressed, the effects are the same, providing all the more reason for the child to hate himself and to feel exaggerated guilt for the slightest failure, misbehavior, or disappointment he inflicts upon his already rejecting parents.

Once learned and internalized, the offender uses the same ruler on himself through adolescence and into adulthood. Whatever he tries, he already has two strikes against him; considering his fear of failure, it is easy to see how all he can remember is failure after failure. Even an acknowledged success is mitigated by these feelings and cannot possibly balance the already overloaded scales of negative factors that he has accumulated over the years. Finding ways for him to succeed and accept the positive rewards for his success is a long and difficult task, not only for the therapist but also for the treatment team.

Since this guilt is pervasive, it affects every aspect of his existence: cognitive and behavioral, physical and athletic, educational and artistic, social and personal, moral and religious. Thus, a holistic approach in the treatment planning is needed (see Chapter 15).

RUDY, whom I will discuss more fully later in this chapter, when ten or eleven years of age, slept in a bedroom next to his parents' bedroom. Unbeknownst to his parents (or they did not care), Rudy could hear everything that went on, especially when his parents were fighting or having extremely loud sex. He often masturbated during these latter times with fantasies of having sex with his mother.

One night, he awoke to one of his parents' regular Friday night arguments. He leaned over toward the adjoining wall to listen and soon realized that they were discussing him, specifically a meeting his mother had at his school with his teacher, the principal, and the guidance counselor. Apparently, from what he could glean, he was considered a severely emotionally disturbed child, and they were discussing putting him in a boys' school.

His father's reaction shocked Rudy. He heard him say, "If only that damned rubber didn't break, we wouldn't be going through all these problems. I told you you should have had an abortion."

Needless to say, Rudy was shocked, angry, and depressed, all at the same time. From that day on, he withdrew from the world and created a world of his own. His catatonic-schizophrenia was born.

RULERS AND SUBJECTIVE JUDGMENT MEMORIES

One of the traits that is most resistant to change and that can be found in all sex offenders is the *use of two rulers:* one from the past (usually belonging to or learned from one of their parents or another authority figure) and one from the present (their own adult self). I call these "subjective judgment memories," and they always produce an irrational form of guilt. Box 5.1 presents a summary of the factors involved in this phenomenon.

Hypocritically, sex offenders continue for years on end to use their personal ruler on friends, associates, and even strangers that they do not particularly like. However, in all judgmental instances where they evaluate or analyze their own behavior, thinking, or personality, they use the ruler from childhood that is at least twice as large and demanding: the subjective judgment ruler.

5.1

Unresolved Guilt Problems and Their Consequences: Subjective Judgment Memories

- Subjective judgment memory: a value judgment about a past behavior based on parental or authority values (rulers) that are not the values of the present child/adult.
- Perfectionism develops—failure is assured.
- Self-punishing behavior results and affects motivation.
- Severe guilt persists and affects all aspects of life.
- The same behavior in others is considered acceptable.

A good example of how subjective rulers work can be found in Chapter 2, where I discussed the inadequate personality structure of the sex offender. It was stated that if the individual scored a 90 percent in a test and this was the highest score in the classroom, it would still "not be good enough." When praised for the accomplishment, the response would be something such as: "It should have been 100 percent." The problem, however, is that a score of 100 percent would elicit the response that: "The test was too easy." In this no-win situation, the sex offender appears driven to see himself in a negative light and refuses to permit a positive interpretation or evaluation of his works or actions. If, however, a classmate and friend of his scored only a 75 percent, he would immediately come to the classmate's defense, tell him the test was unfair, tell him he would help him prepare for the next test, and so on.

In interviewing and treating these individuals, the common theme of parents who could never be satisfied occurred over and over. No matter how hard he tried—and try he did—there was never any praise or reward for the child, and since acceptance and love were dependent on pleasing the parent(s), hurt, rejection, and ultimately self-blame occurred.

In discussing this with one twenty-seven-year-old male offender (incarcerated for a series of some fifty to sixty rapes before he was caught) Kevin stated, "It would be difficult to give up their [parents'] rulers if I felt doing so would cause me to lose them and end up feeling alone." When Kevin was asked how this translated into later life, he replied, "I'll only be loved and accepted if I am what he [the father] wants me to be. In other words, if I live by his rulers. This didn't just apply to my father, it applied to every relationship I ever had until recently and even [in] the recent ones, it's there in certain areas—most important the emotional ones." Here, as in other areas already discussed and areas yet to come, insight is excellent but no change occurs.

Throughout these discussions, the "inadequacy of insight" as a solitary goal in sex offender treatment will be stressed continually. Although it does answer many questions for the offender and explains much of the causality of the behaviors, *insight alone has never, in my experience, produced a single change.* This is quite a strong and potentially controversial statement that will need to be demonstrated over and over again, in case after case.

Another factor associated with using the two rulers is that of resulting perfectionism. As the child who earned the 100-percent grade on a test was dissatisfied, feeling that he should have done more, the offender feels this dissatisfaction about everything he does. A major treatment objective is to change the negative self-image of the sex offender. His trend toward perfectionism, however, prevents this goal from being achieved. Rational or cognitive methods fail in this endeavor, and it becomes apparent quite early in therapy that only the offender himself can change this condition by utter destruction of the parent-imposed ruler.

The irrationality and illogic of this condition needs further clarification by way of an example.

Todd's Big Secret and His Use of His Ruler

After many years of both group and individual therapy, TODD (serving thirty years for a very brutal and sadistic rape), with a great deal of hesitation and obvious pain, related to his group (fifteen mixed offender types) that during his very lonely and isolated early adolescent years, he had first masturbated his dog and then eventually taught the dog to mount and sodomize him. As happens in groups of this type who have been together for many years, several other group members (six or seven) admitted to similar sexual experiences with their dogs. Following their confessions, there was a great deal of emotional release with what appeared to the therapist to result in a successful session with much gained by all.

Todd had appeared calm, talked openly about his feelings, and expressed appropriate empathy and compassion for his fellow group members who had also "confessed" to this terrible sin. That evening, however, in an emergency individual therapy session that he requested, Todd told me that he still felt that what he had done was "sick, disgusting, unforgivable, sinful, and rotten."

Nothing I tried worked, and although Todd was happy for the others who had obviously gained from the experience, his guilt had increased. He then decided that he would quit therapy and finish the twenty months he had to do on his sentence. No matter what approach was tried by several therapists and all of his friends, both in and out of the group, he never returned to therapy. A short six months following his release, he was caught in the act of attempting to rape a handicapped woman in her home and is now serving a heavy sentence in one of the state's prisons, not in the treatment center.

Todd is only one of many failures in which the therapist was unable to break/replace the original ruler, although the offender's own ruler that is used on everyone else, but never on himself, is positive and forgiving.

Mark

MARK, another rapist in Todd's group, after many years of therapy (approximately twelve) and after hearing another group member discuss his ruler problem, requested an individual session. After much hemming and hawing and a great deal of obvious distress, he stated that in all the years of his therapy he had hidden one deep, dark secret that was producing a large amount of irreconcilable guilt. After much encouragement, he told the therapist the following.

From about the age of eleven or twelve, he began peeping on his mother either when she was undressing or when she was in the bathroom. He would become sexually aroused and masturbate, either on the spot or back in his room. As the peeping episodes increased, he developed the fantasy of having intercourse with his mother, and in the fantasy, they both enjoyed the experience. Eventually, in these fantasies, he would replace his father in her life and especially in her bed.

The guilt from this experience had never been resolved and, even in the present time frame, when very lonely and/or depressed, he would revert to this forbidden fantasy, masturbate, and then experience incredible guilt for weeks at a time, even to the degree of contemplating suicide. When he recovered emotionally to some extent, he was asked when he felt he could discuss this in his group and, as with Todd, his reply was that he would rather max out (complete his sentence) without therapy (some fifteen more years).

The astonishing thing about Mark's reaction was that in his group there were several other individuals who had "confessed" to the same or similar fantasies. His best friend in the institution had actually been involved sexually with his mother for several years during his adolescence and later adult, married life. Mark saw no problem with understanding, accepting, sympathizing, and being compassionate with his friend and never considered becoming judgmental with him or dissolving their relationship. Where his peeping/fantasy behavior was concerned, it was judgmentally labeled "perverted, disgusting, unforgivable, and sure to result in condemnation and rejection by the group" (the irrational thinking of individuals with subjective-judgment problems). As with Todd, there were obviously two rulers, one from someone (possibly his older brother) who had reacted with disgust and accusations of perversion when Mark told him about his fantasies. The second ruler was his own adult, empathetic, and forgiving value regarding sexual misbehavior.

When a sex offender verbalizes these contradictory, irrational values and concepts at the same time in the same conversation, and agrees that it does not make sense, the depth and extent of the problem and be easily seen. Where Mark was concerned, a year of intense individual therapy followed this confession with absolutely no change in behavior, attitude, or value system. The original parent-child instilled ruler remained intact.

Kevin

Where Kevin (mentioned several times earlier) was concerned, his dual desire to be a girl and have sex with his father (he had witnessed his father and his sister having sex) resulted in a ruler (source unknown) that measured him to be a "pervert, unnatural, sinful, bad," etc. The resulting guilt remained from age six or seven, when all of this began, until his present age of twenty-seven, with, if anything, an increase in degree rather than any decrease or resolution.

Kevin used these memories to punish himself whenever he did not live up to one of his many perfectionistic standards. In contrast to the other cases mentioned, he brought his secret to group "to cause rejection and degradation," which never occurred. In his mind, however, he would read into group members' facial expressions or using his own "crystal ball" would put feelings and thoughts into the group members' minds and actions toward him that absolutely did not exist. This continued for over ten years of treatment and only recently has begun to be resolved to a limited extent.

The Empty-Chair Method

I use a method called the "empty-chair technique" to determine the existence of subjective-judgment memories and a dual-ruler problem. During either an individual or group session, I place an empty chair next to the individual that I suspect of having this problem. I then ask him to be the therapist for an imaginary patient (the age he was when the parental ruler was born) I am treating in my home office and who is sitting in that empty chair.

I next describe a scenario as close as possible (but never exact) to the individual in question's secret or subjectively unacceptable behavior. Next, I ask the individual playing therapist to counsel "this poor kid who hates himself, is feeling severe guilt, and is experiencing depression and social maladjustment because of what he had done or thought."

Amazingly, every time I have used this technique on a sex offender with this suspected syndrome, whether in my home office or in a correctional setting, the results are the same. The offender does amazingly, counseling the kid in the empty chair as well if not better than some professional therapists would. His adult rulers kick in, and his empathy and understanding of the specific type of problem produce these positive results. This technique lays the groundwork to begin the value-change necessary if this offender is to change and succeed.

I have actually used an ex-offender in my home office to help me with a difficult teenager who went through very similar abuse and circumstances as the ex-offender. The results have always been terrific. Just knowing that someone else who is not a therapist understands and can forgive has indescribable results. (*Note:* This is the rationale behind paraprofessional groups as well as self-help groups and should be utilized wherever possible in treating sex offenders, in or out of correctional settings and regardless of age.)

GUILT AS A BLOCK TO THERAPEUTIC PROGRESS

It is safe to state that *guilt prevents any permanent or meaningful therapeutic progress,* since progress would be an ego-positive and self-esteem-enhancing occurrence. The individual with pervasive guilt feels that he does not deserve success of any kind nor should he behave in a way that would be seen by others as well as himself as positive. Until the guilt is permanently identified, ventilated, and (most important) *let go,* the client will not permit positive feedback from anyone including himself. If the therapist errs, at this point, the results can be disastrous.

RUDY arrived at the treatment center in a state of remission from a severe catatonic-schizophrenic episode (manifested by mannequin-like poses and behavior when frightened). The other offenders were very supportive and made Rudy feel safe and comfortable. Little by little, Rudy began to make friends and, after more than eight months of therapy, began to say a few words during his primary group. He even took the floor one time and did well for a first experience.

From one of his friends, it was learned that he had some background in electronics and that he was interested in working in the video studio complex that I supervised. After some time (almost a year), he became really good at editing videotape, a difficult and tedious task. Believing it would be a positive reinforcement, I went out of my way to meet Rudy in the control booth where he worked and to compliment him on what a terrific job he was doing. I said, "Keep this up and someday you could be the head of the studio complex!" Rudy said nothing and simply continued to do his work.

The following morning when I arrived at work, I was informed that there had been a problem in the main studio control booth. When I entered the booth, I was informed that there had been some $5,000 worth of damage done to the videotape recorders. Someone had deliberately destroyed the recording heads and put the equipment out of alignment (a very serious and costly repair problem). Rudy arrived at work on time, and when asked what he knew about the damage, he confessed to being the culprit, without explanation. As he was being led away to lock up (punishment cells), he stopped, turned around, and said to me, "Now tell me how good I'm doing and what a great studio director I would make!"

Needless to say, I learned an important and quite expensive lesson. Positive feedback, while the client is still in his negative self-image stance, especially when guilt is the cause, will produce poor to tragic results, including regressive behaviors and even suicide attempts. There are also times when a client will quit therapy due to positive feedback occurring too soon or too strongly while he feels undeserving. It is therefore essential to carefully evaluate the progress a client is making and to assess exactly where he is at any given point in his therapy before taking the risk of making any positive comments. A safer method is to ask the offender his evaluation of his progress or of some behavior that the therapist feels merits praise.

This is also not the time to insist on risk-taking behaviors. All concentration must be focused on the source of the guilt and its elimination to a degree that makes positive feedback palatable. Thus, once again, this demonstrates the importance of the need to "assess readiness."

The subjective judgment phenomenon is a constant and persistent barrier to letting go of either the past or present guilt that sex offenders, such as Mark and Kevin, experience and that prevents them from progressing in therapy. Quite often, with compulsive sex offenders, when progress appears to be impeded and no visible or current explanation exists, the phenomenon of subjective judgment memories may be (and usually is) the problem.

"Subjective judgment" here refers to a judgment based on a personal value reaction which, in turn, is based on a value learned somewhere from birth to the time of the occurrence. The distinguishing characteristic of these judgments is that they do not apply to anyone else, only to the individual himself.

The sources of these learned value systems include parents, relatives, school, religion, law, TV/movies, and any other childhood influence. Then, in adolescence, the source becomes the individual's peers.

Basically, what appears to occur in this phenomenon is that the adult, remembering an event or traumatic occurrence, is unable to separate his present value system from that of the child who, at a specific age, experienced the event or traumatic occurrence and then reacted to it judgmentally, usually in a negative manner. An example that clearly demonstrates this phenomenon follows.

Harry and the Elephant

HARRY is a twenty-nine-year-old violent rapist, highly motivated for therapeutic involvement and change. During his first interview and subsequently in one of his first group therapy sessions with fifteen other offenders, he was able to openly discuss the offense for which he was incarcerated.

Late one evening, in a popular park in his hometown, Harry hid in wait and eventually grabbed a female jogger, pulling her into the brush. He viciously beat her while calling her every derogatory and filthy name he could think of, then ripped off her clothing and violently raped her, trying to hurt her as much as he could with his penis. Unsatisfied after his orgasm and continuing to deride and humiliate her, he then sodomized her, again trying to inflict as much pain with his penis-weapon as possible. Following his second orgasm and still unsatisfied, he sat on her chest and made her lick the feces from his penis while continuing his verbal onslaught. Only then did he feel he had accomplished his goal and quickly left. The woman passed into unconsciousness and, when found the next morning, needed to be hospitalized.

Following medical treatment for a week or more, she was transferred to a private psychiatric facility where she remains in treatment to this day.

Harry was able, although with some shame and guilt, to relate this story without apparent fear of rejection from his peers. Therapy for Harry progressed at a steady rate, but the primary therapist assigned to the case continued to feel that there was something wrong in the speed of Harry's progress. Harry, during the next five or six years, continued to grow and mature but never seemed *quite* ready for release to the community as safe.

In his sixth year of therapy, Harry requested an individual interview with his therapist and quite sheepishly and ashamedly stated that he had not been fair to the therapist since he had hidden a secret. He then went on, head down, to relate the following. One summer, when Harry was eleven years old, he spent the summer working with an uncle who was a zookeeper. Very lonely and having no friends to play with, he became friends with a male pygmy elephant that he cleaned and cared for. He spent all of his free time grooming and talking to the elephant. One day, in an aroused sexual state, he began to masturbate. The elephant watched and then came over and began to fondle Harry's genitals with his trunk. Harry noticed that the elephant had an erection and, on impulse, reached down and masturbated the elephant.

As his story ended, Harry was crying and hiding his face with his hands. The therapist then asked why he felt this badly about something that had happened eighteen years before, and Harry vehemently stated, "That was the dirtiest, filthiest, sickest, and most disgusting thing that anyone could possibly do."

The therapist then asked when Harry planned to bring this story to his group. Harry responded angrily, almost shouting, that he would never tell this story to anyone else, ever again. If that meant his doing the rest of his sentence (fourteen years remaining), he would refuse further therapy and do the fourteen years.

It appears unreasonable to believe that the twenty-nine-year-old adult who was able to relate the story of the violent and vicious rape would have a value system that would not allow him to face his peers with the story of an event that occurred when he was eleven years old. To confirm this hypothesis, Harry was asked to imagine being in group and hearing this story told by his closest friend, Bob. When asked how he would react and what he would say to Bob or feel about what Bob had done, Harry became his usual sensitive, empathetic self, stating he would have felt sorry for the young boy who was that lonely and desperate. In regard to the adult Bob, it would make no difference in their friendship nor would he feel any of the disgust he felt about his own eleven-year-old self.

What appears to occur in these instances is a *dual value system*, one that existed at the time of the event/trauma and one that exists today in the now adult person. As is true in other areas with sex offenders, the inability to let go occurs here as well.

When a disguised version of the story was told in his group the following week, more than 90 percent of the group admitted by a show of hands that they also were hiding a subjective judgment memory, but not one of them would share the memory with group members. Several wrote to the therapist and offered to relate the memory privately, as long as it would remain confidential from their peer group.

Several more groups were surveyed with the same result, including an aftercare group of released offenders in the community. Here again, although not one of them would share the memory in a group setting, several volunteered, *in fact requested* to discuss the memory in private with the therapist, as long as they were given the assurance that no one would ever find out.

The range of these subjective judgment memories appears unlimited and includes

- masturbation fantasies of sex with mothers,
- religiously prohibited behaviors,
- large amounts of bestiality,
- involvement with urine and feces, and
- murder.

Here, again, as in other areas of the sex offender personality, this information would never come to light unless the therapist, in some directive fashion, asks the right questions or suggests the importance of the child maintaining control of the adult's mind.

JUDGMENT VERSUS CURIOSITY

When dealing with the subjective judgment memories phenomenon, a new theory/hypothesis became necessary. As in all other areas involving treatment of the repetitive compulsive sex offender, a concrete and graphic method and/or explanation had to be used. In dealing with this problem, it was postulated that *self-judgment stops all therapeutic progress* (see Box 5.2).

Thus, whenever a client (sex offender or survivor) goes into a judgmental mode, it is easy to see why little or no therapeutic progress oc-

5.2

Consequences of Judgmentalism
in Assessing Events of One's Past Life

1. Guilt and the attending emotions
2. Feelings of being
   - inferior
   - different
   - sick/perverted
   - abnormal
   - relationally unacceptable
3. Isolation
4. Distrust of self and others
5. Fear of rejection
6. Depression (from mild to suicidal)
7. Activation of the classic defense mechanisms, especially denial, minimization, projection, externalization, and, if the trauma is severe enough, repression

curs, even after several years. In my experience, I have had sex offenders in this mode for as many as twelve years, especially when an unrevealed subjective judgment memory was involved. The therapist, with either the offender or the victim, must stop this practice as early in the treatment process as possible. In contrast, *curiosity* or the "I wonder why?" approach opens all doors to therapeutic progress on a very rapid and ego-satisfying level.

In order for the curiosity approach to work, the patient must be taught "distancing" techniques. The simplest method of accomplishing this is to promulgate and insist on the "I'm no longer that person" perception. An easy method that has worked successfully for me, both with adults and children, is to use a different name for the child who experienced the trauma. It is best to ask the patient the nickname he was given by parents and friends and answered to as a child (Billy for Bill, Red for John, etc.). If he still uses that nickname, then the client is asked to pick a name he now feels suits the child he was or one that he always liked and wished were his. When this is done, the chosen name often reveals a great deal about how the patient feels about his past self. Names such as "The Jerk," "The Fuck Up," "Stinky," "Thing," "Fatso," and other derogatory choices all reflect the persistence of negative feelings about the child within. In the "Now" technique (see Chapter 18), the patient refers to the person in the mirror as *you* rather than *I* to effect this necessary distancing. Once distancing is effected, the patient can (1) become more objective, analytical, or empathetic, or make connections to developmental behavior or to present problem focus, *or* (2) effect a "makes sense" conclusion.

THE CHILD/ADOLESCENT SEX OFFENDER

Again, the topic of this chapter refers to a child's identity and value choices. As with most children, values are learned from parents, siblings, relatives, and others in his immediate world such as teachers, fellow students, police officers, priests, and ministers.

Naturally, the most influential and important value-source are parents. A child's normal insecurity and need to be wanted, loved, and cared for are the primary reason for the child to adopt parental values. In his mind, "Pleasing parents provides security."

Independence and self-actualization occur much later for the normal child and may never develop for the inadequate personality without professional intervention (i.e., specialized treatment).

In all of the cases presented so far, parents and siblings were the source of the offenders' value choices. Sex offenders notoriously respond to a test item asking "I want to be like . . ." by answering with "my father" or "my big brother" or some other individual they idolized as a child or adolescent. I have never seen a response indicating a desire to be like himself or a better and more successful self. In response to a test item asking "I see myself as a . . ." the responses are 95 percent negative and derisive: fuck up, failure, piece of shit (the most common response), worthless, a disappointment to my parents, below all my friends, unloved, unwanted, friendless, etc. Positive responses to this item are rare or nonexistent from sex offenders.

All of these feelings, thoughts, and self-perceptions result from guilt, real or implanted there by others. In most of the cases presented thus far, this guilt involved who the child was as perceived by others, especially the *never-satisfied parent(s)*. For a significant percentage of sex offenders, the guilt results from committing some "unpardonable sin." Although he was taught that a specific behavior (e.g., masturbation) was wrong, dirty, sinful, etc., he was never taught how to deal with the resultant guilt or how to "let-go" of the past. Dennis and other examples still to be presented will clarify this type of "letting-go" problem.

From the previous discussion, it should be clear to anyone that *guilt is the most destructive force in the universe.*

Chapter 6

Relational Issues

PASSIVE AND AGGRESSIVE PERSONALITIES

The next characteristic to consider in our long list is the sex offender's inability to be assertive. He remains and has been for most of his life either "passive" or "aggressive."

Whenever I do training with teachers and school administrators on this subject, I ask the fifth grade teacher in the audience to raise her or his hand, and then I ask the teacher to think about two boys in his or her classroom who never play or associate with their classmates (peers). I then suggest that one will go to the third grade boys, where he will become the "leader" since he is older, stronger, appears to know more, and can easily control third graders. This is the "deny-er." The other boy goes to seventh and eighth graders where he becomes the "mascot." He never has to compete with them but can become the batboy or locker room towel boy and receive protection, acceptance, travel with the teams, even wear the letter of the team, yet has to give little or nothing in return. This is the "accept-er." The teachers are able to immediately think of the boys in their class who fit these descriptions.

Most sex offenders fall into one of these two categories: accept-ers or deny-ers. What appears to happen is the basis for the theoretical framework upon which our treatment techniques are founded: As children, sex offenders appear to have been basically inadequate personalities as described in Chapter 2. Part of this lifelong adjustment pattern is a fear of any emotionally laden situation, especially if confrontation is a part of it. The overall effect is either a totally *passive* (wimpy) manner in dealing with everyone, especially authority figures or peers from whom they perceived threat/danger, or a totally *aggressive* manner in dealing with situations. The aggression can either be verbal or physical, or often both. It is easy to see, then, how the former go to children with whom they feel safe and in control. The latter use aggression on everyone to constantly maintain control.

"Control" then becomes a major issue in all dealings with sex offenders, as we saw in Chapter 4 with the case of Bobby. Whether the control is used by the deny-er or the accept-er, it will always be there, and it must work in order for any satisfaction from the behavior to be realized. Even the flasher (exhibitionist) exerts control in his act. Try not to look when he flashes; it is literally impossible. Once the intended victim does look, a smile covers his face that says "Gotcha!"

For pedophiles and hebophiles, getting the child to cooperate in the seduction, no matter how minor, provides the same control-produced satisfaction. Remember Howie (whose case is discussed in Chapters 2 and 7), the compulsive pedophile who was so frightened that he never actually touched his victims? Howie's control came from the fact that, without saying a word, his smile alone told the children what pleased him and how they could get his acceptance. He was able to get them to pose nude and also to pose nude with erections, although he had never asked them to or discussed sex with them. He was a master manipulator who with a smile and a "My, my!" or "Wonderful!" was able to teach the boys what he wanted and how they could get invited on another weekend camping trip. Not only did this satisfy Howie's control needs but also assuaged his highly punitive conscience. He easily rationalized that "the boys were only doing what they wanted to and posed in the manner they chose."

Thus, Howie excused himself from all responsibility and guilt. Throughout his interrupted treatment, he never actually accepted blame or guilt for what he had done, nor did he ever agree that his behavior was damaging to the children.

In sexually assaultive behavior, the control elements are more than obvious and are often more important than the sexual gratification. In fact, there have been many cases of attempted rape in which, once the submission and total control are accomplished, the sexually assaultive person (SAP) leaves and does not complete the rape itself.

More Evidence of the Importance of the Control Issue

Harry, a violent rapist (whose case was discussed in Chapter 5), needed "absolute control" in order to achieve any satisfaction from his rapes. If he suspected that the victim was enjoying the act (pelvic movement, moans, etc.) or that he was not producing enough pain, he would perform other acts that he knew would cause pain. When he was finished, his last sadistic act was to force the victim to say that she enjoyed what he had done and that he was a great lover (under threat of further violence and/or harm).

Bobby (see Chapter 4), on the other hand, could stop himself from going any farther once he felt in complete control. Once he had the victim undressed and he was exposed and erect and felt that he had achieved the control element in the rape, he would tell the victim to get dressed and he would run away. If, at that point, he did not feel that control had been reached, he would complete the rape. If after the rape, he *still* did not feel that control had been reached, he would do something more until he reached that point of absolute control.

Each sex offender develops his own control method. These methods are as varied and different as are the offenders themselves. Pedophiles, for example, feel absolute control when they manipulate the child into initiating the sex, at least one time, with no hint or suggestion from the offender. To them, this equals conquest and proves their superiority and mastery over the victim. As additional examples are presented, this control need, especially in the relationships of the offender, will be clearly seen, regardless of the issue being discussed.

SEVERELY IMPAIRED
INTERPERSONAL RELATIONSHIPS

An often-missed characteristic of the repetitive compulsive sex offender is that although he may and often does appear to be quite a sociable person, the fact is that he relates only on a *surface level*. He never really becomes intimate or involved with anyone, even his wife or closest friend. His inability to trust and/or to become vulnerable persists throughout his life, especially if he was sexually molested or traumatized as a child and never resolved it. Although he desperately wants acceptance and closeness, he is unwilling to risk being hurt and thus maintains a distance in all his relationships. Should the other person involved appear to be getting too close, he will push the person away in any manner he can, even to the point of deliberately destroying the relationship. *Safety* becomes paramount in all of his dealings with other people, and he will choose loneliness rather than risk any further chance of being hurt, betrayed, or rejected—the fears that control his behavior daily.

It is easy to see, therefore, why the repetitive compulsive sex offender becomes involved with so many victims. Pedophiles and hebophiles rarely have only one victim. Here, as in his adult relationships, the fears remain and, as soon as he feels himself getting too close, he pushes away and rejects before being rejected.

Frequently, due to this fear of vulnerability, the repetitive compulsive sex offender will say that no matter how hard he tries in a relationship, he gets rejected. It often takes quite a long time to get him to see that in some subtle way he destroyed the relationship.

KEVIN (whose case is discussed in Chapters 3 and 5) has gone through this cycle literally hundreds of times. In each instance, he truly and sincerely wants the relationship to succeed and all starts out well. Then, in an almost paranoidal cycle, he begins to set the other person up by putting expectations and demands on the individual that no one would allow. A single missed phone call, an item missing in a gift package, a disagreement over even the most trivial factor, and the process begins. A record of these occurrences is kept, and each one adds to the proof that either the individual is not sincere with him or in some way plans to use him. It is impossible to show Kevin that in reality it is he who is using the other person or that his expectations are unrealistic and/or inappropriate. Unconsciously, Kevin wants to believe the worst since only separation or loss of the relationship will bring him back to his needed state of safety. The pain, hurt, and sorrow he feels when the relationship ends and the resulting loneliness are prices he is willing to pay (or so he says). Until he no longer is willing to pay so high a price, no change will occur.

THE SEX OFFENDER'S INABILITY
TO RELATE TO PEERS

As early as the lower grades of grammar school, this factor can be detected and a referral made before it is too late. The inadequate personality that may or may not evolve into a sex offender personality cannot, even at very early ages, relate to his peer group. As stated, what usually occurs is that he becomes either a leader or mascot in relation to other children in his younger years and to adults as he grows older. Which type he becomes is dependent on his ego strength, his self-esteem, and his ability to deal with his inadequacy.

For both types of children, this coping mechanism works through grammar school and before puberty. Once puberty is reached and the all-important psychological shifts occur, especially that of wanting to please peers rather than wanting to please adults, a crisis occurs that changes and affects the remainder of his life, if not detected and treated. Being *different* now becomes his primary preoccupation, and the negative judgments occur in rapid succession. Selective perception runs rampant.

DENNIS (an accept-er) has never felt that he was like other children his age, beginning at his earliest memory at age five to six. No reasons can be elicited from Dennis, but if pushed he will use terms such as "sissy, fraidy cat, nerd, weirdo, etc.," while looking at the floor and being obviously upset and appearing depressed. When he entered grammar school, the situation worsened, and he became both an object of ridicule and a punching bag for the older boys. He increased his isolation, running home immediately after school or watching other children play from a safe distance.

High school and the onset of puberty produced depression close to suicidal levels. He literally stuck out like a sore thumb, simply attending school, sitting in the back of the room, never volunteering to answer questions, and if selected by the teacher to participate, standing, head down and silent until released. College produced changes in that he was accepted in a fraternity where he became a slave to his fraternity brothers and an even greater object of laughter and ridicule. One evening, as the brothers were drinking beer on the fraternity house porch, the fraternity president, drunk and in a nasty mood, walked over to Dennis, unzipped and urinated on him as the other brothers laughed hysterically. Dennis sat there through the incident, saying nothing and feeling that this was a price he must pay for his membership in the fraternity since he certainly did not deserve it. Being used as a chauffeur, lending money that was never returned, doing laundry, buying tickets for sports events, paying checks at restaurants, etc., all continued as payments for their acceptance.

After a year or more of therapy, Dennis could admit to the reality of his being used and that these were not his true friends, but retorted, "If I give this up, there will be nothing and no one in my life! It's better than nothing!"

Until Dennis's self-image and self-esteem improve, his life will remain the same, that of a true nerd and wimp, being taken advantage of by anyone who offers the illusion of being his friend. Guilt prevents any change from occurring, and to date, we have been unable to uncover the source of the guilt.

KEN (a deny-er), on the other hand, was a sociable, popular child from his earliest years and the favorite of both his parents. From his first days at school, he was popular and liked by his peers, the teachers, and the staff as well. He was always a success at anything he did and appeared quite happy in his life. At age fourteen, he committed his first rape but convinced the victim that no one would believe her since she was unpopular and not really liked by anyone. She agreed and left the school instead.

The rapes continued until he was finally caught and sent to the treatment unit at age thirty-one. Again, the pattern continued: he became a leader in everything, including his therapy group, was the most popular man in the unit, was given the best and most trusted job in the institution, and prospered. Within two years (of a thirty-year indeterminate sentence), he earned entrance into the parole process. This meant that he was approved and recommended by his primary therapist, a group of therapists serving as an examining board, and a civilian review board from the community, all before even seeing the State Parole Board, who also unanimously approved his parole.

Fewer than four months back in the community, he visited me one night in the hospital where I was undergoing some tests for a possible ulcer (a perk of prison work!) and asked me for a recommendation to graduate school where he hoped to become a psychologist and work with children of sexual abuse. I was thrilled and happily signed the forms.

At the end of visiting hours he left, promising to see me the following week. Driving out of the parking lot with a large number of other visitors, Ken was behind a pretty young lady in a convertible and, without thought or planning, followed her a short distance as she drove behind an apartment complex into her garage. When she shut the engine of her car off, Ken entered the convertible, robbed her of her jewelry, and raped her.

All of this occurred fewer than thirty minutes after his visit to my room. It should also be noted that he was engaged to be married at the time. In less than an hour, I was awakened by a supervising nurse and informed that two local detectives wanted to see me. They told me what happened and then related that after the rape, Ken walked down a main highway toward the police station. Ken knew where he was and where the police station was located. He easily could have gotten away by driving in the opposite direction toward a major interstate highway since the victim had not seen his car. Once back in the treatment unit as a parole violator waiting for his new rape charge to be processed, Ken, crying and depressed, finally told me that he had never believed that other people really knew who he was or liked the real Ken, only the social image he portrayed and the actor he had been all of his life. The reasons for Ken's self-hatred were never uncovered, and after a few months and his new sentence, he again became the actor.

A therapist who specialized in classical behavior modification techniques took over the case (I withdrew since I had been completely fooled the first time) and within a short period of time Ken was once again paroled as "cured." This time, the therapy for his *rape problem* worked.

THE DANGERS OF SYMPTOM REMOVAL

As a result of Ken's behavior, we quickly learned the dangers of "symptom removal." In just under six months, Ken was rearrested and is now serving a life sentence for conspiracy to murder his wealthy uncle, whom he felt was humiliating, berating, and depriving his mother of her true inheritance (his own delusions, according to his mother).

Deny-ers are the most difficult type of sex offender to work with and to assess for real or true change. Although Ken was a very dramatic failure, he was only one of many of this type for whom therapy was never effective until new techniques were finally developed that do work with deny-ers. These techniques are discussed in Chapters 9 through 19 inclusive.

REPRESSION AND TRAUMA-INDUCED COMPULSION

Many of the sex offenders that we have treated complain of a "driving compulsion" that, no matter what they try, will not cease.

DENNIS arrived at the office for his first interview, visibly upset, depressed, and close to suicide. He could not look the therapist in the eye and related that he could no longer endure living with his problem. Slowly, the following compulsion was described: Dennis goes out looking for young boys with their shirts off and with a slightly protruding stomach. The boy also must be thin, inadequate looking, and weaker than the other boys he is with. He then fantasizes that one of the other boys is punching the weaker boy in the stomach and this gives Dennis an erection. Dennis then quickly rushes home to his bedroom and "fucks a towel" with the fantasy getting more and more violent. Following his orgasm, he becomes grossly depressed and wants to die.

He also related the following facts: he is a virgin (has never had sex with any other human being), has never masturbated with his hand, and cannot masturbate to any other fantasy but the one described here. Dennis also fails persistently at work and in all relationships. His "friends" all belong to his college fraternity and treat him like a "dip" (his term), making him a servant and degrading him publicly to the extent of urinating on him in front of the whole group.

Regardless of treatment modalities used, no real change occurred in over a year's involvement in therapy. His fantasies continued to increase in frequency as well as degree of pathology (recent fantasies include the victim being brutally murdered). There is no doubt in the therapist's mind that Dennis was sexually molested as a child and that some element of the molestation resulted in severe guilt that he is unable to expiate, resulting in his self-destructive behavior.

He now realizes that his problems at work and in all of his relationships are self-induced and utilized to punish himself. When asked why, he does not consciously know the answer. In his dreams, more and more material has begun to emerge, including an incident in the park where an older man in dark clothing takes him away from his friends. The age is most probably seven, as all the children in the fantasy are age seven also.

Although the age is known, the event remains repressed, and until we can break through the defensive barriers (even hypnosis did not work) and bring the event back into consciousness, the compulsion will continue and unfortunately will also increase in both frequency and severity. A different type of case will clarify the concept.

Mike: Deviation and Connection to Molestation As a Child

MIKE was an advisor to a boys' group. He was employed as a lieutenant in the Navy Reserve, working toward a promotion to captain. Mike was married and had three young children: two girls, ages five and seven, and a new baby son, nine months old, named Timmy. His wife, Jane, was a loving mother and good wife to Mike who reported "a good marriage with a wonderful husband who was caring and who doted on his children." Although they had always wanted a son, a serious change occurred in their lives when Timmy was born. Mike became more nervous, agitated, and short-tempered than ever before and appeared to have lost his interest in sex, at least where his wife was concerned.

Mike called for an appointment, indicating that he had a problem having sex with his wife and needed help. During the first interview, he related that although impotent with his wife almost all of the time, he was masturbating more and with firm erections. He dated the onset of the problem to his wife's return home with their newborn son. It was obvious that Mike was not telling all. This was discussed as being a problem and barrier to my helping him. After protesting that this was not true and that he was being completely open,

Mike became angry and abruptly ended the session without making another appointment.

Two weeks later, Mike called and made an appointment for the same evening. From the moment of his arrival, it was obvious that he was agitated, emotionally upset, and frightened. I helped him to relax, telling him to take his time and to use his own words. Mike began to cry and slowly related that while helping his wife with the children by changing and bathing his son, Timmy, he was getting more and more interested in Timmy's penis and was having erections just staring at it. He was also masturbating to thoughts of masturbating little Timmy, and this frightened and disgusted him. He said he would rather die than molest his son or any of his children. He also related that this had never happened when he changed or bathed his two daughters.

Crying and sobbing for several minutes, Mike then said that he was willing to tell me his "biggest secret." He related that on an overnight campout with a boys' group, he awoke in the middle of the night, noticed that one of the boys had kicked off his blankets (a boy he had been obsessed with for some time but in a nonsexual, paternalistic manner), went over to cover him, and saw that he was exposed and had an erection. Without thinking, Mike masturbated the boy to orgasm and ejaculation. The boy did not appear to wake up (or pretended not to), and Mike was immediately filled with disgust and revulsion. That evening, when he returned home, he was arrested and bail posted. This occurred just after the birth of his son and the bathing incident. At this point, I asked Mike if he really wanted to understand the problem and alleviate it. He insisted that he would do anything to have that happen. I then asked him to tell me about his own sexual molestation. He immediately began to deny it, saying it never happened to him, and I simply kept asking the same question for the next fifteen to twenty minutes. Suddenly, he sat up and yelled, "Oh, my God! It did happen! I remember!"

As a child, a boarder his mother took in following his father's death molested Mike. They had a consensual and reciprocal sexual relationship for over two years, and the roomer became the substitute father Mike never had and always wanted. The adult bought him clothes and other presents, took him on trips, showed him physical affection (hugging, tousling hair, etc.), and became an idol. These were the happiest years that Mike could remember, since his own father was an alcoholic who died when Mike was only nine years old.

At the end of the two-year period, the roomer disappeared, and Mike felt abandoned, rejected, betrayed, and used. Shortly after this, the family moved to another city where the grandparents lived. Mike made new friends who discovered that he was an adolescent virgin and quickly remedied the situation. Mike began a heterosexual period that lasted through adolescence, into his marriage, and up to the time that he molested the young boy.

The next few sessions were used to explore and ventilate this repressed memory fully. We began to explore the effects of the molestation and repressed trauma throughout Mike's life from the abandonment to the present.

Mike quickly perceived and understood the molestation of the boy on the camping trip. He was depressed at the time; was anxious and frightened by the idea of having a son but did not know why; was having problems with a superior at work; and, finally, had no real male friends, which he wanted but feared. The next hurdle was his conclusion that the memory of the two-year homosexual relationship with the roomer, coupled with his molestation of the boy on the camping trip and his attraction to his son Timmy's penis, all made him a queer and that he'd rather be dead. Sex education followed, and Mike accepted the fact that he was *bisexual,* but that did not mean he had to act on it. Following the session where this acceptance took place, he was able to again have sex with his wife with no trace of the impotence.

EMOTIONS SUPPRESSED OR DISPLACED

Another extremely difficult area to work with in sex offender therapy is that of emotions. Although some sex offenders can emote easily and spontaneously, others simply cannot show any emotion except anger. Even their anger release is minimal and overly controlled.

Tracing emotions back into childhood can be difficult if not dangerous. Repressed memories, usually containing one or more traumas of either a sexual or nonsexual nature, may take many years to uncover. Some of these memories are so deeply repressed that even hypnosis cannot break through the defensive barriers. When, and if, they break through, the amount and intensity of the accompanying rage is impossible to predict. Therefore, precautions for the safety of both the patient and the therapist must be prearranged.

Regression techniques are useful in dealing with this problem but can be dangerous and require a great deal of training and experience before they are utilized. Complicating the entire area of emotions in the sex offender is a system of "defective values," usually surrounding the concept of manhood. Since this is a highly sensitive area for sex offenders, the defective value system must be exposed and resolved before any attempt to deal with the emotional constriction and suppression or repression. The double standard of the sex offender (see Rulers and Subjective Judgment Memories, Chapter 5) applies and confuses matters more. One sex offender may be highly supportive of another sex offender who is emoting and even congratulate him on releasing the deep feelings that have been held in check for so long. However, when it comes to doing it himself, nothing happens. He intellectually verbalizes feelings of hurt, pain, disappointment, and sorrow, but behaviorally nothing occurs.

Repression and all of its effects play a major role in blocked emotions. The more intellectual the individual involved, the harder to break through the barriers. Some of the sex offender's reasoning involved is valid: "If I allow myself to *feel,* I might remember what happened to me or what I did. Then, I'll either hurt terribly or have to feel guilty about what happened, and I don't want to do either."

Here, again, Kevin comes to mind (his case was discussed in Chapters 3 and 5). After many, many years of therapy that produced major positive changes in Kevin's personality, he was still unable to spontaneously emote. He stated that he wanted to emote and felt emotions beginning, but then they were choked off. Concurrently, Kevin suspected that he had been molested, possibly by someone very close to him, but could not "remember" it happening. Each time this was discussed, he became visibly sad and depressed and looked like he was about to cry, but neither the memory nor the emotion ever surfaced. Every method possible, including hypnosis, failed, but there remained too many unanswered questions and unexplainable behaviors that could only have resulted from sexual trauma. For over ten years of combined therapy with several therapists and in many modalities, the search continued but was never successful.

Another method the sex offender uses to avoid dealing with emotions is "displacement." Like a small child (which emotionally the sex offender often is) he projects/displaces the emotions or the reasons for his emotional reactions onto others:

- He made me mad!
- She hurt my feelings!
- It wasn't my fault; if he had not gotten me angry, I would not have hit him.

Getting the sex offender to accept responsibility for his own feelings and reactions is a difficult and long-term task. The use of "I" statements applies here. Maintaining a therapy rule, for both individual and group, that the offender must start all explanatory or judgmental sentences with the word *I* puts all the responsibility on him and usually prevents blame from being projected or displaced.

I often use the following example with clients to explain this concept:

- Wrong: "She hurt my feelings when I asked her for a date and she rejected me."
- Correct: "I got hurt and felt rejected when I asked her for a date and she said no."

THE CHILD/ADOLESCENT SEX OFFENDER

Development of the ability to relate to others has its beginning in childhood and then becomes exacerbated in adolescence. More important, problems in forming or keeping relationships are one of the easiest indicators to find in early childhood and becomes even easier when the child enters school.

From the earliest memories and observations of parents, relatives, and even neighbors and teachers, these children are seen as unable to interact normally with other children. Some of the clearly observable behaviors include

1. an inability or lack of desire to make friends;
2. problems playing with and interacting with other children of a similar age;
3. the tendency to become either a passive follower or a bullying leader;
4. hiding and isolating at the smallest hurt by other children, (these children are unable to express their emotions or, if they do, the expression is inappropriate: temper tantrums, assaultive behavior, etc.);
5. spending an abnormal amount of time in fantasy, reading, watching TV, laying on his bed and staring at the ceiling, etc.;
6. rarely, if ever, raising his hand to answer a question in school;
7. not joining in recess play with his classmates and, instead, wandering over to younger children or going to older children where he becomes their "mascot";
8. answering direct questions with single words or the omnipresent "I don't know" either expressed or signified by a shrug of the shoulders;
9. secretive behavior both in school and at home; and
10. resistance to joining in family activities.

Forced therapy, at this point, would fail since he is not ready to deal with any of his problems, even if he is aware of them (see Chapter 9 on Treatment Issues). In my private practice, I have had too many cases of this type, either parent referred (and forced) or court mandated. I learned early in my career to refuse such cases until the child/adolescent himself calls for an appointment without bribes, threats, etc.

JEFFY (who was introduced in Chapter 1), was brought to my office, following the sexual incident with the neighbor's young son. It was obvious from my interview with his mother that her motivation was to avoid his being sent to a reformatory.

From his first one-on-one session, it was obvious that the story of the sexual incident was well rehearsed and that he was not going to change a word of it. He denied problems, denied deviant sexual fantasies, attempted to manipulate the therapist into telling the courts "it was all a terrible mistake," and used every manipulation he could to cut down on the number of therapy sessions as well as their length.

After three or four of these sessions, I terminated his treatment. I explained why and told him bluntly that I did not believe his story and felt that he did have problems that he needed help with. He appeared happy that "it was over" and informed his mother that I had found no problems and that he was not a sex offender (I was told this by her when he went to court).

Jeffy received probation, was assigned to a new, young, female probation officer, and went full force into his "act." He quickly manipulated her into believing that he was innocent and was able to manipulate her over missed sessions, being constantly late, etc. He also convinced her that he did not need therapy, and she agreed.

Three years later, I received a call from him. He had just been released from the state reformatory where he had spent two years for violation of probation. He explained that he was assigned a new probation officer, a male who had been in the position for ten or more years. When he tried his manipulations, they were rejected, and eventually he was violated and sent to the state's juvenile reformatory.

I then asked why he was calling me. He stated that a condition of his parole was therapy and since I "knew him so well" he would feel more comfortable seeing me.

In our first interview, I explained that I did not trust him telling me that "I'm a new man. These two years taught me a great deal and I've changed." Needless to say, I did not believe him and if we were to work together, he would have to *prove* everything he told me with behavioral examples. (The reader is again referred to Chapters 9 and 10, specifically, to the section on "Show me, don't tell me!")

Jeff (no longer Jeffy) agreed, and he is making great progress. There are no longer attempts to manipulate the therapist; he is open and initiates subjects to discuss in therapy. No matter how many times I test his sincerity, he passes.

Of utmost importance to prevent these children and adolescents from becoming repetitive-compulsive sex offenders is the need for *early identification.* Training parents, teachers, coaches, ministers, and anyone else who is involved in any way with children or teens is the only answer. I have run training sessions of this type with PTAs and other parent groups, church organizations, professional groups, social workers, psychologists, and even priests and ministers. It continues to amaze me that they appear shocked at this information. Many have expressed their appreciation but also have related that they know several children who behave this way and did not know what to do about it. The answer I give is always the same: "Refer them to a professional who is trained to handle this type of problem, not just to someone in the phone book or in a listing or just because he or she is a professional counselor."

More follows on this subject as I continue exploring personality traits in Chapter 7.

Chapter 7

Sexual Performance Problems

STRONG PERFORMANCE NEEDS

Sex offenders, for the most part, have never had sex just for fun and enjoyment. All of their sexual behavior, whether masturbatory or with another person, serves a purpose, and that purpose, most of the time, is to make them feel better about themselves by either proving something or denying something. There could be other motivations as well since this is the most complex of the psychological groups that I have encountered. These additional motivations include control, identifying with the victim, regression to an earlier age, possession of the victim, escape from an unbearable life, and making themselves feel better.

THE SEX OFFENDER'S USE OF MASTURBATION

Masturbation, from the time it was first learned accidentally, discovered naturally, taught by peers or adults, or performed on them by an older, more sexually knowledgeable individual (including molesters), carried a meaning other than pleasuring which immediately became *imprinted* (see Chapter 11). The most common self-learned masturbatory motive was to feel better when rejected, punished, lonely, or depressed in relation to a specific event. Parents should consider this when they send a child to his or her room as punishment for any number of reasons.

KEVIN (see Chapters 3, 5, and 6) was the last of six children and was six years younger than his nearest sibling, a sister. Kevin was not a planned child, and his arrival placed an additional burden to an already burdened family. His father was a workaholic who was rarely at home and when home was always tired and not to be disturbed. From his earliest memories, Kevin felt alienated and rejected by most of his family, except his mother. He wanted acceptance from his father desperately but never received it. Usually, when he asked his father to help him with homework or some other task, his father was busy sleeping or reading the newspaper. He received similar rejection from his older siblings most of the time. Kevin, thus, spent a great deal of time alone in his attic room in fantasies of all types: from hero fantasies to anger and revenge fantasies where he would punish the entire family.

Rubbing against the mattress one day, he discovered the pleasant feelings it produced in his penis, and this became a ritual whenever he was alone. As he grew older, he began manipulating his penis with his hand, and this quickly replaced the mattress rubbing. His masturbation pattern had developed and now, regardless of the negative occurrence, off to his room he would go to "make myself feel better." School problems and social difficulties were added to the list of reasons to masturbate, and his frequency went from once or twice a day to five or six times a day. On a really bad day, he would masturbate a dozen times or more, and the fantasies became increasingly angry and punitive.

Even in adult life, when married, his compulsive masturbation continued, often after he had completed sex with his wife. Kevin cannot recall even one time that sex was for enjoyment only or when sex occurred when he was in a good or positive frame of mind. (More about Kevin appears throughout our discussions.)

MARK (see Chapter 5) was ten years old when he was sexually molested by his older brother, whom he admired and from whom he desperately wanted acceptance. Prior to this occasion, he had no sexual knowledge and had not discovered masturbation. On a camping trip alone with his brother, Mark was talked into going skinny-dipping and then lying nude in the sun on the shore to dry off. Pleasantly tired and dozing off, he felt his brother move closer to him, begin rubbing his chest and stomach, and then touch and fondle his penis. Frightened and pretending to be asleep, he allowed his brother to continue and, when erect, his brother masturbated him to orgasm. Mark had never felt anything like this before, and although still scared and confused by his brother's behavior, he enjoyed the experience and said nothing. His brother then told him to stop faking since now it was his turn and placed Mark's hand on his penis and told him what to do. Some minutes later, fully aroused, his brother told him to turn over, got on top of him, and without explanation penetrated him anally. Although there was a great deal of initial pain, Mark soon found himself enjoying the sodomy and becoming highly aroused again himself. Very little was said, and when his brother finished with him, Mark was told to go into the lake and wash himself and not to tell anyone what had occurred or his brother would never let Mark go anywhere with him again.

Mark was extremely confused at this point: On the one hand, he intuitively felt that he had done something he should not have and that he did not want anyone else to know about; on the other hand, he enjoyed being masturbated by his brother and also enjoyed his brother sodomizing him. However, his feelings about himself dramatically changed. Over the next few weeks and months, the brother's attention to Mark increased, and in addition to giving him presents, the brother showed Mark all the affection he had always wanted from his father (who had deserted the family).

Mark's mother was ecstatic about his new and closer relationship with his brother and encouraged it as strongly as she could. As can be expected, the brother planned another camping trip only two weeks after the first, and Mark somehow knew that it was time to pay for all the gifts and the attention. This time, the molestation took place at night when they were preparing for bed, and the brother told Mark that he knew that Mark enjoyed what he had done to him. He also mentioned their new relationship and the gifts and attention and then (the brother was now naked and erect) asked Mark "to play their game again." Mark's intuition of payment was now confirmed, and since he desperately wanted the affection, love, and presents, he agreed. Their games went on for several years, until one day the brother announced his engagement, much to Mark's shock and horror. By now his love for his brother was more than brotherly, and Mark, needing the sex more than the brother did, had become the initiator. Mark went out looking for sex and a new "brother." Being a good-looking, slim, and clean teenager, he had few problems in finding more than one adult to play the now-lost role of his brother.

Sex now became a *payment* for love, affection, and material gain in Mark's new and distorted value system. Mark was now a male prostitute, and no matter how hard he tried to rationalize his behavior, he realized it. All through these years, Mark understood that he was gay. Being gay, however, was taboo with his mother, his friends, and everyone he associated with except the adult males he was now servicing.

His self-image deteriorated, and he often allowed painful or forced sodomy to be performed on him in order to punish himself for being abnormal. Finally, in a desperate attempt to salvage his manhood, he began dating girls with the hope that by having sex with them he would be magically converted to heterosexuality. The problem was that all the time he was in bed with a woman, in order to perform he was fantasizing about being with a male. Also, in his masturbatory behavior, he was obsessed with inserting objects into his rectum to simulate being sodomized, which had now become an unwanted obsession. His self-hate and the blame he projected onto his mother, who should have protected him from his brother instead of encouraging their inappropriate relationship, finally resulted in rape.

It is interesting to note that in all of his rapes, after intercourse was complete, he forcibly sodomized each victim. In fact, as the rapes continued, he eliminated vaginal sex and proceeded directly to the sodomy, which he tried to make as painful as possible.

For similar reasons and based on the principle of imprinting, every sex offender that I have met and treated had *some distorted sex value* that remained from the first incident of sexual orgasm to the time of his offense. Some of these include the distorted values that sex equals love, revenge, comfort, payment, an equalizer, manhood, acceptance, or a rite of passage. All of these distorted values grossly affect the overall composition of the developing inadequate personality and add a sexual dimension that slowly but surely becomes "compulsive."

First, an *obsession* with sex begins and may last throughout an entire childhood, adolescence, and into adulthood. This was the case with Kevin. Playing with friends, his first school experiences and all social contacts were tainted by sexual obsession; this was followed by compulsive masturbation, graduating to exposing himself at every possible opportunity. Finally, it ended in sexual molestation and sexual assault.

The direction of later behavior appears directly linked with the initial sexual experience. Both Kevin and Mark ended up as sexually assaultive persons but arrived there by totally different routes. It is helpful to look at each path and the differences in the two boys' development from sexually abused children into rapists with multiple victims and severe blocking to all therapeutic effort.

Kevin's path hinged almost totally on his father's rejection. Why, then, did he not become sexually assaultive against males? The answer may lie in *where* the child places the blame for his condition. In the majority of young children, the mother figure is the protector and the one who should look out for all of the needs of the growing child—both physical and emotional.

Females in Kevin's life were always his problem and the group on which he placed all blame for his condition:

- His father preferred his sisters—females—over him and showed them the love that Kevin wanted.
- His mother then showed more attention to the sisters than to Kevin and his brothers (who were independent and did not need it).
- Since his mother rejected him, in Kevin's distorted thinking, she also rejected his penis (his maleness).
- His mother used embarrassment to deal with his misbehaviors, and this increased his rage and anger.

- His attempts to meet and date girls in school all ended in rejection and humiliation.
- His wife was not pretty and did not satisfy him sexually. She did not accept his requests for deviant sexual acts, including "play rape" (his term) and bondage. He also suggested water sports, but she refused.
- When he flashed girls and women, they laughed and made comments about his flaccid penis size. (He wanted them to come over and fondle him and then offer themselves for sex.)

From his earliest memories, there was an inordinate amount of anger toward women, with only two or three examples of anger toward males, mainly as a result of his brothers' rejection and his father's rejection as well.

Women constantly thwarted his compulsive sexual needs, especially for fellatio as acceptance of his penis. Then, in his first incarceration, he became entangled with an older man who introduced him to homosexuality (the older man fellated him regularly and finally fulfilled his need). Kevin developed an intense need to deny his homosexuality and to deny the fact that he now masturbated to fantasies of fellating other men in the treatment unit. Upon release, his need for sex with women became totally compulsive, and his large number of rapes resulted.

Mark, on the other hand, developed a totally different path to his rape behavior:

- His father rejected Mark from birth. His mother was weak, alcoholic, and nonsupportive of his needs.
- At age ten, Mark was raped by his older brother who told him that he was "better than any woman he had ever had." From this experience, Mark developed strong doubts about his masculinity and suspected that he was feminine and gay.
- Mark never had any close friends. After the rape by his brother, Mark, in his first incarceration as a juvenile, became a *kid* (submissive younger male to an older inmate) to an older and stronger inmate who showed him concern, affection, caring, and protection. In return, Mark became his "woman," and this further confirmed in his mind that there was something wrong within himself

and that he was at fault for seducing his brother as well as his friend in prison.

- Mark blamed his mother for all of his problems: his poverty and lack of emotional support; his embarrassment over her drinking and bringing men home for the night; his rape by his brother that he was sure she condoned; and ultimately for not being the mother he wanted and saw at his friends' homes.
- In attempting to deny that he was homosexual, he attempted to have sexual relationships with as many women as he could. However, after each affair he felt dissatisfied and used. None of the relationships lasted. (He made sure of that!) He could not accept responsibility and projected blame for all of his problems on one or another woman in his life.
- Mark had a strong need to *destroy* the woman inside him, and he did this through his victims, although he was not conscious of that fact until years into therapy.
- He could not accept the concept of being bisexual and, therefore, had to prove his masculinity through heterosexual behavior, including rape.
- Being an abused child himself, whenever he saw a woman abusing children or animals, he became enraged and immediately chose her as his next possible victim. One of the woman he raped he had witnessed abusing her little dog in the backyard. He knew from that moment that he would "get back at her his way."

As in the case of Kevin, Mark's self-hate and totally negative self-image were major barriers to therapeutic progress and did not change for fourteen years. Only the development of the self-confrontation technique (described in Chapter 18) had any effect on him. He has now begun to change and to develop a more forgiving and positive self-image, although prognosis remains guarded.

THE UNREALISTIC SMALL PENIS COMPLEX

The majority of sex offenders I have seen in therapy will, at one time or another, "confess" that one of their unchangeable and most serious problems is that they have a small penis. When this occurs, if the therapist asks them how big a normal penis should be, repetitive compulsive sex offenders invariably will either not know or give some outrageous measurement that they have either heard from peers or seen in some pornographic context (either pornographic books or videotapes).

Second, when asked in what context he has compared himself to other males of his age group, the repetitive-compulsive sex offender invariably will name a shower, locker room, nude-swimming situation, group-physical line, etc. In these situations, the comparison is made to *flaccid* penises and, as the reader may be aware, this comparison is invalid due to the difference in retractability of the male genital organ. Penis size also depends a great deal on factors such as genetic background and race. What the offender is unaware of, due to lack of adequate sex education, is that smaller flaccid penises tend to erect to a greater extent than larger flaccid penises do.

Here, again, the sex offender has compared himself *upward* (see Chapter 2 and Ronny in Chapter 3) and through selective perception has ignored the other males in any of the comparison groups with either equal or smaller flaccid penises than his.

More important than his conclusion that he has a small penis is the value or importance that he attaches to it. In his distorted value system (see Chapter 18) a small penis makes him less of a man; unable to satisfy either a woman or a man; a failure (from birth); or justifies his deviant behavior.

If he is a pedophile or hebophile, he rationalizes that he will become involved with males of similar penis size (i.e., children or young adolescents). If he is a sexually assaultive person, then his use of force will prevent the woman or man from making comparisons or judgments about his organ size (especially at night or in the dark). He makes sure that they never see his penis by using blindfolds, hoods, etc. (Untrained investigators will usually connect these behaviors to his concern with being identified.)

Lack of parental communication and lack of adequate sex education are both involved in the *misinformation* and *street or locker room* knowledge that the sex offender brings to therapy. Thus, the importance of sex education programs in the overall treatment of this individual becomes obvious, especially in a group setting, since *it was at a peer stage that the damage was done and it should be at a peer stage that the damage is corrected.* Many self-help type sex education books are available today that will dispel sex misinformation while replacing it with the accurate and important facts he needs and wants to know. (A list of some of these may be found in the Bibliography.)

Penis size, a preadolescent/adolescent comparison behavior, is not the only sex education area where these individuals are misinformed and need to be reeducated (see Chapter 15). However, it remains a prevalent and extremely important problem to sex offenders as a group. Another example will clarify the crucial role of penis size.

BOBBY (introduced in Chapter 4) was in treatment for at least one but possibly more rapes of adult women. There was neither excessive force or brutality involved nor any sadistic injuries, but he did complete the rape and definitely traumatized the victim. An interesting element of his rapes was his insistence that the victim keep her eyes closed before he undressed and until he told her to open them after he redressed. He was not concerned about his identity, as the detectives investigating the rape suspected or surmised. He simply did not want the victim to see his penis. Other rapists with the same problem and concern accomplish the same end by raping in the dark, insisting that no lights be turned on, or by blindfolding the victim. Again, the unknowing believe that this is only to protect the rapist's identity.

After many months in establishing trust and rapport in therapy, Bobby asked for an individual therapy (IT) session. As with other cases we discussed, it was time to reveal his big secret, which turned out to be his shame and embarrassment at having a *small penis.* When asked what a *small penis* is, he was unable to answer except to say that in his comparisons to his teammates in the gym locker room and in the showers, he did not match up to any of them in size. These comparisons were made while he was in a flaccid state (the major error in this type of comparison by both teens and adults). I suggested that Bobby enroll in the next sex education course, which was just about to begin a new semester, and he did.

In teaching sex education with sex offenders, special emphasis must be placed on areas that especially concern this group more than others. These include penis size, manhood values, responsibility for arousal and sexual behaviors, responsibility for pregnancy and sexually transmitted diseases (STDs), the origin of their sexual values and how to change them, and sexual preference versus sexual identity.

After the second session, BOBBY returned to my office, told me that he had listened to the range of normal penile dimensions, and said that "his six inches was normal and okay with him." From that day on, his whole attitude changed; he became more assertive and became competitive in sports (especially weight lifting), and his overall demeanor indicated a happier and more normal adjustment. Had this been done in grammar school or junior high school, the possibility exists that the rapes may have been averted. Creating an atmosphere in which children and teenagers can talk about *anything* to parents or other adults they trust and respect is paramount in the prevention of sexual assault and abuse.

Pedophiles handle the small-penis complex through distorted perception and delusional thinking. Even when they believe they have a small penis (and a large percentage of them do believe this), they rationalize, quite accurately, that it will look larger to a small child by comparison. It is not too farfetched to believe that a percentage of them chose children as their victims from this type of thinking and motivation.

HOWIE (whose case is also discussed in Chapter 2) believed that he had not only a small penis but also an abnormally small erection. This became a motivating force in his never allowing his victims to see him naked, except when they went skinny-dipping, and even then he remained in the water most of the time. When he was photographing them with erections or masturbating, he again was fully clothed and admired and envied their penises and wished "his was as beautiful and large as theirs."

When, after several years of therapy, Howie had his first sexual experiences with other men, nothing they did could get him erect, although alone he had no such problem. In writing therapy, which was the only modality in which he felt sufficiently comfortable to expose his feelings, thoughts, and fantasies, he attributed his psychogenic impotence (his diagnosis) with other males to his fear of ridicule and laughter at his small erection capability. This fear and impotence remain to this day, and there is no way to know whether his fears are real or imagined.

Finally, there is FRANK (introduced in Chapter 2), who was told he had a small penis and would never be a real man, first by the baby-sitter who molested him, then by his sister. During his rapes, he also never permitted his victims to look at his penis but did make them tell him what a great job he had done and how great a man he was.

The *small penis complex,* when it originates early in childhood, leaves a definite imprint that lasts throughout life until resolved in therapy. Many of the adult males that I have treated for sexual dysfunctions (usually impotence), after several sessions admit that this is one of their major concerns. Only part of a session is needed to correct this erroneous belief. Self-help books with illustrations of the variation in size of the normal adult penis are a tremendous aid. Counselors and therapists who may be uncomfortable dealing with sexual issues will often overlook this area. Without resolution of this problem, the rest of the therapy efforts are often wasted, and the danger of recurrence of the deviant behavior or sexual dysfunction continues to exist.

DISTORTED SEXUAL VALUES

One of the most common traits or characteristics of the repetitive compulsive sex offender is his long-term value belief that *sex equals love*. This is the most frequently seen and most destructive of all the distorted values found in sex offenders.

In both pedophilia and hebophilia, the most often used rationalization by the offender to the victim when asked a "why" question about his sexual behavior is some reply containing the word *love:*

- I'm showing you *love.*
- We're making *love.*
- This is how two people show each other *love.*
- I want you to feel good because I *love* you.

The importance of uncovering this distorted, confusing, and all-justifying value lies in the fact that what he has done (i.e., the sex crime or perversion) is therefore all right since he was *only showing his victim love,* not trying to harm him or her. This is especially true where the pedophiles and hebophiles are concerned, although I have heard it quite often from other sex offenders as well.

In their distorted perceptions and their overwhelming need to justify and/or rationalize their behavior (which they intuitively know is wrong), the belief that they love their victims is essential to alleviating the tremendous amount of guilt that they feel afterward (assuming they are not sociopathic). This word—love—is used over and over in their contacts with their victims. It becomes imprinted in the victim's mind as well, since the victim, after returning for the second, third, and more contacts, is also experiencing guilt and needs his or her own rationalization to assuage the guilt. Thus the merry-go-round begins and, if not corrected through therapy, will be used in later years by the victim when he (without intervention) becomes the offender.

In a great many other sex offender case histories, a common thread in the offender's own molestation is the phrase "I'm showing or proving that I love you" in response to the child's question as to what the adult is doing to him or her. Especially when the child is lacking in all sexual knowledge and the molestation is his or her first encounter with genital sex, the *imprint* occurs immediately and lasts for life unless corrected in therapy.

JIMMY (an incestuous pedophile) was molested by his father from ages nine to age sixteen when he, in turn, began molesting his brother and sister, as well as several younger children he baby-sat for. The first night, his father woke Jimmy some time after midnight and took him into the spare bedroom. He undressed Jimmy and then himself (Jimmy, frightened, believed he was about to be beaten). He then began fondling Jimmy's genitals and ordering him to do the same to him. When Jimmy asked what was happening, his father told him he was teaching him how to become a man and how to "make love" to a woman. He promised him that when he was good at sex, he would let him have sex with a real woman. Jimmy, having peeped at his parents having sex, was excited by the thought of "making love" like they did, so he cooperated.

When, after years of sex with his father and then with his younger sister (for "practice," under the father's direction), the promised sex with a real woman never occurred, Jimmy, feeling angry and betrayed, used any child he could manipulate and control, including two young boys he baby-sat for. Ironically, when his father was finally arrested for molesting his children, Jimmy was arrested a few months later for molesting his siblings and was sent to the same institution where his father was sentenced.

Their first session in therapy together was quite dramatic and extremely painful for both. Jimmy, although admitting he molested his younger siblings (both brothers and sisters), insisted that not only did they enjoy the sexual activities, but also it was the "best way I knew to show them that I loved them."

As will be discussed in Chapter 17, the *source* of this value must be found before any change can be effected. Thus, it is necessary to consider how repetitive compulsive sex offenders learn values such as this one.

In those sex offenders who themselves were molested, the answer is obvious: They learned it from their molester who used it to justify his or her behavior toward the child, and now they are using it in exactly the same way. This is the easiest to understand.

However, there is an even more insidious way is which this value becomes ingrained in young people today. Only in the United States is the euphemism "making love" used to describe the act of sexual relations between two people. We still appear to be so sexually neurotic and puritanical that to use any other phrase of a more direct nature to describe sex is either forbidden, too embarrassing, or too guilt provoking to consider.

Imagine the effect on a seven-year-old child, Ernie, who accidentally (or otherwise) catches his parents in the violent throes of intercourse with accompanying audible dramatics and asks what they are doing, only to be told "We're making love!" Now imagine some few days later when mother comes into his bedroom to find Ernie and his sister naked in bed "making love," and his mother's violent reaction. This actually happened to Ernie and his sister Laura. Mother began hitting Ernie with anything she could get hold of, while castigating him with epithets such as "disgusting, pervert, sickee," and menacing him with threats of impending doom when his father came home. Ernie's father was even more violent and destructive in his reaction, literally beating Ernie into semiconsciousness and threatening to have him put in prison (a seven-year-old) for "making love" as he had witnessed his mother and father doing. Needless to say, Ernie never forgot the incident, and his attitudes and values toward sex were colored for life. Ernie became a violent rapist and is in prison today.

DEVIANT AROUSAL PATTERNS

Still another unique trait or characteristic of the repetitive compulsive sex offender is the obsessive-compulsive nature of his *deviant arousal patterns* for masturbatory or other sexual excitability needs. When the compulsion is active, the sex offender is unable to get aroused to a normal sexual stimulus or fantasy regardless of how hard he tries. If he does get erect, and a large percentage do to anything that contains nudity or sexual suggestion, he is unable to reach orgasm unless he changes the fantasy to include his own subjective deviant stimulus pattern.

When KEVIN watched his first sexually explicit film of a heterosexual couple in both foreplay and eventual intercourse (his choice of film), no matter how hard he tried to masturbate to orgasm nothing worked until in his own mind he altered the content of the film to include force, submission, and both fear and disgust on the part of the female. He then had an almost immediate orgasm and relief.

JIMMY, likewise, while watching a sexually explicit film of two adult homosexuals in foreplay, fellatio, and eventual mutual anal sex (his choice of film), masturbated for over an hour. It only made him sore, and he was no closer to a climax then he was during the first five minutes. He then switched the fantasy in his own mind, making the younger looking of the two males a thirteen- or fourteen-year-old teenager, and immediately reached an orgasm.

There is a persistently seen resistance to *giving up the old stimuli subject* in both the pedophile/hebophile group and in the sexually assaultive person (SAP) group, as well (see Box 7.1). They appear to prefer the security of their old and deviant fantasies to the risk involved in making changes. Their insecurity regarding new situations surfaces persistently, especially when *change* is the goal.

Attempting to *force* change through threat, success motivation techniques, or through classical behavior modification techniques, in my experience, simply does not work. All that it accomplishes is confirmation of the offender's failure system and results in frustration and loss of confidence in treatment. The Clockwork Orange syndrome has been seen in hundreds of cases where noxious odors, mild electric shock, or other aversive behavior-modification techniques had previously been tried.* The additional danger here is that the confidence of the offender in treatment itself may be shaken, and the new therapist then has an additional resistance barrier to overcome before any meaningful therapy can begin.

As stated many times before, there are opposing views to mine, and the reader is once again referred to Pallone's coverage of alternate treatment techniques and their successes for other therapists (Pallone, 1990, Chapter 5). As will be discussed in Chapter 14, I have found from my own experience that a specific form of *masturbatory reconditioning* appears to be the best method of dealing with this problem when used in conjunction with the value change techniques discussed in Chapter 17.

A major caveat in dealing with masturbatory homework assignments is that they deal with "self-report," the least reliable source of

---

*A *Clockwork Orange* is a novel by Anthony Burgess, published in 1963, which became a powerful film under the direction of Stanley Kubrick. The work is the psychological history of Alex, a delinquent fifteen-year-old in London at some unspecified future date, who has been conditioned to behave violently whenever he hears the strains of Beethoven's Ninth Symphony. Much of the dramatic conflict concerns the application of "Ludovici's Technique," a variant of aversive counterconditioning, which becomes a matter of public controversy between members of opposing political parties. (For an analysis both of the public policy and the clinical issues, see Pallone [1990], Pallone and Sol [1990], and Coleman, Dwyer, and Pallone [1996].)

7.1

Factors Active in Maintaining Sexually Offensive Behavior

1. Excessive arousal to deviant stimuli
2. Deficient arousal to normal stimuli
3. Lack of social skills
   - Lack of assertive skills
   - Lack of heterosexual skills
   - Lack of sexual knowledge and skills
4. Lack of coping skills
   - Low self-esteem (faulty cognitions)
   - Poor relaxation skills
   - Inability to control impulses

accurate information, especially where the sex offender is concerned. In the aftercare treatment I have conducted with paroled and maxed-out sex offenders for nearly thirty years, there has never been a single individual who has not admitted to me at some time in his aftercare treatment that he had lied during inpatient therapy, either directly or by omission. This occurs most often when the return of a deviant fantasy had occurred, especially if he was somewhere in the release process. The most commonly used justification is that he will handle it when he is released and that if he admitted it at the time it occurred he would be punished by being removed from the release process and delayed another year or more. It is only when the problem begins recurring in the community where real victims, not fantasy ones, are available that he panics and decides to admit it in an aftercare session. These factors necessitate aftercare for all sex offenders, regardless of how successful their treatment appears.

The possibility that the offender has lied during therapy must be foremost as a consideration in evaluating the sex offender for possible release from incarceration or termination from treatment in private practice. A rule of thumb I have used for many years is to *believe nothing that the sex offender says unless it can be demonstrated behaviorally.* Where masturbatory reconditioning is concerned, this cannot always be applied, and the therapist's decision must remain a judgment call, based on his or her experience and therapy knowledge of the client.

THE CHILD/ADOLESCENT SEX OFFENDER

Sex and sexual performance problems are rooted in childhood or adolescent experience over 95 percent of the time. Children have a natural, inborn curiosity about everything. Once they begin leaving the immediate confines of the home (as early as preschool) and come into contact with other children, this curiosity accelerates to an incredible degree. These are the "why" years.

If, at this point in his development, the child is not confident that he can get answers to his questions from his parents, he will go to either peers or other available adults for the answers. Pedophiles and hebophiles are acutely aware of this factor and use it to their advantage. As can be seen from the cases presented in this chapter, the results can be disastrous.

Sex education should begin at home at the earliest possible opportunity. When the child's curiosity about anything sexual is observed, this is the time to begin, but only on the child's level. Simple answers to the question asked works best. For example, seeing a baby of the opposite sex having its diaper changed can be used as the first lesson, especially when the child notices different genitals and asks about them. Also, when a cousin or friend visits with an anatomically correct doll, the time is right to begin.

The most important principle in this early sex education is that *only the question asked should be answered.* This is not the time for a full sex-ed course, the historical "birds and bees" lecture. Another perfect opportunity is when, during bathing or changing, the child is observed playing with his genitals (a totally normal behavior). An incorrect reaction at this time may close all further communication on the subject, especially if the reaction is negative or threatening. The behavior will simply become secretive but not be discontinued. In all the child and adolescent cases I have seen in my practice, I have never had one where, due to a negative reaction to early caught sex play (including spanking or worse), the child gave up the pleasurable practice. This is especially true where boys and masturbation are concerned.

Correcting misinformation gleaned from peers (at school, at sporting events, camping, etc.) is paramount in preventing a maladjusted or deviant sex behavior from beginning and then becoming imprinted. However, in situations where communication between parents and children has not been established beforehand or where minimal communication does exist and is poor, the child would never be able to share such misinformation or even consider asking about it.

Special Considerations for Adolescent Sex Offenders

Adolescence is a period of special confusion, especially in trying to discover a true identity. As stated elsewhere, the major change from childhood to adolescence is the shift from needing the approval of parents, adults, and authority figures (teachers, priests, ministers, scout leaders, etc.) to needing approval from and identity with his peer group.

It is easy to see the problem here for the inadequate personality. He sticks out and both appears and functions like an *alien* to other teenagers. This usually begins in middle school (although it may occur as early as grammar school) and explodes in high school. Due to his inability to hide, he becomes the object of ridicule, jokes, tricks, and even harassment from the "jocks" and bullies. The result is an even more damaged self-image, and depression often results. An incredible amount of anger is either directed at the true source of his problems (i.e., the jocks and bullies), or, more often, is self-directed. His already-existing tendencies—to be a loner, to avoid social interaction, to spend inordinate amounts of time alone and in fantasy—become even more pronounced.

A resulting behavioral trait that often develops is for him to search for another "wuss" or "nerd" (their terms) to team up with for survival. In these cases, if the anger is directed outward, the result could be another Columbine.* Conversely, if the anger is directed inward, he becomes an easy pray to hebophiles (possibly teachers or other school personnel) searching for just such prey. Depression and suicidal fantasies, as well as actual suicide attempts, also surface in this group of teenagers.

As repeated continuously in this work, parents, teachers, and other adults in this adolescent's world need to be more observant for these symptoms and also need to be prepared to do something about it. The best decision, in my opinion, is to refer this type of student to a well-

---

*Columbine High School is outside of Denver, Colorado, where two teenagers, Dylan Klebold (seventeen) and Eric Harris (eighteen), plotted revenge on the "jocks" and shot and killed classmates and teachers.

trained and well-motivated guidance counselor in his school or, in the absence of one, to outside professional help. There are high schools where the brighter and more assertive students, themselves, take on this responsibility as peer mentors (necessarily under supervision), and this should always be appreciated and applauded.

Sexually, the inadequate adolescent experiences his worst nightmare. He most likely is still a virgin, probably has never even been alone with a girl, and, if the opportunity presented itself, would not know how to approach a potential partner.

Some aggressive and jocklike girls, unfortunately, also use these teens in many negative ways: to make a boyfriend jealous or more attentive, to belittle them in front of other students, to be slaves for their every need and whim, etc. When they discover that they are being used, both fear and embarrassment occur, and they then magnify their fear of the opposite sex to a greater degree than was already present and look for a way to "get back" at females for what they did to them. The obvious dangers from such a traumatic experience include pushing them into homosexual involvements, making them easier prey for hebophiles, or increasing already-experienced rage fantasies and pushing these fantasies into behaviors, i.e., sexual assault.

In summary, of all the stages of development, adolescence must be considered the most important one. It also must be the one where observation, guidance, and proffered aid are paramount in the behaviors of parents and other adults involved with these teens if deviant or criminal behaviors are to be prevented.

Chapter 8

Remaining Characteristic Deficits in Sex Offenders

DEFECTIVE GOAL-SETTING PATTERNS

Typically an extremist, the sex offender avoids middle-of-the-road norms. Where goal setting is concerned, he sets his goals either too high or too short, ensuring failure on a persistent and repetitive level. This pattern also appears to have been learned in early childhood, usually from perfectionistic and well-meaning parents.

Report cards were particularly traumatic when school began, and in my experience in my practice and from speaking at PTA meetings or meeting with teachers, parents continue making the same errors in the 2000s as they did when I was a child.

Remember the example in Chapter 2 of Billy and the seven-A's and one-C report card? His father's immediate reaction was "What's that C doing there?" The average child would extricate himself or herself from the situation easily by saying something to this effect: "Dad, that teacher wouldn't give her own son an A; getting a C from her is almost a miracle! By the way, how about a dollar for each of the seven A's?" The future sex offender, however, immediately feels guilt, shame, and fear, becomes apologetic, and promises that he will improve by the next report card (although he does not believe that this is possible).

These well-meaning parents, wanting their child to excel, *focus* their child's perception on the *negative.* When this occurs, each time the inadequate child is in a situation that can be rated or compared to a norm, he develops a permanent *negative self-perception* or focus. This becomes most damaging and dangerous if it continues into adolescence where comparison to peers is a primary activity. Constantly rating himself as below or inferior to his peer group contributes to the already high levels of inadequacy and low self-esteem mentioned earlier (see Chapters 2 and 3).

In addition, his motivation is negatively affected as well, and eventually (usually sooner than later), he may give up trying. Trying for him means taking the risk of failing, and since the pain of failure is too great, it is safer to simply not try. Thus, he will remain below potential in school, sports, and social situations. Either anger (for the sexually assaultive person) or a nostalgic return to an earlier, happier time (for pedophiles and hebophiles) then dominates his fantasy life. *If sexual trauma exists,* he becomes more prone to commit either sexual assault or pedophilia/hebophilia as an *undoing* phenomenon.

Allowing the child the opportunity to react to his performance, whether on a report card, in a competition (sports, drama, science projects, etc.), or anywhere he is involved in competition, will give the observant parent an immediate clue that this process of *defective goal setting* has begun. Should *he* focus on the one C and seem to forget about the A's and if *his* reaction is one of self-blame and guilt to an unusual extent, then a problem certainly exists and needs to be paid attention to. The opportunity then exists to take corrective measures before the pattern becomes permanently ingrained. The longer the pattern has been there, the longer it will take to correct, and in some cases, although the resulting perfectionism seems to be diminished or controlled, it appears that it cannot be totally erased without professional intervention.

Easily Discouraged—Quits

Becoming easily discouraged and quitting is a major barrier to change and frustrates most efforts to help the offender to alter his past and present poor functioning. Most sex offenders have lived a life characterized by "failure." These failures were either real failures or normal first-time attempts that others, primarily demanding, perfectionistic parents, characterized as failures. As observed with Billy and his report card in Chapter 2, parents, whether well meaning or simply perfectionistic, can set patterns of negative reference and focus for the child that may last his whole life. This especially applies to weak, passive, and inadequate personalities such as the sex offender. When the therapist meets one of these clients as an adult, with as many as twenty years of perceived failures and feelings of never quite being equal to his peers in anything, the problem is extremely difficult and complex to resolve. As with all of the other traits/characteristics of the sex offender, where the overall basic inadequacy results in less than normal functioning, so it will in this area also.

From the first meeting with this type of client, the focus must be on positives, and the ambiance of the therapy milieu must be totally positive *while remaining realistic*. This is a difficult task at best, one that requires a great deal of training and experience. Motivating the sex offender to take risks at attempting anything is a difficult and at times impossible task, whether it is to take the floor in his group, to expose a secret, to join an athletic team, to return to school to learn to read or write, to get his general equivalency diploma (GED), or to take his first college course. He automatically sees failure, his greatest fear, as the outcome, regardless of his efforts or how hard he tries. He can readily quote his track record to prove his assumption.

Attempting to change this pattern without first getting him to understand its origin is frustrating and bodes failure on the part of the therapist. Analysis of his attempt patterns is essential and often uncovers the basic problem pattern. Usually one or both of the following goal-setting problems emerges.

Setting Goals Too High

In his need to deny/forget/change his perceived gross imperfections, the sex offender often tries to become perfect. *Perfectionism* thus becomes a major problem that must be exposed and dealt with. Where goal setting is concerned, the offender will set a goal to go from a C or D to an A rather than a C+; from striking out in a baseball game to hitting a home run, rather than simply not striking out or possibly getting a single; from never having spoken in group to taking the floor for the whole session and making it the best floor the group has witnessed. He becomes involved in a constant *besting* process where peers are concerned. In reality, he never believes that he can accomplish any of these goals, nor has he taken the time or concern to evaluate his potential in each of the areas involved. Again he has *set himself up to fail* and thus returns to feeling sorry for himself and denigrating his abilities. It also becomes a prime reason to never try again, an excellent resistance factor for therapy.

FRED, a thirty-nine-year-old severely assaultive rapist (and possible murderer), applies for a job in the unit's computer center. During an interview with the supervisor, he lists several computer languages as his forte and insists that he needs no training and wants to help in any way he can. The supervisor is quite impressed and asks if Fred thinks he can handle the construction of a totally new program in a fairly complex computer language. Fred immediately and enthusiastically volunteers for the task and says that he will have it completed in a month (the supervisor anticipated at least three to six months for completion). Fred begins the next day and at the end of a week presents a typed outline of how he perceives the project. Once again, the supervisor is quite impressed, although by now the supervisor has received word from other programmers in the computer center that "Fred is all talk and no action" and that they do not believe that he is capable of completing the project, since he appears completely unfamiliar with the terminology of the language required (Pascal). Three more weeks go by, and each time the supervisor has contact with Fred, Fred tells him that everything is going well and that he will meet his time frame.

As the supervisor had suspected since a consultation with Fred's primary therapist, the deadline is not met, and what work has been done on the program is useless. When questioned in the presence of his therapist, Fred tells the supervisor that he wanted so badly to succeed and please the supervisor and the treatment unit that he convinced himself that he would be able to quickly learn the language, even though he had had no prior experience with Pascal (an impossible task).

In therapy, Fred's group brought the subject of this failure up and eventually got Fred to confess that this was a pattern of his since grammar school and had cost him both friends and employment as well as caused punishment at home. In relating his story, Fred stated, "I guess my father was right. I am a failure like he said I was, no matter how hard I try!"

Fred was unable to see his part in setting himself up to fail. Once he did, Fred began to tell the truth about his skills and abilities, and he set goals that were lower than his appraisal of his abilities. Thus, he began to succeed.

The therapist must always be alert to this self-defeating pattern with all sex offenders (adults or adolescents), not only in employment or educational abilities but also in relationships, social skills, athletics, and every other facet of life. If the pattern of failure is not aborted as quickly as possible, new failures will confirm his feelings of being worthless and will prevent the necessary new risk-taking behaviors that successful treatment requires. An even more tragic result is that he will quit therapy and not come back. Thus, learning to set realistic goals becomes a priority in his list of treatment goals.

Setting Goals with Too Little Time to Complete Them

In his quest for success (often confused with perfection), the sex offender sets all-encompassing goals. For example, if he is going to learn to read, the goal will be to be able to read by the end of the first week; if weight loss is the goal, it will be fifty pounds in one week; if smoking is the problem, the goal is to quit the next day; if social relationships are the problem area, the goal is to meet and acquire many new friends the same day or by the end of that week. His unrealistic, black-and-white thought processes continue from childhood, and failure is most often the result. Thus, through a *self-fulfilling prophecy* he sets himself up to fail and then can use each of these failures as an excuse to never try again, since the pain of failure is too great.

This problem of setting himself up to fail will occur in almost all aspects of his life, including therapy. Persistent failure becomes a way of life and a good alibi for feeling sorry for himself and doing something stupid or self-destructive as a kind of self-punishment.

MARK, who was discussed in preceding chapters, was practically a nonreader and nonspeller. This condition bothered him a great deal and produced shame, embarrassment, and avoidance of any situation that required either task. Since it badly affected his self-image and self-esteem, the therapist tried to encourage him to attend school during the day, for which he would be paid. The treatment unit had several excellent teachers, trained specifically in remedial work. One female teacher, Miss Laura, took a special interest in Mark. Together with the therapist, she was able to get him to sign up for classes at least six times in a three-year period. Mark would start each course motivated and excited, but the first time he did not perform up to his demanding, perfectionistic expectations, he would quit. Regardless of the reality of his progress (which was quite normal for this particular class of nonreader, nonspeller), he perceived failure. When his quitting was discussed both in individual therapy and in his group, he admitted that he knew he was going to fail before classes ever began, and regardless of what his peers in the same class offered as positive or comparative feedback, nothing changed his mind. Nothing Miss Laura tried could keep him from quitting the class.

Nothing worked until his self-image and self-esteem began to change through *self-confrontation therapy* (see Chapter 18). Also, Mark's goal-setting problems became a priority. Once these changes began, Mark returned to school and became one of the best and most successful students in the class. Within a year, he was reading and spelling at least six grade levels above where he began and, as a result, was able to get a highly technical job in the Video-Studio-Complex where reading instruction and maintenance manuals and submitting written reports and purchase orders were primary tasks.

IDENTITY CONFUSION

In the previous seven chapters, I discussed the individual traits and characteristics of the sex offender. *Identity confusion* summarizes the total of all the other traits and becomes the overall identifier and main treatment consideration. This trait/characteristic of the sex offender is the important and often unrecognized fact that *he does not know who he is.*

If you give him a blank sheet of paper with the title "Who Am I?," the response will contain a list of demographics but nothing about the persona of the individual. Name, age, sex, nationality, occupation, educational level, prior work experience, marital status, prior criminal history, and possibly parental history will all appear, but there is no response to the real intent of the question. This is not resistance or evasion, as in other questioning, but a true lack of pertinent self-knowledge.

For the majority (if not the entirety) of his life, the sex offender has been what he perceived other people wanted him to be or, at best, a poor imitation of a peer or adult he admired and wanted to be like. If it worked and got him the attention, acceptance, or other responses he wanted and desperately needed, he would assume the personality traits of anyone he had seen who had obtained satisfaction of such needs: a brother or sister, a friend in his neighborhood, or a fellow student in school. This is one of the main reasons he can be so easily taken advantage of and/or abused without resistance.

An example from one of our already-mentioned offenders will clarify the concept.

KEVIN came from a family with both parents, two brothers, and three sisters. He perceived that the five other children had the acceptance and love from his parents which Kevin so desperately wanted and needed. He first tried to imitate his older brother who, when brought home by the police for some minor infraction, received attention, forgiveness, and love from both parents. Kevin tried flashing (exposing himself), but instead of receiving love and acceptance, he was punished and rejected. Confused, he next tried to imitate his sisters, going so far as to cross-dress, and again was rejected and punished.

Later, in school, when he tried to imitate the more popular boys, he again was rejected and ousted from the group he wanted acceptance from most. No matter what he tried it did not work, and by young adulthood he was totally confused about his own identity. He developed a chameleon-like personality, imitating anyone and everyone he felt was popular or accepted. In this personality, he used a persistent, almost seductive, smile to "make other people want me with or near them." Anger continued to ferment during all of these episodes and became directed toward females, whom he perceived as most rejecting. As early as eleven years of age, he began fantasizing rape and attempted his first rape during a flashing encounter when the girl laughed at his penis—an episode he perceived as her laughing at him.

A major treatment issue became, and still is, one of identity.

THE CHILD/ADOLESCENT SEX OFFENDER

Identity begins as early as two years old. The first "No!" or "Me" are important indicators of this process beginning. How the child defines his identity is much more complex. From my experience, how he identifies himself is closely linked with his personality. Using our premise that all sex offenders, regardless of age, are inadequate personalities who are either accept-ers, adjust-ers, or deny-ers, which of these three types he is defines the remainder of the process.

The *accept-ers* choose an idol that they perceive as nonthreatening, passive, or compliant. The idol must contain traits that they feel they can emulate and become equal or similar to as they mature. Quite often, this idol is someone in their peer group who is somewhat like them but who has traits they wish they had.

The *adjust-ers* choose future developmental goals for themselves that they feel capable of reaching. Idols exist in this group, as well, but the individual does not attempt to emulate them. Rather, they choose traits they want and set their goals on achieving them. If they find along this developmental journey that a particular goal is unattainable, they modify the trait to more realistic levels. They do not give up on themselves.

The *deny-ers* set goals that are unrealistic. They capitalize on strengths that they possess and *use* anyone and everyone to deal with unattainable traits. They are heavily into denial and blame all failures on outside elements, rarely, if ever, taking responsibility for their own failures. A SAP, for example, blames his victim for his rape: "She came on to me," "She consented and then changed her mind," "If she wasn't so seductive, nothing would have happened," etc.

Change for the accept-ers and deny-ers is a difficult process unless they are discovered and referred to treatment while these traits are still forming. Then, therapy can be positive and prognosis greatly improves.

Here again, parental involvement, teacher and other adult observations, and the insight of close relatives or other family members are all critical. The old "He's just going through a phase" too often becomes a way of avoiding responsibility or taking action. The unfortunate result will be another maladjusted teen or adult. In all my years in this field, the percent of such early referrals is less than 10 percent, a sad statement for prevention.

Before proceeding into the Treatment section of this work, it is necessary to consider the additional traits of adolescent sex offenders that have not been covered to this point. To begin with, I would like to give the reader a comprehensive typology of adolescent sex offenders to use as a reference.

TYPOLOGY OF ADOLESCENT SEX OFFENDERS

Type 1: Naive experimenter. Tends to be young (eleven to fourteen years old), with little history of acting-out behavior. He is sexually naive and engages in one or only a few sexually exploratory acts with a younger child (two to six years old), using no force or threats.

Type 2: Undersocialized child exploiter. Evidences chronic social isolation and social incompetence. His abusive behavior is likely to be chronic and includes manipulation, rewards, or other enticement. He is motivated to offend by a desire for greater self-importance and for intimacy.

Type 3: Pseudo-socialized child exploiter. Has good social skills and little acting-out history and is apt to present as self-confident. He may be a victim of some form of abuse, which is likely to have been going on for years. He tends to be motivated by a desire for sexual pleasure through exploitation, tends to rationalize assaults, and feels little remorse or guilt.

Type 4: Sexual aggressive. Comes from an abusive, chaotic family. He is more likely to have a long history of antisocial acts, poor impulse control, and substance abuse, His sexual assaults involve force. He is motivated by a desire to experience power by domination, to express anger, and to humiliate his victim.

Type 5: Sexual compulsive. Family is usually emotionally repressive and rigidly enmeshed. His offenses are repetitive, often of a compulsive nature, and more likely to be hands off (e.g., peeping or exposing). His motivation may be the alleviation of anxiety.

Type 6: Disturbed impulsive. Likely to have a history of psychological disorder, severe family dysfunction, substance abuse, and significant learning problems. His offenses are impulsive and reflect disturbance of reality testing (i.e., sees things in a distorted, personalized manner).

Type 7: Group influenced. Is apt to be a younger teen with no previous delinquent history who engages in assault in the company of a peer group. The motivation is apt to be peer pressure and the desire for approval.

When working with or treating adolescent sex offenders over a period of time, all of these types will eventually be encountered.

Additional Traits of Adolescent Sex Offenders

In Chapter 1, I presented Distinctive Characteristics of Sex Offenders. Although many, if not all, of these traits also exist in adolescent sex offenders, due to their complex and constantly changing development, the following additional traits need to be recognized and dealt with as well (see also Box 1.3):

- Needs to be accepted by peers at any price
- Uses negative means to attract attention
- Has difficulty postponing pleasure needs
- Exhibits serious empathy deficits
- Lacks a religious/moral value system
- Demonstrates incredible sexual naïveté
- Feels unloved, unwanted, alone
- Displays strong belonging needs
- Has damaged self-worth, self-image
- Develops unrealistic negative body image
- Fears being compared to peers
- Shows symptoms of attention deficit disorder

- Engages in little, if any, communication with adult figures
- Is emotionally immature
- Utilizes all defense mechanisms
- Performs self-defeating/self-punishing behaviors
- Has difficulty trusting
- Uses manipulation and pity mechanisms
- Acts out sexually
- Has a need to control
- Successful therapy is a long and difficult process

Looking at this list, as a whole, one could easily attribute most, if not all, of the list to the adult sex offenders as well. The difference is that these traits are still *fluid* in the adolescent group, whereas in the adult group they have become fixated. The importance of this factor lies in the fact that, if true, this group has a much more positive prognosis for change and for a close-to-normal adult life. This list is also an excellent way to define our concept of the inadequate personality.

As in the adult group, the question then becomes "Why sex?" This must be the focus of the therapist and the treatment. With these same characteristics, these adolescents could have become killers (and some do!), thieves, terrorists, slaves to more aggressive "friends," gang leaders, and many other types of antisocial, acting-out individuals. Untreated, they also have the potential of becoming the adult sex offenders of the future.

Adolescents Involved in Gangs

While in California, I spent several days with a group of special police who were known as the "Gang Squad." We found and talked to several of the main known groups at the time. The group members identified by the police as "followers" possessed all of the traits listed here. When leaders of these groups were shown the list of additional traits, they admitted that they specifically chose a percentage of the group membership specifically because they fit the list perfectly. This was especially true among the gangs at war with other gangs who were responsible for the many, many drive-by shootings that accounted for so many innocent citizens, including children, being killed or seriously injured.

Especially remarkable was that when the followers were separated from the rest of the gang members and literally on their own, they fell apart and reverted to the weak, scared, pitiful individuals that they truly were.

As could be expected, the saddest factor uncovered was that these teens had little or no family life, no support in the neighborhood (except from the gangs) and were mostly school dropouts or social promotion to graduation types.

Looking at the list, the gang leaders, as well as pedophiles and hebophiles, easily met the needs presented.

- The first eleven traits are part of the group culture. He is accepted by his peers; he will certainly attract negative attention; there will be no need to postpone his pleasures; empathy in the gang is nonexistent; religious and moral values are not society's values but are those of the group he joins; he no longer feels unloved, unwanted, or alone, once accepted he certainly belongs; he receives a new type of self-worth and immediately adopts a new self-image (taken from the gang); if sexually naive before he joined, the gang will cure this problem almost overnight.
- If attention deficit disorder existed, it will have no meaning in the group; there will still be little or no communication with his parents or authority figures (especially the police); as a follower he can remain emotionally immature (the gang leader will prefer it that way); defense mechanisms will increase and be accepted by the gang; self-defeating behaviors will be justified by his loyalty to the rules and mores of the gang; trust will exist only for fellow gang members.
- The remainder of the list automatically is taken care of. He can act out all of his negative sexual and anger needs and feel as powerful as he wishes with impunity and protection from the gang (until caught).

From this presentation, it becomes even more urgent that these individuals are discovered as early as possible, certainly before they are completely taken over by a gang. Adolescence itself is a "gang time" in the life of a developing individual, so it seems natural for young males and females to join a gang if one exists in their neighborhood. In parts of some larger metropolitan cities, joining a gang is a survival need since nonmembers are some of the most frequently targeted victims by all of the gangs.

Adolescents Not Involved in Gangs

Not all of the adolescents that become sex offenders were or are involved in gangs. There is a distinct group that isolates and is filled with loners. Some of these teens are easily seen since they do not attempt to hide this trait; another group of teens *appears* normal and socially involved, but, in their own minds, there is a persistent feeling of being rejected by their peers and of not belonging. These individuals are harder to find, and, unless parents, relatives, friends, or teachers really earn their trust, they will stay hidden until they do something that puts a spotlight on them. Only then are they exposed. Jeffy (introduced) in Chapter 1 was this type of teen.

At school and in the neighborhood, JEFFY was considered both highly social and a ladies' man. Jeffy trusted no one from the time his father first deserted the family, including his mother who made him grow up on his own and who cared little about what he did unless it affected her life and comfort.

After his first run-in with the authorities, he was sent to me for treatment. Within the first one-hour session, it became apparent that there was a wall between us. He was *too* polite, acted *too* friendly, and gave me all the right answers (as he perceived them).

After a lengthy session with his mother (who was overtly seductive and intimated that she would do *anything* to get her son out of trouble), it was obvious to me that she knew very little about her son, his school behavior, his friends, etc. It was also obvious that she cared little about him and saw him as a burden on her life and freedom.

The wall that Jeffy constructed was simply too high and too thick to penetrate. After an evaluation indicating that he did not pose a sexual threat to any other children, his case was terminated. It took two years in the state reformatory for boys, several years later, to collapse the wall. The trauma of his first incarceration was sufficient to return him to therapy highly motivated to straighten out his life.

It was at this time that his isolation and social performance was related to me. He had isolated at the reformatory and acted "crazy" (a typical defense behavior in institutions for the purpose of being left alone by staff as well as other inmates), and it worked. No one bothered him in any way, and he did his two years alone with his thoughts and plans for the future. It was then and only then that he realized he had problems he could not solve by himself and he needed professional help.

Dom in Chapter 1 and Howie in Chapters 2 and 7 are the opposite type. Their isolation was out in the open: Dom was a special-education student, and Howie's mother was on the staff at his school. Both were openly isolated and identified as loners and "different," but no one did anything about it. No one tried to help either of these teens, and the result was attempted and seductive child molestation. This is where society and parents fail. Had either or both of these teens been referred to a well-trained therapist, the outcome may have been different. Both responded well when therapy was forced on them by the courts.

Adolescent Sex Offenders from "Good Families"

Over the years, I have been asked what the most surprising fact was that I learned in my work with both adult and adolescent sex offenders. I would honestly have to say that after meeting both the adolescent and his family, the most surprising fact was that these teens did not all come from poor or conflicted homes, nor did they come from run-down and crime-ridden neighborhoods. The majority I have treated came from middle-class to upper-middle-class homes, and a small percentage came from wealthy homes.

The only common denominator I found was that regardless of the social level they were raised in, *communication was minimal or did not exist.* A surprisingly large number of these teens literally raised themselves. There was little supervision in the home, often both parents worked, and, where monies were available, they were either given an unusually high allowance (e.g., one hundred dollars per week) as a "payoff" to take care of themselves and not bother their parents or had a paid nanny. In other homes, both parents worked and from an early age these teens were "latchkey" children who came home from school (if they bothered going) to an empty house where they could do as they pleased.

Both groups of parents, when interviewed, rationalized (excused) their absence based on economic pressures that kept them at work or at meetings (often social occasions) until late in the evenings. Fathers, in positions where travel was part of their employment, were seldom home and rarely (if ever) attended school functions, such as parents' night or sports events, in which their teen was involved. Both groups reported few (if any) occasions where they had dinner together or sat and talked with their teens about their daily lives, educational problems, or goals. The most striking missing element in both groups was that the parents could not identify their teen's friends or, when they did know them by sight or by name, they knew little or nothing about who they were or what they were about.

In many of these cases, the lone teen had sex (including rape) parties where drug and alcohol use were common. Pornography parties with sexual visuals (either on VHS tape or computer-generated porn) were the focus and led to group sex and "gang bangs" (rape of one girl by a group of boys). Also, many of these parties and events too often occurred on school nights under the covering of "studying" or "writing a paper together." Parents rarely (if ever) questioned these explanations for what they found upon returning home late in the evening. When parents were traveling, these parties became two- and three-day affairs, often with accompanying truancy.

Another surprising factor to me was that when their teens became involved with the law and were placed on probation, very few (if any) parents went with them to their reporting meetings with the probation officers or reported their behaviors to that agency. It always appeared that whatever their teens did would rub off on the parents and damage their reputations. Self-centeredness was a major trait in these parents.

Of course, exceptions existed. There was a small percentage of trusting, sincere parents who truly cared about their teens but had tried to regain control *too late* in the development of their offspring. By the time they realized they were being lied to and conned by their teens, it was too late to begin giving direction or to mold their value systems. Here again, fear of being judged bad parents prevented many from seeking professional help. They rationalized that this was just a phase that the teen was going through and soon it would be over.

It is impossible to stress the importance of communication at the earliest age and also of teaching values both directly and by example. Many (as high as 90 percent) of the teens I see in treatment for a sexual problem that led to legal problems reported (and parent interviews confirmed) that there was never any communication in their homes. They also admit that they had wanted to just sit down and talk with their parents but that the parents were never available.

THE REMAINDER OF THE ADOLESCENT
SEX OFFENDER TRAIT LIST

Most of the traits listed in the Additional Traits of Adolescent Sex Offenders section have already been covered in the preceding chapters since adult sex offenders have similar or identical traits. In this section, I discuss only those traits which are distinctive to adolescent sex offenders and which have not already been described.

Uses Negative Means to Attract Attention

Although this trait can exist in some less intelligent adult sex offenders, they have usually learned through painful experiences that using negative means to attract attention does not work. In fact, by the time the adult sex offender is caught and in the court system, many have found positive means of gaining attention including sports, success in employment, and excelling in social activities. All of these overt behaviors are "fronts" to cover their true personalities.

Teens, during all of the developmental stages, might try some of these means of gaining attention *if* they recognize that they have something positive to use. The majority find that only in negative behaviors (alcohol, school misbehaviors including truancy, drug use, sexual promiscuity, violence, petty crime, etc.) are they recognized and seen as "special" or "famous" by similar teens that they interact with. These negative behaviors form their new identity as a denial of the person they really are and fear others will discover them to be. Most are rebellion behaviors, and many are overcompensation for felt deficits.

Internally, these negative behaviors do not satisfy the majority of teens, unless they already are sociopaths. Guilt often results and includes a form of self-hate which may lead to suicide or such blatant acting out that incarceration is assured. Jeffy, introduced in Chapter 1, is this type of teen. In his first few incidents with the law (including the child molestation in Chapter 1) he was able to con his probation officers with his seductive and overly polite manner (all control mechanisms) and could literally get away with almost anything. It took a new probation officer who was able to see through his manipulations to put his foot down, and that is when Jeffy, still believing he could get away with anything, *goofed* and ended up spending two years of his young life in a correctional facility. Fortunately, he used his time there well, did a great deal of thinking and introspection (using methods we had discussed in therapy before his failure), and was able to turn his life around. Today, he is a new person (yes, I tested him over and over again) and on the road to a new life. He works daily; has dropped most of his old friends, both male and female; makes all of his own decisions; and is constantly planning for the future.

Attention Deficit Disorder Often Present

The controversial diagnosis of ADD is still debated by many psychologists who believe it does not exist. One of the major symptoms of ADD is the inability to focus on a single topic or subject for any length of time. In school, they are easily distracted, forget what they hear almost as fast as they hear it, live minute by minute with no long-term planning, are easily distracted by other students, occurrences outside the windows, their own thoughts, and fantasies which are always present. As a result, they are in constant conflict with teachers and supervisory personnel. Often they are transferred to special-education status and then really are lost and unproductive. This is exactly what happened to Dom in Chapter 1. He often was told by teachers to leave the classroom and he would simply walk the corridors of the school almost in a daze. He learned little in these classes, and only when his parents insisted he be returned to "mainstream" status did he graduate. Today, on his own, he is in college and earning Bs and Cs.

Little or No Religious/Moral Value Systems

Referring back to the section on Adolescents Involved in Gangs, it is not difficult to see how pliable and easily manipulated this type of adolescent would be when approached for membership in a gang. With little or no religious or moral values to fall back on, these teens are easily convinced by gang leaders, that the end justifies the means and that the gang dictates the religious and moral values of its members.

This is especially true in the realm of the satanic cults. Here, whatever the teen did learn about moral and religious values as a small child are now exactly the opposite. What was supposedly *good* in the past is now *evil* and, conversely, whatever was *evil* in the past is now *good* and desirable. Loyalty to the gang is the paramount value. In these cults, revenge replaces forgiveness, "take whatever you want" replaces honesty. Members are told to lie to protect themselves, the other gang members, and to act out all impulses (especially sex and violence). The message is do whatever *Satan* wants you to (as dictated by the gang leader), and he will reward you both now and in the afterlife. Chaos in both thinking and behaving results.

By the time parents realize what is happening, it is too late. This is another reason that daily communication and knowing what the teen is about and with whom he is associating is a must. In the recent past, this problem became more than clear when a teenage boy, deeply involved in satanism, sacrificed two young boys in a brutal and sadistic manner to "please his master." His sexual problems revealed themselves when he castrated both young boys.

The rest of the list applies to both adolescent and adult offenders and has already been discussed. These traits will be referred to again and again in the remaining chapters of this work.

This chapter ends the who section of the book, describing the personality and behavioral makeup of both adult and adolescent sex offenders. Chapter 9 begins "Treatment" issues, problems, and techniques.

A final caution regarding the use of published statistics. All statistics are made up of *reported* cases only. As has already been discussed, where sex offenses are concerned, the reported cases are only the tip of the iceberg. A very large percentage of victims of sexual offenses choose not to report. Their existence is only known from counselors and therapists who treat them.

SECTION II:
TREATMENT OF SEX OFFENDERS

Chapter 9

Treatment Issues: Overview

INTRODUCTION

Before discussing the specific treatment issues that have worked for me for over forty years and that I promulgate in all of my training seminars, it is important to take a brief look at the current overall sex offender treatment picture elsewhere in the field.

It seems to me that almost everyone called upon to treat sex offenders develops his or her own specialized treatment techniques. These include:

- individual or group techniques;
- verbal techniques alone or in combination with psychotropic medication;
- rational emotive techniques;
- behavior modification techniques;
- cognitive-behavioral techniques;
- psychodynamic therapy;
- psychiatric treatment with medication;
- self-help groups; and, finally,
- chemical castration or physical castration.

Each of the items on this list has many variables and modifications made by individual "treaters." Some treatment personnel use a combination of several techniques. Individual programs use an endless variety of techniques that they insist work. The bottom line appears to be use "whatever works best."

There is no doubt that the frustrations of dealing with this population stimulate "experimentation" in a search for a technique that produces results. The problems with this type of approach is that, as I have already stated several times, sex offenders are highly manipulative individuals who are always "psyching out" their therapists and often are one step ahead of them. They respond with what they perceive to be the wants and goals of the program they are in. It is a difficult often impossible task to defend against these manipulations, and only experience and prepared precautions against this type of manipulation can prevent a total "con job" from occurring.

To defend against these con jobs, professional programs should include a second opinion by another therapist who has not had contact with the offender, use of the offender's group to evaluate his progress, and "proving-change" techniques as I will soon discuss.

A word on castration, either chemical or real: In my experience, these techniques do not work for two simple reasons.

1. Testosterone replacement is readily available.
2. Once the behavior is compulsive, the offender will still find ways to satisfy his needs.

Loss of erectile response does not prevent the offender from acting out on the victim (e.g., masturbating or fellating young boys or using objects to rape women). I have had many offenders who acted out in this way even after castration for testicular cancers. Several also were still able to masturbate to their deviant fantasies with an injection of male hormone (provided by the prison system). While at a conference in San Francisco, I personally interviewed several pedophiles who were on Depo-Provera (chemical castration) in order to maintain probation. The majority admitted, in confidence, that they were purchasing testosterone for self-injection from a black-market pharmacist. Two also admitted that they were still seeing their former victims and having sex with them.

To prevent errors and manipulations from occurring and in order to provide an effective method of dealing with sex offenders, "specialized treatment training" is a mandatory pre-requisite, since too often this topic and these techniques are not included in the individual therapist's professional schooling.

THE IMPORTANT FIRST CONTACT

Treatment must begin with the *first contact* and continue until the *last contact* in outpatient treatment programs.

In the very first contact with a sex offender, whether in an individual setting or a group setting, a "psycho-educational session" should be held. Although some of these individuals may have had contact with some form of therapy before, the majority have not and do not know what to expect or what is expected of them.

The primary topic in this session is a discussion of the therapist's *confidentiality.* This includes a statement of the laws that the therapist must abide by, including the mandatory reporting of sexual abuse cases and all future crime threats or statements.

The second type of confidentiality is the subject's confidentiality. This should include a discussion that everything discussed in the session or anything that happens in the session must remain there. This is most important where groups are concerned. In my own experience, both in institutions and in private practice, I inform my patients that I tolerate no security breaches. As soon as one occurs, treatment is terminated (my personal decision).

The third factor is that in this first session a personal questionnaire be distributed and filled out there. The specific reason for this procedure involves spontaneity versus planned answers and self-answering versus getting help from others. This is especially a danger in an institution or in an outpatient group situation where the members of the group often have contact with one another outside of the group session. Here again, the emphasis must be on honest answers and confidentiality. Besides offering some initial insights into each patient, the questionnaire becomes a *ruler* at a later time to see changes by redoing it again. I usually do this on a six-month schedule. A copy of the questionnaire that I use is included in Appendix B.

The remainder of this session should deal with the mechanics of therapy: what happens, what are the roles of the therapist and, more important, of the patient, what rules (if any) are to be followed, and, finally what is the overall goal of treatment. The only goal I espouse for all of my patients is that when we finish they will be more knowledgeable about who they were when the problem occurred, who they are now, and who they want to be in the future.

The remaining major rule I impose (in addition to confidentiality) is that the patient must not lie. One method of preventing lying is to give all patients permission to state "I don't want to talk about it today" or "I'm not ready to go there yet" (with the understanding that someday they will have to talk about it). Everything must be exposed eventually during treatment if any positive results are to occur.

CLINICAL INTERVIEWING PRINCIPLES

In order to expect to be effective in the treatment of sex offenders the prospective "treater" must have mastered the clinical skills necessary for practice in one of the mental health professions of psychology, social work, psychiatry, or counseling. Even so, typical training programs for these professions rarely provide a sufficient base in specialized knowledge and clinical technique to permit the neophyte practitioner to plunge headlong into the task of treating sex offenders. Indeed, before considering treatment principles and specific techniques particularly applicable to the treatment of these offenders, it is important to *know what we do not know.* Among the issues that must be dealt with prior to clinical interviewing in counseling or therapy with sex offenders are such concerns as these:

- Personal traits and characteristics that are essential for the counselor or therapist to possess if he or she is to work successfully with sex offenders
- Treatment or therapy orientation/modalities that produce positive results with this population
- Personality traits and defense mechanisms in both offenders and victims that facilitate or impede both disclosure and effective participation in treatment
- Specific barriers (defenses) to revealing the therapist's own personal sexual molestation as a child (if one occurred)
- Means of assessing the reality or illusory character of purported changes in the offender
- The function of *ritual* and *imprinting* in the pathology of the offender
- Prognosis for effective treatment among the major offender groups: pedophiles, hebophiles, incestuous fathers, and sexually assaultive persons
- Distinguishing characteristics which boldly identify the personality of the true incestuous father and which differ substantially from pedophiles/hebophiles

- Needs unresolved in childhood that interfere with the relationship between the offender and his therapist, regardless of the sex of the therapist

Cardinal Principles of Clinical Interviewing

The ten cardinal principles in Box 9.1 cover the consistent problem areas I have encountered in supervising therapists new to this field—issues that should be dealt with in some detail.

Readiness

Readiness on the part of both the client and the therapist is a must prior to any interviewing attempt. In my experience, the client will let the therapist know when he is ready to get into the deeper or more serious issues, either by directly stating so or by using leading statements and body language, indicating that the client wants the therapist to ask questions or introduce more serious topics. Once this readiness is observed, the therapist needs to be ready for very heavy and emotional sessions.

Confidentiality Issues

As touched on previously, before any serious or factual discussion can take place, the issue of confidentiality must be thoroughly addressed. In the state where I practice, child abuse of any type must be reported, although all other sex offenses remain confidential unless

9.1

Cardinal Principles of Clinical Interviewing

- Readiness
- All the nitty-gritty details/facts
- Listening
- The less said by the therapist, the better
- Hope
- Body language, choice of terms, adjectives, and emotional reactions
- Emotional reactions
- Sensitivity to lies or manipulations
- Assume nothing!
- Confidentiality issues

the information poses a clear and imminent danger to the community. This law or any other legal factors or implications that could affect therapy must be explained to the client. The client must then be allowed to ask questions regarding these issues and must be given time to consider all of the ramifications before proceeding any further. My own preference is to cover this issue in the first session, before any serious material is discussed or accidentally related. The client then has at least a week to consider the issue and to make a realistic decision.

Where very young children are concerned (my youngest patient was five years old), this issue must be discussed with the primary parent (the one bringing the child to the therapist and most involved in his or her care).

Another major confidentiality issue, where all minors are concerned, is *confidentiality from the parents*. Since this touches on the parents' rights area, it must be made clear from the first contact that the child is the client/patient and that parents have no right to know what is discussed in the therapy sessions. Where children and adolescents are concerned, I exaggerate this issue by promising that I will not reveal anything they tell me without their specific permission, and I use a "Release of Information" form to concretize this agreement.

A connected and related issue involves obtaining an agreement with the parents that they will not "grill" the child about what was said in the session. Without the agreement of both parents (or one in single-parent situations), I will not accept the case.

Plunging into the area of the abuse and insisting on answers to detailed questions about the abuse will almost always lead to a cutoff of trust (rapport), a heightening of defenses, and a definite loss of free-flowing communication. In many cases when this type of demanding, authoritative approach is used in the first session, the victim will either stop speaking or get up and leave, never to return.

Readiness issues should be discussed in the first session with both the offender and the survivor. It is imperative to give the patient the permission "not to be ready" in the first several sessions to discuss sensitive and traumatizing materials. However, the therapist must be positive the patient understands that these discussions must take place at some time in the treatment process.

In my experience, until a positive rapport is established that includes trust and testing, these areas will not be willingly brought up or exposed. Forcing or demanding that these issues be exposed when the therapist wants them exposed assures lies, deceptions, and ultimately failure.

The therapist's readiness is also crucial. One never knows what the patient/client will disclose. These disclosures are graphic, ugly at times, and possibly even nauseating. Murder may also be confessed. Finally, the language used will be raw and disturbing. If the therapist reacts with shock, revulsion, or insult, therapy is over.

All the Nitty-Gritty Details/Facts

It is necessary to obtain all the nitty-gritty details of the client's past history the first time the client is willing to talk about it. I strongly recommend that the therapist not allow generalities or vague and suggestive statements to substitute for the truth, or else the same areas will have to be gone over again and again to get the total picture.

It is quite common for children, adolescents, and even adults to try to get away with telling as little as possible about their true problems, since telling the therapist all the terrible and traumatic details of their past and present problems means they must hear it again themselves and therefore relive it, to some degree. They also fear being "judged" by the therapist and possibly being rejected.

Often, the client's opening statements resemble these:

- I had sex with him/her.
- We did dirty or bad things.
- I touched him/her.
- We, you know—did it.

Through encouragement and support, the therapist must elicit the rest of the material (the nitty-gritty details) in a direct but reassuring manner.

It is not uncommon, in an embarrassing, degrading, or severely painful trauma, for the offender to reveal only the minimum that he feels is necessary. This is especially true in rape cases. Quite often the offender will leave out the words he used, acts that are repulsive or disgusting, the fact that he reached orgasm, or any fact or behavior that still is producing large amounts of personal guilt. To accept minimal details can be misleading and prolong the therapy as well as delay any significant recovery.

An example in which this *almost* occurred may help to clarify.

BOBBY (whose case is discussed in Chapters 4, 6, and 7) openly discussed the rape for which he was convicted with his first primary therapist.
The therapist probed no further and within his first year of therapy wanted to
refer Bobby for possible release from the program. When his therapist became ill and left the treatment facility, I inherited the case (at the therapist's
request) and was willing to proceed with the release process only after I had
had a chance for an intensive interview. From the first fifteen minutes or so,
something bothered me about Bobby's presentation. It was too pat and
sounded very well rehearsed. I informed him that I needed more time to get
to know him before proceeding and also told him quite directly that I felt he
was hiding something.

Several weeks later, after Bobby had attended and participated in several
of my groups, he requested an individual session. The first thing he mentioned was that his former therapy had not been as intense or as deep and
that he felt there were issues that he needed to "confess." What amazed me
was that his former therapist had never asked him about other rapes or sexual assaults for which he was never apprehended. This was the critical area.
Bobby related the following:

"Sure, there were other rapes, mostly all the same type and pattern, *except* this one case." (At this point he appeared visibly frightened and tears
began streaming down his cheeks.)

"This one lady was different from all of the rest. She laughed at me and
said I was too small to rape anyone. I punched her as hard as I could and
then ripped her pants and underwear off, saying 'I'll show you who's too
small!' When I took my shorts off, she laughed crazily while pointing to my
penis and said, 'If that's all you've got, it'll get lost inside of me!' At that point,
something happened and I went crazy. There was an old, broken baseball
bat in the bushes where I had taken her, and I picked it up and kept hitting her
in the face and head with it until I couldn't hit anymore and until she was
quiet. Then I panicked and ran. I never saw anything in the papers about her,
but I think that she was dead."

Bobby had been treated for a year without ever mentioning this
rape *because he was neither asked about other rapes he may have
committed nor motivated to get all of the problems out and dealt with.*
He had been terrified that someone would find out and that he would
be tried for murder, so he never volunteered anything.

Now the total picture of the case changed. Not only was he an angry and dangerous rapist but also a potential murderer (the ultimate
rape) as well. Were he released without this critical information uncovered, he would have raped again and possibly killed again. In following sessions, he made similar predictions on his own to his group.
The fact that his rage had reached points of being uncontrollable and

deadly had never been discovered or treated. Also, and of more importance, his motivations and the etiology of his rape behavior now had to be expanded to include both his body and penis size and important *triggers* that needed to be thoroughly dealt with before any possible return to the community.

Prior to this "confession," everyone who had worked with Bobby believed that the only precipitating factors involved in his rape behavior were his father's outrageous rejection and physical abuse and his mother's impotence at helping him (see Chapter 4). His good looks, likable demeanor, and the sympathy and empathy everyone felt about his terrible childhood made it easy for him to hide the true extent of his pathology and rage.

In trying to explain this essential factor to both therapists and new clients, I have often used the metaphor of making an appointment with a physician to discuss an embarrassing problem. If the patient leaves out specific and graphic details due to fear of judgment, punishment, or rejection, the doctor may make a wrong diagnosis and then prescribe the wrong medication and treatment. The patient will then be worse off than if he or she never went to the physician in the first place. Even young children are able to understand the significance of this metaphor.

It is also important for the therapist to define for the client his or her own role and to assure the client that the therapist will not be judgmental or punitive.

Listening

In supervising many new therapists over the years, one of my most frequent criticisms has been that they have never learned to *listen*. Lecturing, preaching, interrupting, rapid-fire questioning, taking notes during the session, answering telephones, and other forms of distraction replace the art of listening to what the client needs and is trying to tell the therapist.

Lack of the necessary patience to wait until the client is *ready* to speak or to continue often disrupts his or her concentration and train of thought or, even more frequently, gives the client an excuse to *forget* what he was relating in the first place. As stated in prior sections, the offender will use any excuse or alibi to get away from a sensitive, embarrassing, or guilt-provoking area, and, too often, the therapist provides the way out.

I have experienced pauses of as long as three to five minutes, a seeming lifetime of silence in a therapy session. Usually the wait is worth it, because the client is fighting with himself about revealing something difficult, betraying a confidence, or identifying an abuser. The *pause* often identifies the crucial areas and/or subjects for the therapist, if he or she is paying attention.

The Less Said by the Therapist, the Better

In order to accomplish good listening skills and yet keep the session moving, I suggest the use of a few,well-placed cue words, which will be discussed more fully in Chapter 10 under the section on Confrontation.

- *Because?* For statements/feelings without reasons.
- *And?* There must be more to the thought/statement.
- *Pzzzzzzzt!* A shocking I don't believe you.
- *Picture?* I don't understand. Make me see it.
- *Tilt!* You're off the subject. Get back to it.
- *Belly Button!* Used where behavioral changes are concerned. Means don't tell me you've changed, prove it to me by examples.

Where this skill is concerned, experience will always be the best teacher.

Hope

At the first opportunity, it is important for the therapist to communicate to the client that

- Although sex offenders have serious psychological problems, this does not mean they are totally bad people; it means they are human beings with a problem.
- The future depends on working through all of the facts and feelings, especially any *anger/rage* reactions that may still be there from childhood trauma.

- Although the full responsibility for the offense is the client's, he can be treated and eventually lead a normal and happy life. In other words, *there is* help.
- The past does not predict or determine the future, and *change is possible and can be permanent.*
- Sex offenders need a return to *reality*—not judgment, punishment, distortion, etc.
- Sex offenders need to identify and resolve *all guilt* for their past and present deviant behaviors to live normal and healthy lives in the future.

Body Language, Choice of Terms, Adjectives,
and Emotional Reactions

Once the therapist has mastered the skill of listening, learning to concentrate and pay attention to anything and everything the client says or does is paramount in importance. A change of position, a change of facial expression, a sudden downward glance or avoidance of prior eye contact, or a lengthy silence all signal to the attentive therapist that a sensitive, painful, or guilt-producing area may have been broached. Depending on the situation, the therapist may choose silence with some form of physical support, such as simply nodding his or her head or moving or leaning closer. The therapist may also choose some form of verbal support, from the simplest "Uh-huh" to "Take your time" or "Are you okay?" or "Do you want to continue?" The therapist, at this point, must know the client and know what is most appropriate for the particular situation.

The therapist's body language is also extremely important. This begins in the way his or her office is arranged. The old formal manner of sitting across a desk from a patient often is interpreted as a distancing from and blocking contact from the client. Placing the patient's chair on one side of the desk allows the therapist to turn toward him or her in an approachable way. Any sudden change in the therapist's demeanor or facial expression is always observed by patients, especially sex offenders, and is usually taken as some form of shock reaction, disapproval, or annoyance on the part of the therapist. Becoming comfortable in an uncomfortable situation is attained only through practice and time.

One important word of caution: under no circumstances should the therapist use the overly used statement "I understand" where sex offenders are concerned, unless the therapist himself or herself has been a sex offender or victim of sexual abuse. Rapport can be lost with this one patronizing statement. Instead of seeming supportive, it will most likely produce anger in the offender and a loss of credibility for the therapist, damaging essential rapport.

I have observed this reaction on videotape countless times, when a new or inexperienced therapist under supervision makes this critical mistake and then cannot understand the client's reaction of anger and hostility. One such case comes to mind.

A young male psychologist, just out of graduate school with his master's degree and fresh out of a clinical internship in a state mental hospital, was conducting his first interview with a twenty-year-old male who was a pedophile and himself had been molested. Early in the first interview, the man stated, "It was terrible! Awful! The worst thing that ever happened to me! I feel dirty and contaminated!"

Without the least hesitation or time to think, the young psychologist replied, "I know, I know! I understand just how you feel." Immediately the client became enraged, stood up, and yelled down at the stunned psychologist, "Oh, yeah! When did you get fucked in the ass?"

The psychologist stammered something so quietly that it was not picked up on the videotape, and the man left the room, slamming the door. The therapist forgot the following important principle concerning survivors of sexual abuse.

Survivors Are Extremely Sensitive to Lies or Manipulations

A more appropriate response by the therapist would have been "It certainly must have been a terrible experience for you. I really don't know what you must have gone through, but I'd like to, if you would share it with me." This example presents support, as well as a chance to gain trust with honesty and to encourage the client to continue and go into further detail in order to get the therapist to understand.

Where choice of terms, adjectives, and emotions are concerned, the therapist will be most effective and miss the least amount of important material if the next principle is followed.

Assume Nothing!

In training new therapists, I always suggest that where any form of sexual deviation is concerned, regardless of the age of the client, the therapists act as if they had just arrived from another planet and need every word, phrase, and term clearly defined and explained by the client. Using the therapist's own background knowledge or personal experiences can cause confusion and lose valuable material while it is fresh in the client's memory. This is especially true in the session where the facts of the abuse are first divulged.

A tragic example can best illustrate this all-important point.

TONY is now a young twenty-three-year-old adult. When he was only fifteen, he was sent to the old New Jersey State Diagnostic Center on a charge of juvenile delinquency involving impregnating his fourteen-year-old sister, Jill. Since both Tony and his sister admitted the charges, the case seemed cut and dry and the only diagnostic or therapeutic work left was to decide on a course of action. The choices were to return Tony to his home under strict supervision or to send him to a reformatory for punishment (since there was little treatment available in those days).

However, my gut reaction was that something was amiss in this case. Tony just seemed wrong for this particular charge, and there was definitely something unusual about the whole family. The social worker on the case was asked to do an in-depth workup on the family while I decided to do some brief therapy with Tony on an emergency basis. Following the principles outlined, I asked Tony to make believe I was from another planet and knew nothing about the reproductive behavior of humans. Smiling, he agreed and thought this would be an interesting game. I then instructed him to take me through the impregnation of his sister, step by step, leaving nothing to my imagination. The following story emerged.

Due to money problems, Tony and the other children were allowed only one bath per week. Since he was the oldest, he went first. To save money, he was not to drain the water but leave it for his sister to bathe in. Being a normal adolescent, he became stimulated washing his genitals and proceeded to masturbate and ejaculate. Jill then bathed, not knowing what Tony had done, and a month or more later announced that she was pregnant. When Tony was questioned by his parents, he admitted to the masturbation in the bathtub, and they told him that was how his sister became pregnant and he was the father.

When I recovered from my shock at the story, I asked Tony about intercourse, and he admitted that the whole family played the "fun games" on a regular basis: Tony with his mother, and his sister with her father. The younger children were allowed to watch and were taught to pleasure themselves with masturbation. When asked about babies, Tony stated that they were a gift of God. He did not connect pregnancy to the "fun games" in any way whatsoever. I then spoke to Jill, who was also at the center, and she readily admitted playing "fun games" with several of the boys on the football team at school. She also discussed her "fun games" with her father.

The social worker on the case was informed and reluctantly discussed the "fun games" with the parents who, surprisingly, readily admitted that this was their only pleasure, since they could not afford TV or other entertainment, and that it was the best way to show their kids *that they loved them.* Needless to say, the parents were evaluated and found to be of borderline intelligence, socially isolated, and retarded.

The real trauma in this case resulted from the arrest, exposure, ridicule by peers and neighbors, and the deriding and callous attitude of the juvenile officers. The family had to be relocated. A total program of reeducation and resocialization training was undertaken, and both Tony and Jill were provided therapy. Jill had her baby and, due to the unusual circumstances, the parents were allowed to adopt the child as their own. Supervision was provided by the then Bureau of Children's Services.

Through psychological testing, Tony was found to be of above-average to superior intelligence and, with a great deal of tutoring, improved in his schoolwork sufficiently to go to a community college.

Without "assume nothing!" as a guide and without following up on gut reactions, the true facts of this case would never have emerged; Tony and Jill would have ended up in reformatories and the rest of the young children would have continued to be sexually abused. It is important to state here that I have encountered hundreds of cases *where the surface facts in no way reflected the true facts of the case.*

TERMS

The client's choice of words can tell the therapist a great deal about how he feels about what happened, how much guilt exists, and how judgmental the client is being about himself. Also, the rapport, trust, and confidence that the client has will be exposed in word choices as well as spontaneous emotional reactions. For example, for an adolescent boy or young adult male to use slang sex terms rather than precise anatomical ones may indicate greater trust and rapport with the therapist and may also increase credibility.

Adding an adjective to a term may clearly indicate the degree of guilt, anger, or pain that the client is communicating. "It was dirty, filthy, disgusting, and sickening" is far different than "It was terrible." Keeping track of these terms and adjectives enables the therapist to measure desensitization and progress over a period of time and indicates when the next level of therapy can begin.

Clients with very low self-esteem and who are resistant to seeing themselves in a better light frequently use minimizing phrases, including

- Sort of
- A little bit
- Maybe
- No big deal

and many others. These phrases are most frequently used in discussing some positive change, risk, or new behavior that the client has accomplished. When asked if the particular behavior is positive, an affirmation is immediately minimized, the head goes down, and the voice deepens and trails off.

Dennis (see Chapters 6, 12, 13, and 14) usually begins all sessions with a litany of failures, errors, mistakes, and homework assignments he did not do because "I guess I didn't want to." When this negative confession is complete, he will then add one or two occurrences that he felt could be seen as positive: "Well, I did call one of my friends and ask him to go to a concert with me. We really had a good time— *but the only reason he went with me is because he had a fight with his girlfriend and had nothing better to do.*" Or: "I went for a new job interview and they hired me. It's quite a promotion and really good for my future—*but I'll probably screw it up like I do everything else.*" In feedback, the therapist who pays close attention to these terms and listens to what the client is really trying to communicate can then use the same terms and inquire as to why they are always appended.

Reverse role-play also helps in these instances. I like to use one of the client's close friends, whom he really cares about, in the role-play. In its simplest terms, the technique involves repeating the same phrases—*as the friend*—and then asking the client how he would respond. The answers are usually right on target. The client now is in a catch-22 situation since if he tries to talk the friend out of the minimizing behavior, the therapist can ask why he doesn't do the same for himself. If he allows the minimizing by his friend, then he really does not care about the friend or want to make him or her feel better.

The focus of all these types of sessions has to be aimed at *reality* and *balance*. With very difficult and resistant clients, the technique I use is to *forbid* them to use a second negative judgment about themselves until there has been at least one positive judgment. Thus, the pattern is one negative, followed by one positive, followed by the second negative, followed by the second positive, etc. Eventually the concept of *balance* takes hold and they are able to relate a week's events in a more realistic manner.

GROUP VERSUS INDIVIDUAL TREATMENT

Of all my major errors (and therefore learning experiences), *emphasizing and depending on individual therapy* was the most serious. The seductive and manipulative personality of the offender should be one of the most important of all therapeutic considerations. These individuals can perform well enough to win an Academy Award and thus the danger of the therapist being fooled, used, or manipulated exists for whatever goal the sex offender chooses (especially freedom).

As a group, however, the members become an ideal ruler to measure the change or lack of change of their fellow group members. Although this is unusual in a correctional or institutional setting and would be considered "ratting" under normal circumstances, the confidentiality imposed on the group relieves this pressure. This confrontive exposure of their peers' behavior appears to serve several functions:

- It helps to assuage their intense guilts.
- They feel it will earn acceptance from the therapist.
- It prevents guilt from occurring should they allow a group member to deceive the therapist, to be released, and to harm another victim.

Group "Musts"

Direct but Don't Interfere

Although the therapist does need to remain in control and direct, new supervisees tend to take over the group and become lecturers or teachers. In fact, I have supervised some who could not run a group without a blackboard. Although some instruction in group procedures may be necessary, once these initial sessions are over the group should be allowed to run pretty much on its own with the following control functions performed by the therapist.

Keep the Focus of the Session or Topic

Groups tend to lose focus quite easily and quite often. Also, the man-on-the-floor may deliberately change the subject when the going gets too emotional, painful, or threatening to his image or security. The therapist's role, at this point, is to keep the group and the subject on course until some conclusion is reached or the subject can no longer continue.

Do Not Take Sides or Become Judgmental

A serious group error that many therapists make is to become the protective parent on behalf of the client who is being confronted, facing anger from the group, or appears totally alone in his views. This is especially true when the stronger bullies in the group are picking on a "seductive little defenseless boy"-type offender. Helping him to grow up, face these negative reactions, and see that he will survive becomes an important therapeutic benefit when the therapist *stays out of these battles between individuals and the group*. If the therapist uses these times and situations to *observe*, he or she will learn a great deal not only about the man-on-the-floor but also about many of the other group members.

Becoming judgmental destroys the rapport and trust that the group and its individuals need in order to believe that the therapist's main motive is to help them. One instance of this type may permanently change the trust between the therapist and the group that is necessary for it to be functional and productive.

Never Give Answers; Ask Indirect Questions

The danger here should be obvious. Due to the strong defense mechanisms of the offender, the therapist will often see answers and insights long before the offender does. At times it is both difficult and frustrating not to *suggest* an answer or direction, but this must be avoided. If the therapist suggests an insight or answer that the client has been struggling with, the offender will usually accept it in order to please and agree with the parent-authority-figure, and the therapist will never know for sure whether the verbalized insight is truly the client's own. *It is more important for the client to find his own answers,* regardless of the amount of time this may take. Each offender, as previously stated, is a unique individual, and although the therapist may sincerely believe that he or she knows where the client is coming from and that he has heard the answer before, the possibility that this is a new and never-before-heard insight always exists.

Also, if a solution suggested by the therapist fails, the offender will place the blame (and rightfully so) on the therapist and refuse responsibility. Since making the offender accept responsibility is a major role of this therapy, the error is obvious.

Early in my work with offenders, I met and treated LUKE, a Vietnam veteran who was married and had a son that he adored. Luke was arrested for performing fellatio on preteen and teenage boys, whom he paid for the act in order to keep them from telling anyone. One of his pickups apparently was more innocent and naive than the others he had molested and went home and told his parents what had happened. Luke was arrested.

Luke was quite a likable individual, and all of his group and quite a few other therapists and staff at the treatment center knew him and felt positively toward him. In therapy, he was open, honest, and a hard worker. He worked with the Vietnam veterans group as well. What was quite obvious was the amount of guilt that Luke was suffering from something besides his sexual offenses (guilt from his violent, sadistic sexual and killing behaviors in Vietnam). After a little over three years of therapy in which I felt Luke had made tremendous progress, I began preparing him for possible release. His family visited regularly, and Luke and his wife seemed to be a loving couple with an adorable and quite bright son whom Luke adored.

Whenever Luke balked at the thoughts of release, I *pressured* him on behalf of his family and assured him that he could continue in an outpatient setting with little or no problem. Luke finally agreed and was released shortly after. He returned to his old job, where he was welcomed by his employer and fellow workers with open arms. He did not have to begin at the bottom all over again but instead was given a promotion. Everything looked wonderful! For a year or so, all appeared well, and in outpatient sessions Luke reported no problems or recurrences of fantasies or impulses.

A week after his first-year anniversary on parole, Luke was arrested, caught in the act with a twelve-year-old boy in his car.

In our first interview upon his return, I asked what happened, and he angrily screamed at me, "I told you I wasn't ready, but you kept insisting that I was! I trusted your judgment more than my own, and look what happened to me and my family." It was later revealed that Luke's first recurrent act with a young boy occurred only a week or two after release. He "played the game" for his wife and child as well as for the friends who had so much faith in him. The guilt from Vietnam had never been resolved. I transferred him to another therapist who worked quite well with him.

From that day forward, I made it a practice to put *all responsibility for evaluation of therapy progress* on the individual. Now, even when a client says he or she feels that he or she is ready for promotion, I deny it and make him or her prove it. "Show me, don't tell me!" has become my stock phrase in such situations. In addition, should the client prove through behavior that he has made significant progress and is ready for promotion or termination (PRN Status), I then look for confirmation from others who have daily contact with him. Without these two proofs, no promotion or change in program is given.

Homogeneity of Groups

One of the persistent areas of controversy in the treatment of the offender is that of "homogeneity of groups." Although I have already discussed the vast differences in the personalities of the different types of offenders (and will continue to do so in the following chapters), their *sameness* is far more important as a treatment issue. Another concern is the danger of their forming a mutual defense block against the therapist. Therefore, mixing types of offenders in groups has been far more productive for me, and has kept the groups alive and interesting.

It is incredible to see the interaction of the different types of offenders and their "self-determined hierarchies." Each feels that the other's choice of deviant behavior is far worse than his own (a minimizing mechanism) and cannot understand the other's choice of victim or deviant act. The most common hierarchies I have encountered are represented in the following statements:

- *Rapist:* "At least what I did was *normal* and with an adult woman, not kids like those perverts!"
- *Incestuous father:* "How could those deviates molest someone else's kid? That's disgusting!—I only used my own kid and I had that right; they didn't."

- *Hebophile:* "I can't understand those guys having sex with six- and seven-year-olds. There's nothing there, and they can't really do anything. It doesn't make sense!"
- *Pedophile:* "It wasn't sex. It was sex education and loving! What those others did was dirty and awful. I only showed my victims tenderness and how to feel good."
- *Flasher:* "I don't know why I'm even here! I never hurt anyone. All these other guys are criminals; I'm not. No one ever got hurt from seeing a guy's penis."

In a group setting, these perceptions of one another play an important confrontational role. In trying to understand one another's deviant behavior, questions abound. As a result, in a well-functioning group, the therapist can almost sit back as an observer; the groups tend to run themselves.

On the other hand, when we tried a group of all pedophiles, the therapy was unsuccessful because they were so passive, frightened, and unable to be confrontive, all that occurred was mutual support, exchange of experiences, and sharing of new fantasies for their nightly masturbation. Little or no progress or change occurred, and resistance became stronger rather than diminished.

Typical Group Errors Seen in Supervision

In almost forty years of supervising therapists with sex offenders and victims, I have witnessed the same errors again and again. The most common mistakes that I have observed are these:

- Beginning the group with an adversarial role on the part of the therapist
- No empathy or observable interest on the part of the therapist
- Threats by the therapist to the group or to an individual in the group
- Lack of education of the group into the concepts of group process or therapy rules/roles
- Use of force by badgering the members of the group or one individual in the group
- Too much interpretation on the part of the therapist
- Ignoring readiness concepts and trying to force admissions/confessions too soon

- Taking control too soon
- Becoming too defensive
- Playing the victim of the group when things do not go the therapist's way
- Alienating the group by demands, too much control, forced topics, or direction
- Too much talking or involvement on the therapist's part

These observations will be discussed in greater depth as I progress in this discussion of the treatment of the sex offender.

THE CHILD/ADOLESCENT SEX OFFENDER

The child/adolescent sex offenders were the primary motivation for my emphasis on group therapy as a necessary treatment modality. Developmentally, this is the "gang-phase," and all emphasis turns from wanting to please and be like adults to wanting to please and be like his peers. The inadequate boy or girl entering adolescence craves the attention and acceptance of (belonging to) their peer groups and will do *anything* to achieve this new goal. This includes drinking, using drugs, becoming sexually active, dressing according to the latest teen styles, etc. The more inadequate the emerging adolescent is, the more desperate this need appears to become.

Individual therapy at this stage will contain denials, minimizations, blame projections, and manipulations, all aimed at pleasing the adult in order to shorten the therapy and/or to get out of trouble (especially in court-referred cases). Therapists should consider the principles listed in Box 9.2.

Where the materials in this chapter are concerned, everything presented also directly applies to the child/adolescent sex offender with some minor additions/changes: (1) where children and adolescents are concerned, therapy should begin in individual sessions until "readiness" for joining an ongoing group occurs, and (2) during the individual sessions, the therapist must carefully determine if there are circumstances, factors, or incidents that are inappropriate for exposure in a group. If both the new patient and the group would be traumatically affected by the information, a "cover story" should be established and agreed upon. The only mandate for the cover story is

9.2

Cardinal Principles in Clinical Interviewing and Treatment of Adolescent Sex Offenders

1. Readiness must exist before treatment begins.
2. Believe nothing. All statements must be proven.
3. Listen and do not interrupt. The less said by the therapist the better.
4. Get all the nitty-gritty details/facts. Use "cue words": And/More/Picture/ So!/Because/Why?
5. Constantly observe, especially body language and emotional reactions.
6. Be sensitive yet cautious and be ready for lies and/or manipulations.
7. Assume nothing!
8. Use any and all opportunities to question values, judgments, etc.
9. Let the client set the pace of the session, especially where disclosure is concerned.
10. Never say "I know how you feel," unless you are a survivor of sexual abuse and are willing to self-disclose.

that the dynamics are essentially the same. Acts, behaviors, and sexual conduct including zoophilia (sex with animals), coprophilic behaviors (acts involving feces), necrophilic acts (sex with dead bodies), and any other acts that would severely upset the members of the group.

An example or two of the types of behaviors that should be given cover stories may clarify. An eleven-year-old boy who was sent to me for trying to have sex with younger children, ages seven to nine, related the following sex history.

MELVIN, now eleven years old, began masturbating at age nine after watching his older brother do so on a regular basis. They slept in the same bedroom, and Melvin would pretend to be asleep. Although he could not ejaculate as his brother did, he did have pleasurable orgasms. Naturally, his brother's penis was larger than his and produced copious amounts of semen. Melvin began fantasizing about masturbating his brother but was terrified of approaching him. However, Melvin had a dog named Bunny. Melvin and Bunny were great friends and wrestled a great deal. One day Melvin noticed that Bunny had an erection. Without thinking, he first touched the dog's penis and shortly afterward masturbated the dog. This behavior went on for quite a while until Melvin learned from friends on a scouting trip what "BJs" (fellatio) were. After masturbating to fantasies of fellating his brother, Melvin again went to Bunny to satisfy his curiosity. From there, within a few months, Melvin, naked, knelt on his knees and Bunny mounted him. This behavior continued for several years.

Melvin was quite embarrassed and ashamed of his behavior but stated that "after a while, I just had to do it. I couldn't stop" (compulsion). These revelations took over two months (eight sessions).

I decided that this material was too traumatic to bring to group, not only for Melvin but also for the other group members. Melvin and I worked on a cover story. We simply changed Bunny to a younger nine-year-old friend with whom Melvin had a long-term relationship. We also decided that we would continue individual sessions on a monthly basis so that we could deal with his choice of an animal for a sex partner. It worked well, and today Melvin is married and has several children and two dogs. There has been no reported recurrence of the problem with animals.

Murder cases (usually accidental in children and teens) also fall under this category unless the child/teen wants to bring it to group and is comfortable with the security of the group. I have treated teen cases of both types: two who needed a cover story and one who brought the murder to his group. Amazingly, his confession triggered another group member to confess that he also had committed murder.

Once again, the therapist must be ready to handle these kinds of confessions in both individual and group therapy situations. In my case, these admissions were considered past facts and not reportable materials. However, release consideration had to include a careful evaluation of the individual's potential to repeat this type of violence, especially in a compulsive rapist.

The final consideration in these cases must be the safety of all group members. Where extreme passivity and fear of being harmed are concerned, the therapist must assure that this type of individual will not become a pawn in the group or be misused after the group session by older and more manipulative individuals. This is critical in a correctional setting.

During my year at a reformatory for boys aged seven to seventeen, the danger of sexual abuse was a daily problem. Group makeup there was critical, and some truly inadequate boys were unable to participate in group therapy and had to be seen on an individual basis. There was no doubt in my mind that the older, more sociopathic boys would use these inadequate children and youths for their own material and sexual needs. (More on this in upcoming chapters.)

Chapter 10

The Five Cs of Sex Offender Treatment

Five principles or cautions are readily identifiable as necessary mandates in sex offender treatment. These principles are summarized in Box 10.1. Each of these elements will be considered in some detail with examples where applicable.

CONFRONTATION BY THE THERAPIST

Due to the passivity, dependency, and seductiveness of the sex offender, there is a tendency on the part of therapists to be supportive, gentle, and parental in their approach. In my experience, I have found that none of the supportive, passive therapies (including Rogerian, psychoanalytic, and other techniques of this type) worked. Naturally, there will be divergent views on this point. What I am discussing is my own personal experience with sex offenders.

One reason for my stance is that the offender's denial is so intense and the guilt so great that admitting the offense(s) is too traumatic and is avoided at all costs. As stated before, not all of our colleagues will agree with this stance. For a contrary view, the reader is referred to Nathaniel Pallone's (1990b) excellent coverage of other sex offender treatment techniques in his *Rehabilitating Criminal Psychopaths.*

In my experience, whether in individual or group settings, confrontation appears to be the only method that will reach the core of the sex offender's problems. Whatever the offender says, it must be doubted, and he must always be made to back up or prove his statements. The offender either tends to use vague generalities and/or quickly picks up (from either the therapist or from other group members) and uses psychological jargon as a means of mitigating or minimizing the impact of his statements. After confrontation, the vague

10.1

**The Five Cs of Sex Offender Treatment:
Confrontation, Cautions, Confirmation, Control,
and Consistency**

1. Confrontation
   * Nondirective, passive therapies usually fail.
   * The therapists must be active, take control, confront.
   * Value change is the most essential focus, followed by new self-image formation.
   * Use of questions, not answers, produces better results.
2. Cautions
   * Sex offenders are manipulative, seductive con artists.
   * Rationalization, projection, and denial dominate as the most frequently used defense mechanisms.
   * Explosive reactions are possible—and unpredictable.
3. Confirmation
   * Believe nothing sex offenders say.
   * Use group therapy to confirm changes and/or new patterns.
   * The therapist must be comfortable with sexuality.
   * Relatives, staff, and family are necessary partners to confirm facts, changes, and new behaviors.
4. Control
   * The therapist must maintain control, not the group.
   * This control involves "distancing" on the part of the therapist.
   * Control must be subtle, not total.
   * Control is impossible when the therapist tries to be a member of the group.
5. Continuation/Consistency
   * Aftercare treatment is essential.
   * Emergency access to his former therapist is necessary.
   * Consistent treatment is important.

statement "I molested my daughter" becomes "I forced my daughter to fellate me and forcibly sodomized her."

When using confrontation, it is important not to interrupt the thought processes of the client with long-winded statements and/or questions. Thus, an easily learned and understood "cue phrase" system was developed to prevent this interruption from being used as a means of avoidance by the client.

Although already presented in Chapter 9, these cue phrases are important enough to repeat in this section as suggestions.

- *Because?* I don't understand the motive or reasons for your actions/conclusions.
- *And?* Not enough. Whatever you're telling me is incomplete. Something is missing.
- *Pzzzzzzzt!* I don't believe you, or I don't buy that explanation, reason, etc.
- *Picture?* You're being vague, and I don't get a clear understanding of the situation.
- *Tilt!* You're off the subject or track. Get back to what we were discussing.
- *Belly-Button*—Don't just tell me the changes you've made, give me proof that I can verify.

The principle involved here is that *the less said by the therapist, the better.*

Nondirective, Passive Therapies Almost Always Fail

The sex offender's defenses, especially denial, minimization, projection, avoidance, and evasion, demand a confrontational approach. In my experience, weeks, months, and even years can be spent in frustrating therapeutic contact with these clients with no visible change or improvement when passive methods are used. (Here, again, refer to Pallone [1990b] for divergent opinions on this topic.)

Often, new therapists in the treatment of sex offenders have been trained in these passive-type treatment modalities and insist they will work. I always encourage them to give it a try and, within a short period of time (usually fewer than three months), they return and acknowledge that *these methods do not work with this type of offender.* Then the real training begins.

The Therapist Must Be Active, Take Control, Confront

Until a new group is well trained and can function fairly independently, the therapist must direct, control, and keep the group on track. Since *avoidance* of any painful topic of reexperience is part of the offender's makeup, he will try any tactic to change the subject, go off on a tangent, or lead the group discussion away from the feared topic. The therapist must be alert and constantly keep the group focused on the topic of the man on the floor (the individual presenting his topic or problem to the group).

There is also a danger of the group *harming rather than helping* the man on the floor. Sex offenders become quite judgmental of one another, since they can feel better about themselves by finding someone more deviant or depraved than themselves. It is extremely important that the therapist allow sufficient time (usually ten minutes) at the end of each group meeting for (1) recovery from an emotional session; (2) a summary of what occurred in the session; and (3) each group member to give his own feedback to the man on the floor. During feedback, the therapist should always be last. It is also important that the therapist's feedback show no favoritism or partiality (such as defending the man on the floor from the group) and that plans/goals for the next session be clearly delineated.

Focus on Value Change and Formation of a New Self-Image

All sex offenses are based on seriously defective values, learned from early childhood and distorted to fit the deviant needs of the offender. Value formation and change are discussed in greater detail in Chapter 17. For this section, allow it to suffice that this is one of the most difficult, frustrating, and long-term battles the therapist will face.

Use Only Questions, Not Answers

A common error of the new therapist is giving the client cues and answers. For example:

- That really must have been a frightening and awful experience!
- That really must have made you angry!
- You really must have hated him or her for that!
- You really must feel guilty about what you did to your daughter!

Instead, the therapist should ask questions, such as:

- I've never had that happen to me. Can you help me to understand how it felt to you?
- When he or she did that, how did you feel?
- When it was over and you had time to think about it, what did you feel about the incident?

It is important to remember that asking questions that do not give hints of the expected or desired answers is an art. Unfortunately, there is not enough emphasis put on this issue in the formal training of therapists. *Supervised practice* utilizing videotape (the ideal method) or audiotape is the best way to learn. Tape playbacks, especially videotape, instantly expose errors in the words or facial expressions and body language of both the client and the therapist. Sudden loss or gain of eye contact, a shift in sitting position, head down or suddenly up, tension from a relaxed state, etc., all instantly betray the reaction of the client to any statement by the therapist, either in individual therapy or in group. Although audiotaping is helpful, the *visible clues* are lost, and the supervisor must rely on the accurate recall of the supervisee.

It should be mentioned that sex offenders are constantly *looking for answers* and want the therapist to provide them. They will try anything to accomplish this goal and, if they do, can then deny the answer at any future time and blame the failure on the therapist. Some typical questions that offenders want the therapist to answer include

- What should I do with my life?
- What changes should I make?
- What goals should I set?
- When do you want to see me again?
- Why do you think that I did it?
- What makes me do these things?
- Should I go to Alcoholics Anonymous (AA) or Narcotics Anonymous (NA) or some other ancillary program?
- Should I tell my wife? parents? friends?

Each of these questions is a *trap!* Once the therapist answers the question, all future blame for the consequences of the choice becomes the therapist's and not the client's. If, for example, the therapist suggests that the offender tell his wife of the offense and she then leaves and divorces him, the client may conclude that she left him not because he committed a sex offense but because he told her about it, which is the therapist's fault. The same follows for all of the other hundreds of questions that the sex offender will ask the therapist to answer during the course of treatment.

CAUTIONS

Sex Offenders Are Manipulative, Seductive Con Artists

Most offenders I have met in either private practice or in an institutional setting were nice people. They are polite, gentlemanly, cooperative, well behaved, and very hardworking. They do everything they can to please and be accepted. It is quite common for them to make the therapist the positive parent that they never had and to try to create a personal relationship for themselves with the therapist.

In this dynamic there is also a means of "normalizing" themselves and feeling equal to the therapist. When this occurs, the sex offenders distance themselves from their peers and see themselves more as part of the staff rather than as part of the client population. Once this delusion is accomplished, their normal denial mechanisms take over, and they no longer are the dirty, bad, evil perverts that were sent for treatment. Thus, the therapist must constantly guard against this type of relationship developing.

Female therapists are at even greater risk since, if the offender can delude himself into believing that his therapist *wants* him as a boyfriend, he will misperceive even the most innocent kindness for love and soon become infatuated with the therapist. Usually she is the last to know that this is how he really feels, and when it becomes known, (through love letters, touching, gifts, etc.) it is often too late to deny it, since the offender will find a rationalization for the denial, such as the following examples:

- The authorities made her say that!
- She is worried about her job; but when I get out, we will be lovers.
- She really loves me but has to be fair to the rest of the group.
- She does not know she loves me, but I will convince her.

The dangers here are apparent and must be avoided, even through transferring the client to another therapist's caseload.

Rationalization, Projection, and Denial Dominate As Defense Mechanisms

Although sex offenders tend to overuse all of the defense mechanisms, the three defenses discussed here tend to dominate.

Rationalization, projection, and denial exist from the first contact with the offender and contain the excuses, alibis, and explanations for his behavior: why he could not have done it or why it happened.

The therapist needs to find a method of getting the offender to see and accept the reality of the situation. Because it will be painful for the offender to accept full responsibility for the act, the therapist must take his or her time to avoid making the offender face too much too soon. If the offender's initial experience with therapy is extremely painful and frightening, it is more than possible that he will quit therapy—if not physically then mentally, by lack of concentration or involvement. It is more useful in the long run to allow the original defenses to exist and then, as rapport and confidence build, to slowly break through the defenses with specific questioning and a persistent return to the defended area.

JOEL, a twenty-nine-year-old mechanic and part-time musician, was convicted of child molestation involving two children he was baby-sitting. From his first intake interview he was in total denial and insisted that he pled guilty rather than put the two children through the ordeal of testifying in court. He was one of the best-adjusted individuals that the institution had. He was a gentleman, honest, kind, a hard worker, a good friend to many other sex offenders, and was generally liked by everyone. In group, although a consistent participant in discussions about others' offenses, when he took the floor, he discussed his alcohol and drug problems, his concerns for his family and especially his ailing father, and other situational and adjustment problems—anything but his offense.

If pressed to discuss the details of his charges, Joel strongly (almost angrily) stated that he was not a sex offender. He would then repeat his rationalization as to how he was convicted. After several years of therapy and watching other friends and group members bare their souls and improve both emotionally and psychologically, he took the floor in group and now changed his story. The second version became "It might have happened. I was so drunk and so high on drugs that I really don't remember what happened that night. But I'm still not a sex offender, and I'm definitely not turned on by kids." Although both the group and the therapist did not believe this new version, he was encouraged to keep working in therapy and to try to re-member what really happened that night in his apartment.

More than a year passed, and a third version emerged: "I've begun to re-member something about that night. I wanted to have a party and invited my friends over. This dizzy dame that I can get drugs from sometimes came along with one of my other friends, and the dumb bitch brought her two young kids with her. Eventually they went to sleep on the daybed. After a few hours, we were all kinda high, but the drugs were running low, and she de-cided she would go get some more. She took the keys to my car and left, without even asking. Several hours later, everyone left and I was stuck with her damn kids. I sat near the daybed staring at them and then went over and sat on the bed. I was really horny from the drugs and maybe—I don't remem-ber this part—touched the little girl but only through her clothes, not in her pants like the report says."

Revenge was now his rationalization, and the blame was projected onto the mother of the victims. He was still in total denial that he could possibly have pedophilic tendencies or traits. This level re-mained unchanged for several more years. When asked why he would choose sexual contact as a way to hurt the mother of the chil-dren, he could not answer.

Shortly after this admission, Joel decided to max out his sentence. Although he continued to attend his group, no further therapy prog-ress occurred. Joel completed his sentence and was released. He is currently married, has a good job, and has not had a recurrence. He admits he learned much about himself in therapy, although he chose not to share it with me or his group members.

Explosive Reactions Are Possible— and Unpredictable

The therapist should never become too complacent or comfortable when dealing with sex offenders and their problems. Most offenders have problems in the area of emotional expression and "stuff (sup-press)" their feelings in the present as they have done since they were children. As children, they were never permitted this emotional ex-pression, and usually there is a great deal of suppressed anger that may erupt when the right buttons are pushed. Since the therapist is working in the dark where the past is concerned (only has what is in the record or what the client has shared), he or she can never know when an explosive reaction will occur.

During one of my groups with offenders, RICHIE, the man scheduled to have the floor, did not show up for group. Since he worked on the kitchen crew and had had problems getting off work before, I made a phone call and had him sent to the main studio, where we were videotaping his group. When he arrived, he looked the same as always, and I asked why he had held up the group for more than fifteen minutes. He stared at me for a moment, took off his shoes (a safety rule in the studio), walked over to one of the video cameras (a $7,000 unit on a rolling tripod), calmly picked up the whole camera unit, and attempted to kill me by bashing in my head. He missed me by about an inch and then, roaring, threw another camera through the one-way window between the studio and the control room.

In about thirty seconds, the entire group was up and jumped Richie. He simply threw them around the room as though they weighed nothing. After about a minute and a half, he threw up his hands, said, "It's over!"—and calmly sat on the floor and awaited the officers who had been summoned. Richie had never shown any anger outbursts in his many years of serving time and was always seen as a large but friendly "pussy cat" whose behavioral record was excellent. In checking his record, there were no recorded incidents of violence, and even in his rape (the offense he was in prison for) he was nonviolent and, in fact, took the victim home after the incident (which led to his capture). In the many more years Richie would serve on his sentence, he never again showed any aggressive or violent behavior, and I eventually took him back into my caseload.

This was not the only time I encountered unprovoked or unpredictable explosive reactions, and *caution* is the only protection.

CONFIRMATION

Believe Nothing

As stated earlier in this chapter and in several other places, sex offenders are manipulative and strongly involved in denial, projection, and rationalization. Now add one further defense mechanism to this list: "partialization." I define partialization as the persistent and compulsive practice of telling only part of the story. Sex offenders are overly concerned with acceptance and the concomitant fear of rejection. They also want to get the whole process of therapy over as quickly as possible, with the least amount of exposure and pain. Thus, it is not uncommon for a therapist to sincerely believe that a client has totally exposed himself, when in reality he has only exposed the outer core of memories, incidents, and confessions that he feels comfortable in handling or having the therapist know.

PETER is a thirty-nine-year-old decorated Vietnam veteran who was recently paroled on a rape charge and violated his parole. Upon his return to the treatment program as a violator, he vehemently denied committing the new rape and used all of his savings and his family's assets and even went into considerable debt appealing the charge. No one else doubted Peter's guilt, as the rape occurred in broad daylight and the circumstances made identification easy and unmistakable. Still, Peter's protestations of innocence and his denial continued for seven years. Late one evening as I was finishing up some paperwork in my office, I received a call that Peter was extremely upset and had to be seen as an emergency referral. When he entered the office, he was on the verge of hysteria, crying, wringing his hands, and unable to sit still. He walked around the office in this manner for a while and then regained some composure, sat, and stated, "I can't live like this anymore! It's all been a lie! I not only committed that rape but at least six others since I was paroled!"

Although reluctant to explain his seven years of denial, he finally admitted that "I'm no good, evil, rotten! I belong locked up for the rest of my life, that's why I raped again!" Due to the degree of his emotional upset, no further probing was possible that evening, but a follow-up session was scheduled for the next day. In a much calmer mood and in control of his emotions, Peter told me that he had been involved in one of the most notorious Vietnam massacres. He had raped young women in a village at the order of his platoon leader and then took his squad to another village and ordered each member of his group to rape the village leader's wife and daughter, making the father and other village leaders watch. He then, again on orders of his superiors, ordered his men to kill everyone in the village. To this day, he wakes up screaming with nightmares of the incident and cannot find a way to forgive himself.

The importance of Peter in this discussion is that had this been discovered in his first nine years of therapy, there may not have been another rape victim, and he may not have been additionally traumatized by his own behavior. As it now stands, therapy is at a standstill. He wants to do all of the time on his sentence and, were he released, might again rape and possibly kill to assure that he would never be released from prison again.

The Group Confirms Changes and New Behaviors

In Peter's case (as well as hundreds of others), therapists basing their judgments on the client's input would have made terrible errors and effected many more victimizations. In all cases of sex offenders, whether seen in private practice or in an institutional setting, *the therapist is perceived as having total control of the client's life.* Regardless of the situation, ranging from self-reported deviant behavior to court-action referrals, the client knows that he has broken the law and can be sent to prison for his deviant acts. Developing the rapport necessary for total trust is difficult at best, and in most cases nearly impossible.

However, where group therapy is concerned, especially in an institutional setting where the clients live, eat, and sleep with one another, the group can far better evaluate and judge changes or lack of changes in an individual member of the group.

Paraprofessional Groups

Institutional settings also permit the use of "paraprofessional groups." These are groups led by inmate paraprofessionals, trained and constantly supervised by a senior therapist. These are the only groups where sex offenders are placed by their offense dynamics: a pedophile/hebophile group, a sexual assault group, a group in which alcohol was a key element in the deviant acting out, a group in which drugs was a dominant factor in the deviant offense, an incestuous fathers group, etc. When I supervised these groups, all of their sessions were videotaped and, when possible, monitored by the supervising therapist from his office.

The most amazing factor in these groups is the large number of admissions which are made but which were never made in the individual's primary group, *even though he knew that the session was being taped and possibly observed by a supervising therapist.* This factor demonstrates the value of these groups. *Caution:* Without supervision, these groups could become dangerous and a place of conspiracy.

Behavior As the Only True Proof of Change

It must be noted at this juncture that I strongly believe that *behavior is the only real, concrete proof of true therapeutic change.* As stated before, sex offenders, in or out of an institution, are experts at analyzing the wants/needs of therapists. They learn amazingly quickly, by studying the therapist's reactions, comments, follow-up questions, change of subject, body-language, facial expressions, etc., whether their answers, confessions, or comments are pleasing or upsetting to the therapist. Wanting to please and desperately needing approval and acceptance, they will then pattern their sessions to gain said approval and acceptance.

There are revelations in this type of therapy that will shock anyone, others that appear comical, others that generate immediate anger and even disgust if one is not prepared. The therapist needs to maintain a poker face, hiding all personal reactions no matter how difficult this may be.

The Therapist's Comfort with Sexuality

Early in Chapter 9, the reader was asked to identify the most important personal trait that should be a prerequisite to working with offenders. The best response (from my viewpoint) is *comfort with all aspects of sexuality, in general, and with your own sexuality in particular.* If this condition is met, there will be no prejudgments, no prejudices, no moral imperative or prohibitions, and therefore less chance of a shocking revelation damaging the therapeutic process. Whether the revelation involves masturbating an elephant or a dog, licking feces, molestation by a mother, raping eighteen-month-old babies, or other shocking acts that sex offenders do and need to confess, the therapist who has dealt with his or her own sexual issues will be better equipped to handle the situation without harm to either himself or herself or to the client.

My suggestion for this type of preparation is that all therapists who intend to work with sex offenders or their victims be mandated to attend and participate in an extended SAR (sex attitude restructuring) seminar and training session. The desensitization alone that takes place during an SAR is worth the money, time, and effort. In an SAR, the individual is exposed to a variety of sexually explicit films, several shown simultaneously (depending on the equipment available at the site). In professionally operated SARs as many as twelve screens operate at the same time, allowing the participant to watch or to avoid all significant factors. After each twenty-minute film session, the large group divides into small, randomly chosen discussion groups. Each subgroup has a facilitator who is very carefully trained in this work. The facilitator guides discussion of the films and the participant's reactions to them and then carefully suggests the possible need for further work or counseling in a particular area.

If taken seriously and honestly, these workshops can offer the participant an opportunity to learn a great deal about himself or herself. *Prejudices, fears, moral indignations, disgusts, turn-ons, and turn-offs* can all become quite conscious during both the viewing of the films and the discussions that follow. Reacting or overreacting to what is said in the group discussions is extremely important since the same reaction is possible with a client.

Once the trainee/participant has learned facts about his or her sexual values, prejudices, fears, and doubts, he or she can take appropriate remedial measures before treating patients with any form of sexual dysfunction.

In 1969, I attended a weeklong training seminar in California for certification as a sex therapist. Prior to attending the course, I felt that I was very liberal and nothing sexual could upset or disturb me. After all, I had been functioning as a sex therapist for at least seven years.

After a prolonged SAR with twelve screens displaying explicit sexual behavior between consenting adults, the group was asked to fill out evaluation forms, detailing our reactions, preferences, likes and dislikes, etc. When all of the papers were collected, the mentor/facilitator, a motherly, petite female gynecologist (who subsequently was dubbed "Mom") said to the group, "Now that all of you have lied on the evaluations, who would like to have their paper back and do a new one?" The professionals in the group were highly insulted, myself included, until, from behind each of the twelve screens stepped evaluators who stared at each of us with a clipboard in their hands. They had been watching our reactions during the showing of the films and knew what we avoided, what we did not want to be seen watching, etc. Without a moment's hesitation, I went forward and asked for my paper back and filled out a new and honest one. Later that evening, in an individual session with an advisor, I was asked only one question: "Why did I lie on the first form?" Was it image or was it fear of facing myself?

Today, I mark that training session as the beginning of my being a true sex therapist. I learned a great deal about myself and had enough material to work on personally and with a colleague for more than a year.

Relatives, Staff, and Family As Therapeutic Aides

The group confirmation process can be further enhanced by other outside sources to confirm or deny essential changes in behavior. I have used wives, parent(s), siblings, children (especially in incest situations), employers, neighbors, personal friends, or anyone I could recruit to aid in the treatment of an offender in my private practice. Permission from the client is necessary, and I do not divulge any confidences during these contacts. They are simply for information/confirmation and this is made clear from the beginning to both the client and the volunteer.

Simple questioning techniques are utilized that do not contain psychological jargon or diagnostic terminology. Please note that the volunteer must be guaranteed confidentiality, just as the client is, if one is to expect honest and real answers to questions. This applies especially to wives, children, and lovers who either fear the client or fear losing the relationship.

Potential questions may include

- How has _____ been doing lately?
- What is the current status of your relationship with _____?
- Are you feeling more comfortable talking to _____ lately?
- (For wives/lovers): How has sex been the last few weeks with _____?
- (For children): Are you less afraid of your father now than you were, or are things still the same?
- (For employers or co-workers): Have you seen any changes in _____ in the last few weeks? If so, what are they?
- (For families): Are things around the house less tense since _____ has been coming to therapy?
- (For institutional staff): Has _____ been any different lately? If so, in what way? Also: Has _____ been socializing any more lately than before? If so, with whom and how often?

The last question is important since most sex offenders tend to remain isolated in their rooms until changes begin. All questions should be patterned by the particular circumstances of the case and can be much more directive and pointed than questions used with the offender himself.

VICTOR had spent five years in therapy for sodomizing teenage boys. His victims were usually hitchhikers whom he picked up, drove to lonely parks or deserted factory areas, and then, threatening their lives with a gun, forced to undress and submit to his sexual assaults. He then drove them home, threatening their families with death if they reported him or told anyone. During five or more years of therapy, he based his insight into his crimes on the sexual abuse he received at the hands of an older stepbrother, who was the parents' favorite and who they would believe in preference to him. His therapeutic progress continued positively as did his behavior. He was a clever young man, and everyone tended to be seduced by his wily ways. However, something bothered me about this individual, and somehow (gut reaction) I felt we were being conned.

On a family picnic day, I happened to meet his parents before he arrived at the picnic area and we began to talk. They were interested in his progress, and I was positive in my comments to them. By chance, I asked how Victor's stepbrother was doing. The parents looked astounded and remarked, "You must have us confused with another family, since Victor is an only child. We never had any other children. Victor always wanted a brother of his own. We spoiled him something awful. He got everything he wanted, except a brother." The other therapists involved with Victor were just as shocked and astounded as I was. So was his group when I confronted him with the new information. Smiling (or sneering), he admitted that he "had heard the story work before and decided to use it." He never thought anyone would check up on him.

CONTROL

The Therapist Must Maintain Control

Although often assumed, too often control does not exist in a group due to the therapist's lack of adequate training. This can lead to nonproductive groups or too often to disaster, especially in an institutional setting.

One of the major dangers involved when a too mild, too passive, untrained therapist leads a group is that of potential *conspiracy.* Where any possible positive recommendations by the therapist (promotion, release, court recommendation, etc.) are concerned, this danger is always present. The group members can get together after the sessions (both in inpatient and outpatient groups) and make an agreement to support one another in group in order to obtain some sort of positive gain. I have seen this happen in both my institutional work and in my private practice.

This danger is especially present when *peer-review* is incorporated into the therapy. Although peer-review is a positive and necessary component of sex offender group therapy, the therapist must have sufficient training and experience to know when something is going awry.

During my supervision of therapists in a correctional setting, videotaping of sessions was the tool I employed on a periodic basis. One peer-review session conducted by a relatively new and inexperienced therapist resulted in the therapist presenting two patients for release procedures. Asking only a few questions of the therapist proved conclusively that he knew little of the dynamics of the two patients' offenses and that he simply caved in to the enthusiastic recommendations of his group members. When I interviewed one or two of his group members with whom I had had previous contacts, the conspiracy was readily uncovered along with the leader of the group who was conducting the operation. Needless to say, none of the recommendations for release was followed, and I personally met with the group to let them know their plans were "busted" (exposed).

Peer-review, a valuable tool, should be employed only by long-term, experienced therapists who have worked with sociopathic inmates and know how they operate.

The remaining elements under the control-principle all involve the therapist's knowledge of and acceptance of his or her role in the group. While remaining the authoritative figure in the group and the one person who controlled promotion and or release (both in institutional and private settings), the therapist must not distance himself or herself so far above the group level that the members of the group cannot relate to him or her. This is not always an easy task, especially when the therapist has favorites in the group. When one of these residents is being attacked by another member or the entire group, the *urge to defend* will occur and must be controlled. The therapist must assure that the group is not aware of these favorites, as the cohesiveness of the group will be damaged. Also, the favorites will become the target of remaining group members and either be attacked or used by the more manipulative and sociopathic members. Ultimately, the group will be divided into factions and will no longer perform as a group.

Control Involves Distancing on the Part of the Therapist

In order to achieve the type of control mentioned, there is a critical need for the therapist to distance himself or herself from the group and its members. This involves avoiding pets or favorites in the group and treating all members the same. This, in turn, involves being certain that all members get the opportunity to "take the floor" and to express their opinions equally. Too often, therapists almost unconsciously and automatically choose group favorites or group leaders to answer queries or to give their opinion of the "man on the floor's" presentation.

Once the habit of distancing is established, no one in the group will feel left out. A more important result is that the weaker members of the group will no longer use the same answers or dynamics in discussing their problem that the perceived favorites have already used and were praised for.

Control Must Be Subtle, Not Obvious

There are times when the group has gone off track, is being petty, or is being too negative to the man on the floor. These are times when the therapist must intervene but in a manner that is not dictatorial. The most efficient way to achieve this control is to use questions rather than give orders. Instead of "Get back on the subject!" try "Are we getting lost? I'm losing the original thought of what was being said," or "Where are we going with this discussion? Does it apply to what was being said by (name of man on the floor)?"

Any form of mild, noncondemning questions will work, and the individual therapist will have to develop his or her own style to solve this problem. It really is not difficult.

Control Is Impossible When the Therapist Tries to Become a Member of the Group

The new or timid and inadequate therapist who needs acceptance in his own life will carry this need into his or her group(s). These therapists want the group to like them and to see them as the leader (when in reality they are not). Thus, the therapist never disagrees with what is said in the group, rarely gives direction, and too often gives answers to difficult questions that the group or one of its members is struggling with. The moment the wiser, more manipulative members of the group realize this is occurring, they will use the situation to their own advantage. (Remember that sex offenders are highly manipulative.) This is one of the situations in which that danger is extreme. Now, through manipulation, the group is controlling the therapist, not the therapist controlling the group. Remember the therapist who was manipulated into referring two group members for release?

Control issues are critical in all group therapy modalities and can only be accomplished professionally and positively through specialized training.

CONTINUATION/CONSISTENCY

Aftercare Is Essential

For offenders who are released from an institutional setting, whether private clinic, hospital, or correctional facility, *aftercare by that facility* is essential. In my experience, leaving an institutional setting is in itself traumatic for the sex offender. He has become *comfortable,* has had few responsibilities, has had few or no financial problems, and has been cared for (food, clothing, and shelter) as if by parents. In fact, the institution has become a substitute parent in all these areas, including telling him when to eat, sleep, recreate, etc. In addition, work (if it does exist) is usually foreign to his past experience and artificial in that it usually lasts only an hour or two per day. Now, he has to again become an independent, self-sufficient person.

For those with families and a home to return to, the transition is much easier. However, there is still a feeling of *strangeness* and *not belonging* that must be gradually overcome. Finding a job becomes a major problem. For those without family and home, the trauma is even greater. Finding a place to live and a job at the same time appears impossible. The longer the institutional stay, the harder the problem seems to be. For both groups, the first sexual encounter will be frightening (fear of impotence or failure in satisfying a partner), and for the more passive-dependent types, finding relationships at all seems impossible. Thus, support in the form of aftercare counseling becomes an essential factor for a successful return to the community.

Emergency Access to the Therapist
May Be Necessary

Due to the fears, doubts, and exaggerated reactions that the released sex offender experiences, access to his or her own therapist, at least by telephone, is necessary to maintain the gains achieved in the course of treatment. A different therapist or one not acquainted with the forms of treatment he received may say the wrong things and offer suggestions that are new and foreign at a time when continuation and consistency are crucial.

Consistent Treatment Is Important

This access is necessary on a twenty-four-hour basis, and both private therapists and institutions must have an on-call system or an answering service in place if failure is to be prevented. During vacations, another therapist who is *totally familiar with the client* should be assigned to handle his or her problems. In institutional settings, this continuation and consistency can be achieved easily if more than one therapist is involved in the case, either as a secondary opinion therapist, an ancillary program therapist, or a roaming substitute therapist utilized during illnesses and vacations.

If, upon release, this support must be obtained from a new agency rather than the one from which the offender was released, the task is even more problematic. Most new agencies will want to start therapy all over again, *their way.* Putting the client through his past once again can retrigger the entire problem and often does. I have had released offenders return to me for treatment from as far as two adjoining states because they could not relate to local therapists and did not want to repeat years of painful and guilt-provoking treatment. If the goal of treatment is to integrate the now ex-offender successfully into society and to prevent his victimizing anyone again, these measures, as difficult as they may seem, are necessary and essential.

Sex Offenders Are Never Really "Cured"

Sex offenders are never cured and, therefore, they may experience recurrences both easily and frequently, at least at the thought and fantasy levels. Treatment (usually in a relapse prevention module) must include making the sex offender recognize this fact and preparing him to deal with it should it occur. This requires continual contact with the therapist, support individuals, and groups in the community. PRN status (call in when necessary) in therapy should never be attempted until these factors are adequately covered and internalized.

THE CHILD/ADOLESCENT SEX OFFENDER

Here again, all of the factors listed in this chapter apply to the child/adolescent group as well as to adult groups in or out of an institutional setting, but there are a few exceptions.

Self-Help Group Modality

Remembering that adolescence, and the stages leading to it, is a peer stage, it becomes essential to allow adolescent or preteen/adolescent groups to function somewhat on their own. The self-help group modality, based on the paraprofessional groups discussed previously, fits perfectly. The therapist becomes the *group advisor* and visits the group regularly. Special arrangements must be made to use this modality.

Most groups that I have been involved with, in and out of institutional settings, are what is termed "ongoing groups." This means that there are older members in the group and a regular insertion of new members. This situation makes the self-help modality work. To begin with, there is a single patient in individual therapy. This patient is usually there for a sufficient number of sessions until new patients come into therapy. When I have a minimum of three patients (close in age and with sex problems), I schedule them at the same time for a few sessions to see how they work together. Invariably, one becomes a leader. Once this occurs, I deliberately make myself absent from the group for twenty to thirty minutes with some excuse. I then return and ask what I missed and, again, the leader speaks up and gives me a summary. I now have my *core-group* and suggest that they try a session on their own. If they agree, the *leader* then reports to me on how the group went and any other significant occurrences. I also regularly visit the group as a nonparticipant in order to assure that it does not collapse into "bull sessions."

In these self-help groups, the therapist's control is essential. This is most true in the choice of a group leader who will be the therapist's main contact. The choice must be the therapist's for all of the reasons mentioned. I have attended self-help groups in which the group is permitted to elect/choose its leader/facilitator. The conspiracy dangers mentioned throughout this chapter apply to all groups in which a particular sex offender has even minimal authority or control.

Where adolescents are concerned, self-help groups are a tremendous asset but without close supervision can also become a liability. The copycat explanations for their offenses, the tendency to conspire, and their need to be like their peers in all areas constitute the dangers of this type of group.

Here again, *video monitoring* is the ideal choice of supervision (if this is not possible, audiotaping may be used). There are many occasions in which simply removing the presence of the therapist can be beneficial. Timid members talk more openly; the need to please adults (if it remains) also disappears; language becomes plainer and more open; and peer-group dynamics flourish. Even though they know that the therapist is watching and listening from an adjoining room/office, this does not inhibit their participation or openness. The cost is minimal in today's world of electronics, and the benefits far outweigh the costs of this type of supervised group therapy.

The rewards from working with child/adolescent offenders are far greater than from working with the adult offenders since the prevention-element is greater. This group is usually too physically inadequate and inexperienced to perpetrate the horrific sex offenses that some adults do.

Finally, all of the Five Cs mentioned in this chapter for the adult offenders apply to the child/adolescent offenders as well.

Chapter 11

Sexual "Imprinting" As a Consequence of Early Traumatic Molestation

INTRODUCTION

The *American Heritage Dictionary* (1985) defines "imprinting" as "a learning process occurring early in the life of a social animal in which a behavioral pattern is established through association with a parent or other role model." "Sexual imprinting" occurs when an individual experiences his or her first orgasm with another human being. If the result is pleasant, enjoyable, and with a person who is liked or loved, the imprinting will be *positive;* if the result is painful, frightening, and with a person who uses force, threat, or intimidation, even though an orgasm may occur, the imprinting will be *negative.*

By extension, "positive sexual imprinting" in sexual abuse cases means that when a child (male or female) who is prepubertal and anorgasmic is sexually molested and that molestation results in the child's *first* orgasm (with or without ejaculation), and the child perceives both the sexual experience and the relationship with the abuser as *positive,* a "lifelong imprint" will occur. Even when the abuse later becomes traumatic and is totally repressed (due to negative reactions of parents, authority figures, peers, etc.), the imprint remains and will surface at some future time when *triggered* by an event that, in some way, is associated with the elements of the original abuse. In these "resurfacing events," the *content* of the abuse may (and often does) remain repressed while the *effects* (physical, sexual, emotional) are experienced vividly and to a disturbing degree. These are the "positive sexual imprints."

Imprinting may also be *negative,* especially when a sexual assault occurs with accompanying fear, pain, threat, humiliation, and degradation. These assaults may also produce lifelong imprints resulting in sexual dysfunctions characterized by aversions, frigidity, panic reactions, impotence, or punishing behaviors.

In his new book *Don't Tell* (2002, p. 118), Michel Dorais suggests "ambivalent imprinting" as a third alternative:

> The individual is confused about his sexual orientation. This would explain, partially as least, why some boys will end up as nude dancers or prostitutes in a homosexual environment while describing themselves neither as homosexual nor bisexual but as homophobic.

In the past forty years of treating individuals with sexual dysfunctions, literally hundreds of clients have reported instances of *unwanted, disturbing,* and *guilt-provoking thoughts, fantasies,* or *behaviors* which could not be explained by the client's present values or attitudes or which could be logically seen as the result of consciously remembered sexual traumas.

There are several different ways in which this phenomenon manifests itself:

- Unwanted sexual reactions/turn-ons
- Self-punishing behaviors
- Negative self-esteem reactions
- Unwanted and unexplained isolation behaviors

Each one will be considered separately for purposes of clarity.

UNWANTED SEXUAL REACTIONS/TURN-ONS

CHUCK is a nineteen-year-old, happily married young man. After a year of hard work, Chuck is given a promotion to a vice presidency in the corporation where he works. One of his new perks is a membership in an executive health club where he hopes to lose some weight and meet some new friends. The club is great, and Chuck is as excited as he has ever been about a new adventure. What makes it even better is that it is a unisex club, and he sees many extremely attractive young women that he would like to meet. The first evening goes well: he really enjoys the program of exercises and feels accepted and liked by the other executives. He has already met several new friends of both sexes. Following two hours of happy and hard workouts, the time for his group is up. While the rest of his group goes into the men's locker room to change and shower, Chuck is called to the office to have his picture taken for his identification card. When he arrives in the locker room to change, the rest of the men are in a large open shower, and Chuck catches himself staring at their bodies and, in particular, at their genitals. Concurrently, he feels a stirring in his groin and an instant flush of embarrassment. Shock and panic occur. He quickly pulls his street clothes over his gym shorts and leaves the health club, sure that he will never return.

At home, Chuck lays on his bed, fear and tears welling up, and replays the mental tapes of what has just occurred. To this point in his life, Chuck remembers being interested only in women and has considered himself a normal nineteen-year-old heterosexual male. Now, there are doubts. In a few weeks, he becomes aware of ancillary, strange new behaviors: he is avoiding any possible male contacts; he no longer uses the urinals at work but locks himself into a booth instead; he finds excuses and alibis to get out of any possible male-oriented social gatherings (such as stopping for a few beers after work). Finally, the next time (after the incident) that his wife initiates sex, he is totally *impotent.* After almost six months of this hell, Chuck calls for an appointment and slowly and painfully exposes the incident, his fears, and his present state of isolation, anxiety, and impotence.

This same type of scenario has been heard from girls and women, high school boys, scoutmasters, ministers and priests, as well as other individuals from all professions and walks of life. Consider another example.

MIKE, introduced in Chapter 6, has been married for almost ten years, and his wife has just had the beautiful son he has always hoped and prayed for. Mike is a lieutenant in the Navy Reserve and is in line for promotion to captain. He has had many happy and successful working and socializing experiences with men, without problems. He is well liked and highly sociable. Being community minded, he also is a scout leader and has been on several camping trips with a group of scouts. Shortly following his wife's return from the hospital with their new baby son, Mike's wife asked him to help her give the baby a bath and he willingly and excitedly agreed. While he held and washed his infant son, he caught himself staring at the baby's penis and felt himself becoming excited. He instantly fantasized touching and fondling his son's penis and wanting to make his son "feel good" in that manner.

Like Chuck, he panicked, yelled for his wife, and made the excuse that he feared hurting or dropping the baby. She took over, and he left the room in a state of fear, tension, and confusion. From that moment on, Mike's life changed dramatically: at work, he waited until all of the other officers had showered and were in bed before doing so himself; he backed out of the upcoming hunting trip with several of his friends that he had been looking forward to for several months. He desperately tried to get out of taking his scouts on a scheduled campout but could not, so with trepidation, he went (the only adult on the trip).

The first night, after all the scouts were asleep, he stayed awake until two or three a.m., torturing himself with the memory of what had happened with his son. Glancing over at the sleeping boys, he noticed that one of the boys, Scott, had kicked off his blankets and went over to cover him. When he arrived at the bunk, he was startled to see that Scott was exposed and had a rigid erection in his sleep. Without hesitation, he knelt by the bed and began to masturbate Scott, his only thought being to bring the boy to his first orgasm and ejaculation. He did just that, and it appeared that Scott had slept through the entire incident. Mike covered him up and left the area to torture himself again with recriminations. His fears were well founded. The evening after returning home, two policemen arrived at Mike's home with a warrant for his arrest. Scott had been awake. Due to his excellent record in the community, he was permitted diversion with the agreement of immediate treatment, and that is when I first met him.

Finally, take a look at a case involving a woman.

MARY, age thirty-one, was a very attractive, intelligent, single woman with several degrees. At the time of her referral, she was functioning as a supervisor in a mental health agency that supervised a great many adolescent clients. Mary's primary complaint was that she was anorgasmic. She had recently met and been dating a younger man, Andy, age twenty-six, who was getting impatient with her excuses for not "going all the way," and she feared losing him. One evening, after an hour or more of heavy petting, Andy finally gave her an ultimatum, stating the suspicion that "maybe something is wrong with you." He took her home and promised to call. The call never came.

At about the same time, a new employee was assigned to her department: a young, attractive, and openly friendly young woman toward whom Mary felt attracted. She found excuses to work more and more closely with the new woman and began touching her on the shoulder, rubbing her neck or back, etc. The woman responded warmly and gratefully. Mary felt strange feelings and panicked. She withdrew from any contact with the young woman and concentrated on dating Andy, although she had not heard from him. In the next week or so, Mary noticed several changes in both her personality and her behavior: she became less assertive and had difficulty making decisions; she isolated herself from most of her friends and all of her social activities; and she began to feel more and more attracted to her female supervisees, while avoiding prolonged contact with her male supervisees. In the third or fourth week, she began feeling *erotic* toward the female and panicked. This is when she made her first appointment, deciding not to tell the therapist the real reason for coming to a sex therapist.

The major difference between negative sexual imprinting and positive sexual imprinting is that negative sexual imprinting is *not* necessarily permanent and can be resolved and changed to a large extent through therapeutic intervention. The main treatment technique difference, once the traumatic memory is conscious and ventilated, is to *desensitize* the client to the trigger stimuli that produces the negative or phobic reaction.

COMMON FACTORS FOUND IN IMPRINTING

There are six common factors found in imprinting, summarized in Box 11.1. Each will be explained in this section and applied to the three cases just presented.

The Trigger

This is usually a behavior or event that, before it occurred, was seen or considered to be normal, happy, or positive. In Chuck's case, it was his joining the health club; in Mike's case, it was finally having the son he wanted and dreamed of; in Mary's case, it was falling in love with Andy.

It should be noted that the trigger could be a traumatic event as well, especially if it duplicated the original imprinting cause. This will be explained more fully later.

The Unwanted Behavior

This is usually an act or reaction, *always* with a physical component, that is totally out of the ordinary for the individual and, to his or her conscious memory, has never occurred before. In Chuck's case, it consisted of staring at the genitals of the men in the showers and becoming sexually excited; in Mike's case, it consisted of wanting to touch his son's penis and later, and even more unwanted, his sexual

---

11.1

Common Factors Found in Imprinting

1. A trigger
2. An unwanted behavior
3. A confusion reaction
4. An isolation reaction
5. Guilt and self-recrimination
6. Generalized sexual dysfunctions

molestation of one of his scouts; and in Mary's case, it consisted of becoming interested in her new female supervisee in an erotic way.

A Confusion Reaction

Immediately following the first incident of the unwanted behavior, a sense of bewilderment and confusion occurs. This is primarily due to the fact that the behavior *makes no sense* to the individual experiencing it and does not seem to fit or belong in the individual's life. For example, in Chuck's case, the reaction was the bewilderment and confusion he felt when he became aware that he was staring at the other men's genitals and felt the stirring in his groin. In Mike's case, it was his confusion over the desires and fantasies of touching his son's penis and giving him pleasure through fondling him. In Mary's case, her confusion involved feeling erotic toward her young female supervisee, since she had supervised many other women for many years without such a reaction or feeling.

An Isolation Reaction

In all cases observed to date, an isolation reaction was seen and is considered an avoidance or escape behavior to prevent a second or more disastrous occurrence. All of the clients paranoidally predicted that the next incident would increase the depth or severity of unwanted behavior, usually, as in Mike's case, involving acting out the impulse, fantasy, or desire. This reaction is dramatic, and although the clients continue to work daily and normally in most if not all instances, their social contacts and behaviors are dramatically eliminated from their lifestyle even from their spouses, families, and children.

Guilt and Self-Recriminations

In all the cases I have seen, *guilt* was the major reaction to such unwanted behaviors. The guilt produced damaging behavior as well as a negative self-image, feelings of abnormality, and a dangerous destruction of self-esteem. More than one of these clients had contemplated suicide, and several had actually gone so far as to have made an attempt before seeking professional help.

Generalized Sexual Dysfunctions

In each of the cases seen, there were abrupt changes in sexual functioning. This is usually the reported reason for seeking sex therapy. These changes include *inversion* of the former sexual identity, *paraphilic* behaviors, and *desire-phase* problems accompanied by abstinence. Even masturbation may now pose a threat. This group holds no hope for a return to normal sexual functioning, and this must be a critical therapy consideration.

QUESTIONS ABOUT ETIOLOGY

After dealing with several hundred cases of this type, a theoretical hypothesis was developed to try to explain the *imprinting phenomenon* and to help create a treatment model for those patients in severe distress. The hypothesis was:

> The first pleasurable orgasm in an individual's life produces a positive imprint and will remain with that individual in some form for the remainder of his or her life, either consciously or unconsciously. Conversely, if the first sexual orgasm is painful, forced/coerced, or unwanted, a negative imprint will occur that can be readily treated.

In each case where the imprinting phenomenon was observed, therapy uncovered an early, long-term (versus single occurrence) sexual seduction that was initially experienced as either positive or negative.

The positive imprint appears dependent on a "positive-affect situation"—one in which the sexual seduction occurred in a positive way with many benefits attached: affection, love (paraphilic), both emotional and material support (clothes, trips, movies, physical contact, a port in the storm, a parental substitute, and myriad other benefits that the child wanted or needed).

The negative imprint occurs when sexual assault occurred accompanied by force, threat, pain, and fear. Guilt and aversion to sexual behavior results. Some of these survivors later sexually assault children or adults as revenge, passing on the pain and guilt, needing to find or create someone *lower* than they perceive themselves to be.

In many of the positive-imprint cases, a relationship developed that was *perceived* as positive and beneficial until exposure or separation occurred. For those situations in which exposure of the abuse occurred in a positive manner, no trauma need occur, but the imprint will remain and needs to be explained and dealt with in therapy as soon as possible.

Where exposure of the abuse occurred in a negative manner, that trauma in itself often results in a partial or total *repression* of the event or a "delusional distortion," especially if the seduction occurred in late childhood or early adolescence. This is often precipitated by one or more adults involved in negatively reacting to learning of the abuse. The child then either represses the event totally or changes the reality of the occurrence and adds threat, fear, pressure, etc., that in reality did not exist. A caveat: this only *explains* the behavior, it does not *justify* it.

Years may pass, even an entire developmental stage, during which no conscious memory of the relationship exists and the child develops along accepted, normal pathways. Examine how this theoretical framework fits into our three example cases.

In CHUCK's case, the early seduction was begun at age eleven by a teacher in junior high school. Chuck was a sensitive, quiet, well-behaved boy who did well in most of his subjects but had trouble with mathematics. His father had deserted the family early in Chuck's life, and his mother worked, sometimes two jobs, to keep the family going. The teacher picked Chuck as a potential victim almost from the first day of the new school year. Within a month, he had assigned Chuck as class monitor, given him special after-school jobs, and offered to tutor him in math at his apartment, if his mother consented. The attention Chuck was receiving was everything he had wanted from his missing father, and he literally could not get enough. Chuck easily convinced his mother to allow the personal tutoring and, little by little, the teacher introduced private and special games into their weekend meetings. The games began with strip poker, progressed to measuring penises, and moved on to discussions of sex and finally "sex education" that resulted in the teacher masturbating Chuck to explain erection, orgasm, and ejaculation. When Chuck could not ejaculate at first, the teacher had Chuck masturbate him in order to complete the lesson. Oral sex came next and became their usual sexual activity, often as a reward for excellent homework or for doing well in a tutored lesson.

This relationship lasted until Chuck's final year of junior high school and the imprint was set. He then left for a different school in another part of town. There he met other budding teenagers and joined their activities. Within those three years of senior high school, Chuck had his first heterosexual encounter, a "train" (another name for a gang sexual experience, where the newest or youngest boy is last in line) that he enjoyed. From then on, until the incident at nineteen, his sexual behavior was heterosexual, and the relationship with the teacher was forgotten (repressed). Being nude in the health club locker room with other adult men triggered a forgotten erotic impulse, and the unwanted reactions occurred. The memory remained repressed, hence the confusion, anxiety, and the need for therapeutic intervention.

In MIKE's case, the scenario differed only in the cast. The seducer was a roomer that his mother had taken in to help pay the bills after his father died. The roomer slept nude in the same room with Mike and one night slid into Mike's bed, suggested that Mike also sleep nude, and then reached over, fondled him, and masturbated him. Mike was either ten or eleven at the time, and the relationship lasted until he was thirteen. Mike liked his new friend, and they went camping and fishing. The roomer supplied whatever Mike wanted that his mother could not afford. As with Chuck, the imprint was set. When the roomer moved out, Mike missed him but then began associating more with his peer group. He was subsequently initiated into the wonders of the opposite sex, lost his virginity, and remained heterosexual in interest, fantasy, and behavior until the birth of his long-awaited son. Even after the incident while bathing his son, he did not remember the roomer.

It took six months of therapy before the early memories finally began to emerge, slowly at first and then like a raging waterfall. What was amazing was the depth and the detail that emerged. Once the barrier was broken, memories of words, phrases, feelings, even smells emerged. The most important memory was that when Mike asked the roomer why he was masturbating him, the roomer answered "to make you feel good," later tied in with "because I love you," furthering deepening the imprint.

Finally, MARY, is a slightly different case. Seduction by an aunt when she began menstruating, clitoral stimulation to the point of pain, and a horrifying day when her mother was observed watching them naked in bed were all factors that emerged in the course of therapy. The last one—being caught by her mother—resulted in a plethora of curses, slurs, put-downs, and name calling that ended in Mary being blamed for what the aunt (the mother's sister) had initiated. Mary's imprint was negative and firmly set.

Sex for Mary was labeled as sinful, dirty, evil, the invention of Satan, etc., and Mary was forbidden to ever touch herself *there* again. This produced a negative imprint. As time passed, Mary also repressed this incident but not the admonitions about sex. Although still not remembered (her memories returned periodically in small spurts), there must have also been a warning about men and sex with men. Mary is still unable to tolerate seeing pictures of a naked man for even a split second, nor can she view sexually explicit movies. Therapy will continue for quite some time.

THERAPEUTIC CONSIDERATIONS AND CAVEATS

Naturally, the first therapeutic goal of import is to discover the early event(s) that imprinted, positively or negatively, and eventually triggered the unwanted behavior. Where positive imprinting had occurred, this has been found to be an early sexual seduction that was positive and pleasant over a period of time and that for some reason, traumatic or not, was totally repressed for quite a number of years. Where negative imprinting had occurred, the early sexual experience was painful or forced and was then usually repressed. What remained were the emotions attached to the event that could be triggered by any reference to sex or sexual behavior.

Once the event is totally uncovered and all the emotions, labeling, and revulsion have been ventilated, the therapist can proceed therapeutically as with any recent survivor of a sexual assault. The ambivalent feelings about the seducer in the story must be thoroughly explored and accepted. Often religion, parental values, societal values, and personal belief systems are at play and need to be thoroughly explored and dealt with as well.

Next, sex attitude restructuring becomes a paramount concern. By now, where *inversion* is concerned, the client has labeled himself or herself "queer," "abnormal," etc. In reality, these confused individuals are *bisexual* and must be made to understand that accepting this fact (which I believe is unalterable due to the imprinting) does not mean that they ever have to act out in this manner. Thus Chuck, although he may catch himself sexually attracted to or stimulated by men, can remain heterosexual behaviorally and never become involved in a homosexual act. Knowing that he has this control of his own sexual behavior is an important and comforting therapeutic gain.

Individuals with imprinting problems containing inversion elements feel and believe that once they experience sexual stimulation from a same-sex person, eventually *they must act on it*. This is not the case.

Once CHUCK accepted this fact, he was able to return to the health club, have similar reactions to the original unwanted behavior, but not panic or leave. He has become accustomed to these reactions and is no longer threatened or concerned about them. His former social life has been reactivated, and he has become more sensitive to other men's needs and can even be socially physical (hugging, horseplay, wrestling, etc.) with them without a problem. He is no longer impotent, and his sex life with his wife has been described by both as "fantastic!" He has been out of therapy now for several years and checks in with me at least once a year.

MIKE, since he committed a sexual offense, remains in therapy on a monthly basis at the order of the court and continued for two years before being promoted to PRN status. He is now appealing to the court to terminate therapy with my concurrence. Sex with his wife remains normal (they both went through a complete sex therapy course that they badly needed). Mike now changes and bathes his son without problems, although his wife must be present by court demand. Masturbation fantasies, at rare times, include memories of himself and the roomer, but they are pleasant and erotic due to positive imprinting. Although presently not interested in a male-male encounter, he does not preclude the possibility in the future and has discussed this with his wife, who accepts it, "as long as it does not contain love" (her condition).

In the negative imprinting cases, the therapy is more complex and takes much longer. All of the emotional elements, the negative self-perceptions, self-criticism, as well as the guilt, have to be exposed and ventilated. Most important, a new self-image must be formed. These reactions all occurred in the case of Mary.

MARY, although she understands and accepts what happened to her and the imprint it left, is still in therapy. Progress has been made on a work level where she again is able to function well as a supervisor with both sexes. Her social life remains minimal with no man in her life at present. She has not decided whether she wants to work in that area or to "leave things as they are since it is safe" (her words). As with all clients, the decision is hers, and only time will tell what she will choose. She continues to accepts her bisexual thoughts with little or no guilt but remains sexually inactive. She is learning to masturbate and has had success in becoming orgasmic.

Treatment is identical for both positive and negative imprinting. Simply put, identify the imprint cause and then begin treatment as with a survivor of sexual abuse at an early age and/or exposure. Although often a painful and difficult treatment process, the majority of cases are successful, and adjustment is oriented to the goals that the patient/client sets. Specialized techniques are involved, and I repeat the caveat to my colleagues that they should not attempt these cases without special training and supervised experience. *Note:* More information on imprinting and the survivors of sexual abuse as well as their treatment can be found in my second and third books (Prendergast, 1993, 1996), listed in the Bibliography.

IMPRINTING IN SEX OFFENDERS

Where sex offenders are concerned, an interesting phenomenon has been observed that takes on *ritualistic* overtones. I have found this pattern of ritual in both pedophiles and hebophiles. Choice of victim type, sex, and age, choice of setting for the act, and choice of specific sex act all appear to be determined by the imprint made at the offender's own victimization or sexual seduction.

AL was arrested for sexual molestation of six- and seven-year-old neighborhood boys. The offenses followed this pattern: He would lure the child into his garage where there was nothing except a single chair near a workbench. In the *first* occurrence with each child, he would sit the child on his lap for a few seconds and then tell him to go home. In the *second* occurrence, he would sit the child on his lap and rub his back. In the *third* occurrence, he would sit the child on his lap, rub his back, and extend the rubbing into the child's pants in order to rub his buttocks. In the *fourth* occurrence, he would sit the child on his lap, rub his back, extend the rubbing into the child's pants in order to rub his buttocks, and then reach around the front to fondle his genitals and masturbate him.

This ritualistic behavior occurred with three boys before a fourth boy reported the incident to his parents, whereupon Al was arrested and sent for treatment. Therapy over a six-month period revealed no pedophilic fantasies and no homosexual thoughts or occurrences. Although he denied any conscious memory of being molested as a child, there was a total absence of any memories for the period around age six. Memories before and after this age were as expected. Finally, hypnosis was utilized and on the third hypnotic regression the following story unfolded.

Al, age six, lived next door to a bachelor who had a toy shop in his garage. Al would hang around the open garage door watching, in fascination, the tinkering and seemingly magical production of toys for the next Christmas season. Finally, the toymaker invited Al in, and the following episodes occurred during his next four visits: On the *first* visit the toymaker sat Al on his lap; on the *second* visit, the toymaker sat Al on his lap and rubbed his back; on the *third* visit, the toymaker sat Al on his lap, rubbed his back, went into his pants, and rubbed his buttocks; on the *fourth* visit, the toymaker sat Al on his lap, rubbed his back, went into his pants, rubbed his buttocks, and then moved to the front and fondled his genitals and masturbated him. This went on for over a year unreported and then, without explanation, the toymaker moved.

This exact repetition of the details and events of an original molestation that is later repressed has been seen in literally hundreds of offenders over the past forty years.

If asked why a specific age range is targeted (e.g., seven to nine, nine to eleven, twelve to fourteen, fifteen to seventeen) the most frequent response is "They're the best!" or an equivalent phrase with a similar meaning. If asked why a specific choice of act (e.g., fondling versus oral or anal sex) the response is "That's the one I like best!" or "That one feels best to me!" or some equivalent response.

We have actually, on many occasions, had arguments in groups of pedophiles and hebophiles as to what age, physical build, hair color, body type, act, etc., is best. The "imprint effect" extends also to the place or setting of the seduction/molestation. For example, if their own experience had been in the woods or on a camping trip, this will be the setting they choose for seducing their victims; if in an attic or cellar, that will be their choice of setting; if in a garage (as with Al), this will be the preferred setting.

In some 100 offenders queried (regardless of sex or age of victim), this phenomenon was observed and verified in over 90 percent of the cases. The remaining 10 percent had multiple seduction/molestations, all of different types, with different individuals and with a variety of sex acts. With these offenders, the imprint effect held only for age group and male/female choice.

OFFENDER PATTERNS

The following sequence appears to occur in the *imprinted* sex offender:

- An early sexual seduction occurs which is not discovered or reported and which contains a pleasurable orgasm and also other pleasant elements such as friendship, gifts, money, caring, trips, etc.
- The relationship ends abruptly because the offender moves, the child moves, the child changes schools, etc. This leaves an emotional scarring that leads to or results in a total *repression* of any of the events of the relationship until many years later.
- A *trigger* event occurs and the behavior is reactivated with a *role reversal:* the former victim now becomes the adult victimizer with a child victim who is the same age as he was at the time of his own molestation. For Mike this was the birth of his son; for

Chuck it was the sight of all the naked men in the health club
shower and his becoming stimulated.

- Thoughts and fantasies containing the desire to *reenact* the former scenario begin, sometimes instantly, from the onset of the
trigger event. Although at first these are *obsessive* thoughts and
masturbation fantasies, they then translate into *compulsive* behavior over which the offender claims little or no control, regardless
of the severity of the consequences. Teachers, for example, know
they will never be allowed to teach again; husbands fear divorce;
priests/ministers know they will be defrocked; all fear exposure
and prison, but they do not stop (nor can they). When finally
caught and arrested, there is a sense of relief that is openly expressed early in the treatment process.

- Immediate *behavioral changes* occur: flight, guilt, and social
isolation being the most frequently observed and reported. Chuck
ran out of the health club vowing never to return and avoiding all
social contact, especially with males; Mike ran out of the baby's
room and never again would participate in either changing the
baby's diaper or bathing him; Chuck became impotent with his
wife; Mike stopped having sex with his wife; Mary stopped dating men.

PREVENTION

Prevention appears dependent on reporting or some form of disclosure at the age that the seduction/molestation occurred. I interviewed twenty-five men, molested at an early age, who had reported
the event and received either short-term therapy or were given adequate explanations to handle the associated fear and guilt. The main
personality difference in these men, when compared to sex offenders,
was that they did not put the blame or guilt on themselves but rather
on the offender, where it belonged. Their self-esteem remained intact. They did not change their sexual identity or orientation because
of the molestation. Most of them reported the abuse to their parents or
a teacher/counselor at school. On the whole, they were able to accept
the benefits (whether the sexual pleasure, the gifts, the relationship,
etc.) without feeling that *they caused the molestation* as other traumatized victims do, as in the following types of perceptions:

- I must have been seductive or too attractive or turned him on.
- My body was too nice or too sexual and caused him to do what he did.

The survivors' lives remain unaltered, and their development continues along normal lines. From this group, I learned several important preventive factors that were part of their lives and not part of the usual sex offender's life (see Box 11.2). The importance of a list of such factors is obvious: *If these strengths and educational elements can be incorporated into the lives of all of our children, then the sex offenders will have less chance of success, except by force.* Note that

11.2

Factors in Abused Children Who Did Not Report and Who Did Not Become Sex Offenders As Adults

1. Their self-esteem was strong and positive.
2. They had a fairly good sexual knowledge at the time of the molestation/seduction.
3. There was an important adult in their lives with whom they could discuss anything without fear of repercussion.
4. Their religious education was along positive and forgiving pathways.
5. They had several real friends in their peer group with whom they could discuss anything.
6. Their personality structure was stronger and more positive than the usually quite inadequate sex offender.
7. They were successful in school, sports, or some other area that produced pride, both for their parents and themselves.
8. Their parents were more regularly involved in their lives and activities, attended PTAs and other school functions, and spent as much time as possible with them on weekends, etc. They also traveled and vacationed with their parents.
    - Home life was an important part of their lives. The family ate together, prayed together, and played together. There was closeness between the children and their parents and the children with one another.
    - Their friends were welcome in their homes and they were welcome in their friends' homes. What they did with their friends and where they "hung out" were known by the parents and not a secret.
    - Whatever went on in their rooms and where they roamed on their computers were open to their parents and not "a right to my privacy."
9. They believed in themselves and had large amounts of self-confidence.
10. They were long-term-goal oriented in contrast to the living day-by-day lifestyle of the sex offender.

not all ten factors were present in all twenty-five men interviewed; however, there were at least six of the ten factors present in all of the test group.

The importance of these ten factors (and there may be more) is that they clearly indicate that *if* children could be brought up in a more positive environment and *if* parents could be educated to *accentuate the positives and minimize or utilize the negatives,* fewer children would be so readily available to the child molesters.

Since the molesters themselves experienced negativism, hypercritical appraisal and judgment, and a persistent emphasis on their failings and deficiencies, they know all too well the emotional devastation that results and the tremendous need that is generated for acceptance and love *at any price.* These simple changes could greatly reduce the ever-increasing number of children, especially boys, who are being molested and have nowhere to go and no one to trust or confide in. The numbers of sexually disturbed or dysfunctional adults that exist in today's world attests to this problem.

THE CHILD/ADOLESCENT SEX OFFENDER

The bulk of the descriptions and dynamics of imprinting in this chapter occurred in childhood or early adolescents. Therefore, the entire chapter refers to this group as well as to the adults they become. For clarity, an example of one of my adolescent sex offenders follows.

DOM, first presented in Chapter 1, was twelve years old when I first met him. He was accused of sexually touching a male classmate in the boys' lavatory while the boy was urinating. The boy reported the incident, and Dom was sent home with a note to his parents. The result was that he was ordered by the school superintendent to attend therapy or be expelled.

Although he was seen on a weekly basis for almost six months, he was never open, spontaneous, or totally honest. When taking his sex history, Dom related that on a science hike, a schoolmate, four years older than he, asked him to go with him to "pee." Dom agreed, and when they were hidden in the woods, the older boy exposed himself and asked Dom to hold his penis while he urinated. Dom complied, and this gave him a pleasant erotic feeling. When he finished, the boy told Dom to take his own penis out and he did the same. The only difference was that when Dom was finished urinating, the older boy knelt down and took Dom's penis in his mouth. This was Dom's fist experience with "blow jobs" and it imprinted positively.

On a subsequent science hike, a female classmate asked Dom to come into the woods with her, unzipped his pants, took out his penis, and gave him his second "blow job." Dom was even more thrilled with this experience than with the older male student. The imprint was confirmed and remains to this very day.

The problems began when Dom began asking other children at school to "give him a BJ." None did, and he became known as a "pervert" to most of the students at his school. He isolated, cut off all social activities, and became a compulsive masturbator with the two fantasies of his two best experiences.

When he became adolescent, he could no longer reach an orgasm to the fantasies and began looking for a partner to satisfy his needs. He remembered in the woods how he was initiated, and the referral incident took place.

After almost a year of nonparticipation, I bluntly asked him why he was coming to therapy. The response was, "If I don't come, I'm grounded for the weekend." My next questions concerned his feelings about having a problem. He angrily told me there was nothing wrong with him and that BJs were a normal part of growing up. I asked his mother to join us and had him repeat to her what he had told me. Therapy was terminated.

Update: I received a call from Dom three years later asking for an appointment. He had written a note to his sister asking her to "please give me a blow job!" and the sister gave the note to their mother. There was such an uproar from his brothers (whom he admired and respected) that he came to the conclusion that he indeed did have a problem. Dom remains in therapy up to this writing.

In this chapter, I have discussed my experiences with positive imprinting where sexually unwanted behavior is concerned. I have also observed unwanted guilt behaviors based on negative imprinting from extremely restrictive, punishing experiences in childhood and adolescence, especially those associated with incest. The results of these negative forms of imprinting are just as disastrous as those involving the sexually unwanted behaviors resulting from positive imprinting and will be discussed in upcoming chapters.

Chapter 12

Pedophiles

BACKGROUND

Of the three principal types of sex offenders (pedophiles/hebophiles, rapists, and incestuous fathers), the pedophile is the most complicated and the most difficult to treat. It should also be noted that the number of reported child molestations has been steadily increasing. However, there is still striking evidence (from therapists treating survivors of sexual abuse) that the number of reported cases is only the tip of the iceberg. Many more cases go unreported at the request (and sometimes *demands*) of the patient-survivor. A careful study of both of these groups may afford the opportunity of preventing this increase from getting even greater, since this deviation is almost always (more than 90 percent) traced back to some form of sexual seduction or trauma in the individual's childhood (see Chapter 2). Therefore, it appears quite logical and appropriate to infer that *were these childhood sexual traumas discovered at the time they occurred and immediately treated and resolved by trained and competent counselors or therapists, these treated children would not go on to become abusers themselves, therefore the number of child sexual molestations would eventually decrease rather than continue to increase.*

Broadly defined, adult pedophiles and hebophiles are individuals who prefer, need, and are compulsively drawn to children and adolescents. Among many others who have addressed the topic, Nicholas Groth (1979) has followed the distinction between fixated and regressed pedophiles introduced by Krafft-Ebbing. My own experience confirms Groth's typology but with the caveat that not all of the characteristics listed for each classification are always present. In Box 12.1, I have listed the characteristics of each group as I have seen them over the years.

In the simplest of definitions, the "fixated" pedophile has never had an adult sexual experience but remains fixated in his psychosexual de-

12.1

Fixated versus Regressed Pedophilia: Sources, Dynamics, and Offense Characteristics

Fixated	Regressed
1. Primary sexual orientation is to children.	1. Primary sexual orientation is to age-mates.
2. Pedophilic interests begin at adolescence.	2. Pedophilic interests emerge in adulthood.
3. No precipitating stress, no subjective distress is evident.	3. Precipitating stress is typically evident.
4. Persistent interest plus compulsive behavior occurs.	4. Involvements may be more episodic.
5. Preplanned, premeditated offense takes place.	5. Initial offense is often impulsive rather than premeditated.
6. "Equalization" is the principal dynamic: Offender identifies closely with the victim and equalizes his behavior to the level of the child; offender then is a "pseudo-peer" to the victim.	6. "Substitution" is the principal dynamic: Offender replaces conflictual adult relationship(s) with involvement with the child (or with children); the victim becomes a "pseudo-adult" substitute in the offender's mind.
7. Most offenders are single and have little or no sexual contact with age-mates—although some may have sexual contact with an age-mate of their own sex, usually serving as a substitute for a child partner, with this interaction typically (mutually) simulated by the use of child pornography.	7. Sexual contact with children proceeds concurrently with sexual contact with age-mates; the offender is usually married or living in a common law (heterosexual) relationship.
8. Usually there is no history of alcohol or drug abuse.	8. In a high proportion of cases, the offense may be alcohol or drug abetted.
9. Evidence of characterological immaturity with poor social-sexual peer relationships.	9. The lifestyle is more nearly traditional but with underdeveloped peer relationships.
10. The offense is a maladaptive resolution of life issues.	10. The offense is a maladaptive attempt to cope with specific life stresses.

velopment in childhood; the "regressed" pedophile, on the other hand, progressed psychosexually into adulthood but when strong sexual stress was encountered, regressed to an earlier psychosexual stage, usually in early to midadolescence. The primary importance of distinguishing between fixated and regressed pedophilia or hebophilia is for establishing the prognosis for safety and/or the ability to recommend releasing the offender from institutionalization or community treatment. In court-referred cases, this distinction is even more important because the court is looking for a recommendation for treatment either in the community or in an institutional setting (usually prison).

The following are the characteristics of fixated pedophiles:

- They are harder to treat due to their incredible resistance to change.
- They are convinced, as a group, that what they are doing is good for the children and tend to rationalize their behavior in any way possible. They are supported by international organizations such as the North American Man/Boy Love Association (NAMBLA) and the Pedophile Information Exchange (PIE), as well as by Greek mythology, sociological studies, and several prominent psychologists and sexologists. This makes the therapist's attempts to help them change even more difficult.
- They are much more inadequate than the hebophiles, rapists, or incestuous fathers and therefore are less likely to believe that, for them, change is possible.
- They have never had an adult or peer sexual experience and do not want one since they are convinced that they have found the best sexual world of all.
- They are terrified of sex with a peer adult since they negatively perceive themselves as inferior in all areas when compared with their peer group.
- They are failure phobic and thus take fewer risks or attempts at new behaviors than the other groups.
- By the time they are exposed and either incarcerated or mandated to treatment, they have been actively pedophilic for a great many years and are comfortable in their deviation (happily-maladjusted).
- Their personality deficits are far more numerous than any of the other groups of offenders, and they are aware of this factor.

The regressed pedophiles, on the other hand, have much more going for them in the way of positive therapeutic factors:

- They are usually much more guilt ridden and thus less resistant to change.
- They realize that what they did was wrong and that they harmed their victim(s).
- They are less inadequate than the fixated group and find it easier to believe that change is possible.
- They have had peer/adult sexual relationships and then regressed. Therefore, they know that they are capable of adult sexual behavior.
- They have fewer personality deficits than the fixated group and, therefore, their prognosis is much more positive.

From this discussion, one can see that differential diagnosis with the overall group of child molesters is essential before any treatment plan can be formulated. After working with this differentiation, I quickly came to the conclusion that a second delineation was necessary, based on the victim age-group preference. This need arose when, in several groups composed exclusively of child molesters, I discovered that they disagreed with one another on age choice and also that their overall personalities were grossly different. The result was the differentiation explained in the next section.

PEDOPHILES VERSUS HEBOPHILES

An important distinction involving child molesters is that of the pedophilic versus the hebophilic personality and makeup. On the simplest level, pedophiles are interested in:

- prepubertal, anorgasmic children of either sex;
- young children whom they can mold sexually into the rituals that most satisfy their needs; and
- young, weak, easily led, and intimidated children whom the offender can easily *control* and from whom there would be no fear of physical injury.

Hebophiles, on the other hand, are interested in:

- postpubertal, orgasmic preteens or teenagers who are capable of enjoying sex to orgasm;
- easily led or influenced youth of either sex who can be controlled and who pose no physical threat; and
- sex partners with whom they can have an affair and yet with whom they cannot live, thereby avoiding the risk of failure in a relationship.

The two groups are vastly different, and their prognoses for successful treatment are just as different. The pedophiles have the poorest prognosis of all the sex offenders. Many individuals in this group have never had a successful adult sexual relationship but are rather fixated at a preteen or teenage level of psychosexual development. This group contains the largest number of treatment failures, regardless of approach or environment.

The hebophiles, on the other hand, have usually reached an adult, peer level of sexual relationship but then, due to some real or perceived trauma, regressed to a former age level where they were the happiest and safest (usually in the teenage years). This group has a much more positive prognosis and a larger number of rapid successes. The two groups also differ in personality and characteristics makeup as can be seen in the comparison of pedophiles versus hebophiles in Box 12.2.

PEDOPHILES VERSUS INCESTUOUS FATHERS

Since incest usually involves either children or adolescents, it is necessary and appropriate at this juncture to see the difference between these two groups. Although pedophiles differ greatly from incestuous fathers, as can be seen in Box 12.3, there is less of a distinction between incestuous fathers and hebophiles. In fact, most incestuous fathers are either regressed pedophiles or hebophiles, but the reverse is not true. Here again, the differential diagnosis aids in determining the individual's overall treatment plan and is also essential for proper and safe prognoses. It is safe to state that the incestuous fathers group has the best prognosis of all the sex offenders and is the easiest and fastest to treat.

12.2

Comparison of Pedophiles versus Hebophiles: Sources, Dynamics, and Offense Characteristics

Pedophiles	Hebophiles
1. Victim age preference is prepubertal, anorgasmic.	1. Victim age preference is postpubertal, orgasmic.
2. Age bracket choice depends on the level of inadequacy. A general rule is that the more inadequate the offender, the younger the child victim.	2. Age bracket choice usually reflects the age at which he was happiest, sexually and otherwise. This may be considered his age of psychosexual fixation.
3. Offender is usually fixated.	3. Offender is usually regressed. This group includes the incestuous fathers.
4. Offender's need is to please the child sexually for acceptance and with hope child will continue the relationship. Often uses "sex education" as a ploy.	4. Offender's need is to have a sex partner. Considers his behavior as "having an affair."
5. The sexual behavior is usually one sided with the offender pleasing the child victim.	5. The sexual behavior is usually two sided with reciprocation a need of the offender.
6. The offender is grossly immature and inadequate.	6. This group usually is more mature with a good adult facade.
7. Employment goals are usually below potential. This group prefers passive and subservient positions.	7. Employment goals are age and potential oriented. This group often contains professionals and successful businessmen.
8. Socially, this group fears both their peers and adults. They are comfortable only with other inadequate males or children.	8. Socially, this group gets along well with peers on most levels except sexually.
9. Treatment time is usually a long-term battle for the smallest visible or observable changes.	9. Treatment time usually reflects rapid growth; changes appear sooner and are more easily observed or proven.
10. Prognosis is extremely poor. This group comprises the most failures of all sex offender groups in treatment.	10. Prognosis is good. There are more strengths to work with, and the success rate is relatively high.

12.3

Comparison of Pedophiles versus Incestuous Fathers

Pedophiles	Incestuous Fathers
1. These offenders have usually never had a successful adult sexual relationship.	1. These offenders have had successful adult sexual relationships and then regressed to below peer age levels.
2. Inadequacy dominates in the group, and they fail persistently.	2. This group is more adequate and usually successful in most situations.
3. These offenders lose their jobs frequently. They have no direction in their lives and few or no realistic goals.	3. This group frequently does quite well in employment. Many are successful businessmen or professionals.
4. This group has few, if any, real relationships, and they tend to isolate from social interaction.	4. This group has good relationships at work and socially outside the home. They are often considered model citizens.
5. These offenders are socially inept, primarily due to their pervasive inadequacy.	5. These offenders are more socially skilled and display an excellent social facade.
6. This group usually lacks any real religious conviction.	6. This group is usually more religiously oriented, basically fundamentalist, but hypocritical.
7. This group is weak, is easily controlled, and takes orders both at home and at work. They control no other adult in their lives.	7. This group is characterized by the "King-of-the-Castle" Syndrome: They rule the lives of their wives and children and control all activities in and out of their homes.
8. This group harbors strong feelings of failure that are often realistic.	8. Superiority often characterizes this group. Fears of failure, if they exist, are unrealistic.
9. This group fears anger and avoids expressing anger themselves. They tend to be easygoing and need to be liked by everyone, especially children.	9. This group is openly angry at their mothers and wives. Their anger ranges from mild to assaultive.
10. The major motivation of this group is seduction.	10. The major motivation of this group is anger.

(continued)

(continued)

11. The victim for this group represents the offender in the past or an ideal self.	11. The victim for this group represents his wife or girlfriend substitute.
12. Victims can be of either sex and same-sex sex is considered acceptable.	12. Victims are primarily females. Same-sex sex is considered a "put-down," but boys are also victims.
13. Sex must be enjoyable for the child more so than for the offender. He needs to "please" the child.	13. Sexual behavior is to satisfy his own selfish, sexual pleasure. The sexual needs of the victim play no role.

The "King-of-the-Castle" Syndrome

The major distinguishing characteristic of the incestuous father is his driving and all-pervasive need to function as the "king of the castle" in his home and also in his employment. He controls and dominates the lives of his wife and children and rules with an iron hand, oblivious to his own hypocrisy and double standards.

In contrast to the pedophile, he is usually quite socially adept, assertive in work and relational situations, makes friends outside the home easily, and has the facade of a wonderful person. His *secret* home life is unknown to his relatives, including his parents and his friends. When he is exposed, it is not uncommon for employers, fellow workers, and others in the community (often including the authorities) to disbelieve the complaint and to support the offender quite strongly. As is obvious, this is incredibly traumatic for the victims of his assaults and also for his often passive and inadequate wife.

The incestuous father often works or volunteers in the community and is awarded the highest honors and praise for his work. Many in this group of offenders have important and responsible positions, and many others are self-employed. An example at this point will clarify,

DONNY and JUDY lived in an upper-middle-class home. Their father, ALAN, was a prominent physician and surgeon, well known in the community and active in child abuse functions on both a local and state level. Unfortunately, Alan was a Jekyll-and-Hyde personality who ruled his home as a dictator.

Alan began his incestuous molestations and sadistic, brutal physical abuse of both children when they were approximately seven years old. One particular incident became a crucial traumatic event, the first of many, for Judy. After returning home from a social affair that the whole family had attended, Alan took Judy into the living room, undressed her, and attempted intercourse with her. Judy was only seven years old. During this molestation, Judy's mother came into the living room, catching Alan in the act. By the utmost denial process, she slapped Judy, called her a "tramp and a whore," and accused her of seducing her father and trying to steal her husband away.

From that day on, Judy's mother rejected her totally and would not even speak to her. Shortly afterward, the mother left the home and the children with the "monster," as Judy came to identify her father (quite appropriately). Alan now had the children to himself, with no fear of being caught or stopped in his perverse behavior.

Judy now became the woman of the house, and from that day on she acted as hostess and sex partner for her father, replacing her mother, although unwillingly. Although there were four children (two other brothers), Judy was closest to Donny and learned years later that Donny also was being sexually molested as well as physically abused by their father. The physical abuse was the most sadistic that I have encountered (outside of sex-mutilation murders). Alan forced absolute submission to his will and punished the children in horrible and sadistic ways, resulting in permanent physical damage. Where Judy was concerned, he forced objects into her vagina, beat her with his fists and objects including baseball bats or whatever else was available. He also forced her to perform any and all forms of sexual acts, ranging from the normal to the most perverse.

As a result, Judy sustained multiple concussions, since he primarily hit her over the head. He would then take her to the emergency room of the hospital where he practiced and told the attending physician that "She's a klutz and accident prone and fell down the stairs *again* and *again* and *again!*" The physicians and hospital staff accepted his stories, or more likely protected him because he was a physician. This went on until Judy was fifteen, when she finally ran away from home and was forced to live and survive on the streets of a major city. To this day, the damage done by her father plagues her with a glandular malfunction.

As for Donny, the same pattern emerged. The extent of Alan's brutality knew no bounds, and one night, when Donny had not cooperated to the extent Alan wished, Alan cut Donny's penis nearly off. Donny refused to go to the emergency room with this trauma, and Judy helped him to clean and bandage the damaged organ with butterfly stitches. Now they knew that they both were being used.

They also discovered that the monster, Alan, had played them against each other, knowing of their love and affection for each other. If either one balked at his demands, Alan would threaten to go to the other one to get compliance. To defend their sibling, both gave in on such occasions.

While Judy fought and ran away from home when she no longer could bear living that way, Donny could no longer live the life of a forced sex slave and committed *suicide*. The shock of this almost pushed Judy into a psychotic break, but her inner strengths (that she never recognized) kept her going. She finally made up her mind to confront her father and, if necessary, expose him to the world. Unfortunately, Alan had a major coronary and died before this was possible, leaving a distraught and broken Judy to survive. Her other two brothers wanted to know nothing about what happened to her since they left home as quickly as they were able to and, through extensive denial, were able to mitigate their guilt for not helping either their sister or their brother. Fortunately, Judy has grown and matured on her own to the point where she is now a teacher and soon will finish her education. She then plans to function in some form of crisis counseling, for which she has a natural talent.

Fear and terror tactics on the part of their father, as well as intense shame and guilt for the years of perverted sex with him, prevented either child from reporting him. In addition, Alan convinced them that they would never be believed (a typical incestuous parent ploy that is also used by authority-type pedophiles and hebophiles), and Judy had had enough hospitalizations to see that the doctors believed (or acted as if they believed) her father. This case clearly reveals the divergence in outcome of these cases and also clearly indicates that *the personality strengths and character of the child victim definitely affect the outcome of the case, especially where incest is concerned.*

Judy was a *survivor* and Donny was not. The depth of the effects on Donny are dramatically seen from one of his final journal entries:

> I wonder how it came to be that I was chosen to be the child of an animal . . . of a heartless bastard who comes from the pits of hell. I have spent my entire life in silent acceptance of what has had to be. . . . I never had an option or an alternative . . . there was no way that I could say no. Just grin and bear it. . . . No one would ever know what is at the core of my very sad soul . . . if in fact there is a soul left in me. It's full of crud.

Donny took his own life, alone and in despair, on a hot, balmy summer evening.

TREATMENT CONSIDERATIONS

In the past, even in our own treatment philosophy, it would have been considered essential to return to the original sexual trauma that determined the *victim age choice* and the *sexual act choice.* As this can be a long-term battle, especially where the original trauma is deeply repressed and defenses are formidable, we have since made this goal secondary to immediate focus change. The reasons are obvious:

- Since motivating the sex offender is an essential early treatment task, he must experience some immediate change or relief in order to believe that treatment can help. The constant problem of not remembering the trauma produces frustration and a belief that he is untreatable.
- It is a well-known axiom that with all clients in therapy, the harder the therapist pushes and demands that a task (such as remembering) be accomplished, the less the chance of success.
- There are three essential requirements for change that must be met by the client:

  1. the *desire* to change;
  2. the *belief* that change is possible for him; and
  3. the *belief* that he deserves to change.

I will discuss each of these requirements separately.

The Desire to Change

Because clients come to therapists *stating* that they want to change, therapists often assume that this is true. Too often, this is not the truth. A very large number of clients that I have treated eventually admitted to me in therapy that they really did not want to give up the deviant behavior. The reasons were myriad and included

- I really like what I'm doing and see nothing wrong with it!
- The kids like the sex and keep coming back for more, so it's not harming them. They know what they're doing! (Pedophile/hebophile)
- I've read a great deal, and this behavior is not only normal in some societies but has been *proven* to help preadolescents grow and mature sexually. (Pedophile who is usually a NAMBLA member)
- I know society says that what I'm doing is wrong, but I disagree. It happened to me when I was a kid and never harmed me! (Pedophile)

- Women are always turning men on and then saying "No!" How much do you think a man can take? (Rapist)
- She's/he's my kid, and I can do anything I want to her/him. (Incestous father)
- He/she seduced me! All I did was respond to his/her seduction. What's wrong with that if it's his/her idea? (Pedophile/hebophile)
- My wife, kids, dog, and car were all my possessions. That's how my father treated us, and that's how I treat my family. (Incestous father)
- My rights take precedent over the whole family. After all, I'm the breadwinner and without me they'd have nothing. (Incestous father)

The resistance in these individuals, as well as their defensiveness, is extremely strong and rigid. Care must be taken not to be deceived by their initial protestations of sincerity, especially if the individual has been exposed and is now either facing court action or is already found guilty and is on probation with treatment as a condition.

An important maxim that applies to most, if not all, psychotherapy must be, "Show me, don't tell me!" Once the patient realizes that he or she will not be believed without some form of concrete evidence, especially where *change* is concerned, fewer attempts at manipulation or lying occur. This philosophy/technique must be emphasized in the training of any counselor or therapist, who will be dealing with either the offender or the survivor of sexual abuse.

Masturbation Fantasies

As in many other treatment situations that will be discussed, *masturbation fantasies* will play an extremely important diagnostic role and thus need to be carefully monitored. Even fantasies that occur while the client is having sex with a partner are definite indicators of where the client is in his therapy. The claim that "They (the deviant fantasies) keep coming back. I can't stop them!" translates into "I keep using the fantasies to stimulate me, and I don't really want to give them up. I have a greater orgasm with my fantasies than with so-called normal ones."

Therapists must take special care not to allow the client to know what they are looking for. As stated in Chapter 1 and elsewhere, these are extremely clever and manipulative individuals who are "psyching" the therapist out as much as the therapist is trying to "psych" them out. An accepting, nonjudgmental approach, with homework assignments and self-report, especially about fantasies, appears to be the best choice of technique. Careful note taking *after the client leaves* is extremely important to weed out any obvious inconsistencies in reporting masturbation fantasies over a period of treatment time.

Making absolutely sure that the client *wants to change* becomes a first hurdle and first priority. No further work can or will be accomplished until this desire to change is firmly established.

The Belief That Change Is Possible

Where change is concerned, another often overlooked factor centers around the individual's own beliefs about his ability to change. Although he may sincerely believe that change is possible for other deviates with identical symptoms and behaviors, it is quite possible for him to feel just as strongly that for him change is impossible. This then becomes a self-fulfilling prophecy. Dennis, seen in many chapters, is a perfect example of a long-term client not believing that change is possible for him.

Often there is a complex set of conscious or unconscious mechanisms functioning in this belief. For example, if I really don't want to change or to give up my deviant behavior but cannot acknowledge or admit to this, what better way to accomplish my goal than to convince myself that change for me is impossible? As opposed to the "desire to change" problems where supportive methods are employed to uncover the situation, here *confrontation* may work better. This factor becomes readily visible in noncompliance to homework assignments with excuses such as "I forgot," or "I just didn't have time." When using confrontation methods, these alibis soon become "I didn't want to!" or "What's the use? Nothing works for me."

As a general rule, the longer the practice of the deviant behavior, the more likely the belief that change is impossible for him will remain a barrier to treatment. In cases where the child molester has had more than 100 victims and has been molesting for over twenty years, this factor emerges as the principal barrier to any real treatment progress and must become the principal focus of the therapy sessions.

Likewise, in the case of a rapist who has raped more than sixty women and successfully avoided arrest, this factor will present a serious barrier to all therapeutic efforts.

The Belief That I Deserve to Change

A simple sex offender formula explains

> If I change, that will be positive; I will like myself more and people will also like me more. But I'm no good, bad, evil, etc., and I don't deserve all of these benefits. Therefore, I must not change.

In situations where the self-image and self-esteem are this poor, change is impossible until these negative judgments are modified to more positive ones. These are probably the most difficult cases to work with (even more difficult than the sociopaths). Formal therapy, as such, will produce few or no results. Insight, in my opinion and experience, does little to help and simply becomes an intellectual exercise for many in this specific group.

The only thing that appears to work consistently is to *set up situations and conditions where the client will be forced to succeed and will also be unable to deny the success.* I have used art, sports, home improvement and repair, electronics, and many other related daily activities to *prove* to the client that he is worth something. Beginning with *physical* forms of success, I then move to *social* and *moral* forms of success, for example, developing his body in the gym, helping a friend or neighbor, saying "no" just once to an impulse, or substituting a good behavior for a bad one. Each success is recorded and a list is kept of each successful incident and the *worth* attached to it. The following simple logic becomes an important aid: *Could an evil, worthless, no-good person do all of these highly positive things?*

The first and most desired effect is for the client to begin having doubts about his worthlessness and then slowly to begin to believe that, *possibly,* he is worth something. This slow change method works better than any fast and dramatic improvement and is more credible with the client. The progress will not be linear but will have ups and downs, and these are important treatment topics to deal with. Warning the patient that these ups and downs will occur is essential.

THERAPIST CAUTIONS

When dealing with sex offenders, either institutionalized or in the community, whether self-referred or on probation, therapists have a moral and ethical responsibility to the community and the potential victims that these individuals could harm. It is quite easy for the offender to *rationalize* that as long as he is coming to therapy, he is being treated. This is not always true.

In Chapter 10, I discussed the need for *confirmation* to be the method of choice with these individuals. Several additional factors will be considered at this point.

- *A time limit should be established for evaluating discernible change and/or other indicators of therapeutic progress.*

Dennis attended weekly therapy sessions with no visible or reported change in over six months. When I asked him why he continued coming and spending his money, he replied "Because I need treatment. I'm a sick person."

Then I asked if he thought he was receiving treatment. He stated, "Of course I am. You're a therapist, aren't you?" I then set immediate limits for some positive effort and results and gave him a month to begin making some movement toward change. Surprisingly, he did improve on a social and interpersonal level but *refused to give up his deviant masturbation practices and fantasies,* stating, "There's no way I can stop doing it now. That will take a long, long time for me to stop, if ever."

Each step of the way in treatment with this type of individual is a battle for both control and change. Each therapist must make up his or her own mind as to how long he or she can be the excuse and alibi for an offender who is still free in the community.

- *Therapists working with offenders in the community must realize that treatment strips away defense mechanisms and that the client will, in all likelihood, get worse before he gets better.*

This principle also applies pointedly to Dennis. When he began treatment, his masturbation fantasies involved seven- or eight-year-old boys with only their shirts off standing across the room from his bed. He then fantasized an older boy punching them in the stomach, and that image brought him to his climax. As therapy progressed, the fantasies changed and frightened both the client and the therapist. In the new fantasy, the young boy was now totally nude and the fantasy was of Dennis walking over to him and fondling him. Without the change, Dennis could no longer reach a climax. The dangers are obvious.

- *The therapist must constantly reevaluate each case as to progress, potential danger to himself or herself or others, and the ability of the offender to remain safely in the community.*

There will come a time in many of these cases where the fuse is lit and the danger to the community becomes too great for the therapist to continue with the same treatment. In these situations, options depend on the circumstances.

1. If the client is on probation, that department should be informed of the therapist's concerns *without divulging any confidential material*. There is usually a condition that the therapist must provide regular evaluations on the progress or lack of progress of the probationer. After several frightening cases of this type in my early years of treating offenders, I made it a condition, when I received a referral from the courts, that regular evaluations and progress reports would be required and that the court or probation department would arrange for the legal releases of such reports. Since that decision, I have had little trouble with these cases.
2. In cases where the client is self-referred and not on probation, the problem is a little more complicated but can still be dealt with. Once adequate rapport is established and the client trusts the therapist, he usually will accept the advice that is given. On several occasions I was forced to recommend inpatient treatment at a private facility when the overt dangers to the community became too great. This decision relieved the burden as well as the anxiety of both the client and the therapist. Once a sex offender, whether he is currently committing offenses or not, is removed from the specific source of his temptations, there is a relief that nothing else can provide, a feeling of being *safe*.

3. Finally, in cases of parolees, the problem becomes simpler. Referrals from the parole department automatically involve updates and evaluative reports on a regular basis. In addition, the parole officers usually have the right to detain and arrest parolees who behave in a manner that suggests an *imminent danger of return to their criminal behavior or a threat to the community.*

The need to become involved in any of these situations should remain a major consideration before a therapist decides to specialize in this controversial and responsibility-laden area.

THE CHILD/ADOLESCENT SEX OFFENDER

The earlier pedophilia/hebophilia is detected, the easier the treatment and the better the prognosis for adult adjustment. As can be seen from the previous discussion, the longer this perversion exists, the greater the habituation becomes ingrained until compulsion results.

As stated elsewhere in this book, my experience over the years has been that 90 percent or more of the pedophiles I have encountered (either in prison or in my private practice) were themselves molested as children. Those with an existing homosexual preference may often be identified in their choosing to associate and play exclusively with boys and feeling alien or uncomfortable with girls. In some there also was a preexisting attraction to other boys' bodies, especially an interest in their genitals. These survivors of sexual abuse continue their homosexual behavior with other boys in a particular pattern that I have observed many, many times. At first, the sex play with other boys is age appropriate (zero to two years difference), and then a specific change occurs during adolescence: their own age continues to increase but the age of the boys they choose to have sex with does not, creating an age difference that reaches pedophilic levels. A typical case of this type will clarify.

ROD was first molested at age five by his cousins, ages ten and twelve. They fellated Rod, and he enjoyed the experience tremendously, especially the acceptance he felt it earned him. This relationship with his cousins continued for approximately ten years. During this time period, he was also homosexually involved with two other cousins, ages eleven and thirteen, and a family friend, age fourteen. In the latter relationships, Rod was the fellater and received no reciprocation until age eight when they began fellating him also.

Rod's initiating of sex began when he was ten and the neighbor's son was ten as well. They slept in a tent together in the nude. Although he initiated the sex, the other boy willingly joined in. When he was thirteen, the next boy was ten or eleven. *The age separation had begun.*

In high school, when Rod was sixteen, he seduced a thirteen-year-old boy from his neighborhood. It began with a massage (this behavior continues to this day) and then rubbing his genitals. The boy responded and reciprocated.

In college, when Rod was twenty, he seduced "Greg" age eighteen, and performed his first sodomy. Greg "loved it" and reciprocated. (Rod continues to fantasize about this experience to this day.)

At age twenty-four, he met a sixteen-year-old "who was really hung." Their relationship lasted five to six months and was always reciprocal.

After graduating from college, Rod became a member of Big Brothers "in order to find a little brother." He was assigned to a twelve-year-old whom he seduced at their first meeting together. They had mutual oral sex and then Rod sodomized him. That evening his mother noticed his underpants were really messy and began questioning him. After a week of badgering (Rod's description), the boy told her that he and his Big Brother were having sex. Rod was arrested and sent to prison for treatment with a thirty-year indeterminate sentence.

Update: Today, Rod is in the community on parole, doing fantastically for the past fifteen years. There have no further involvements with underage boys. Rod has accepted his homosexuality and is involved with several adult partners, looking for "Mr. Right." He teaches at the college level and has had no involvement with any of his students. He knows his warning signs; when they occur, he calls for a therapy session. Prognosis in this case is very good.

PREVENTION

Had Rod's own molestation by his older cousins been discovered and had he been seen in therapy, there is an excellent chance that he would never have followed the pattern and become a pedophile. His family was totally unaccepting of homosexuality and was quite vocal about it making it impossible for Rod to talk about his cousins or his sexual fantasies and needs.

Parents, teachers, religious leaders, neighbors, and all of society are responsible for our children's safety. The excuses—"It only happened once!" and "He's just going through a stage!" and "All kids experiment!"—are heard over and over again when parents are interviewed and asked why they waited so long to bring the individual to therapy. This is pure ignorance and self-protection on the part of these adults who know of a molestation and do not report it.

If therapists could become involved in cases where only one incident of molestation occurred (refer to Jeffy in Chapter 1), treatment would be short and end with a very favorable prognosis for normal development and adjustment. When ten or more years have passed since the behavior began (refer to Dennis in several chapters), the therapeutic challenge becomes immense. The latter cases too often end with another molestation and the incarceration of the client.

A major problem in finding these cases is the ignorance of a large part of society about the dynamics and dangers of these children/adolescents molesting younger children and of the availability of trained therapists and counselors who can help in these cases. The information has to be disseminated by professional groups, and judges and prosecutors need to be informed/trained as well.

The trend of incarcerating these offenders is to "lock them up and throw away the key." Regardless of the length of their sentences, someday they will be released and will be even more dangerous than when they were first imprisoned. They network in prison, exchange information, plan how to get away with their next molestation, and even share with other offenders names and addresses of their victims who have not reported. Treatment by trained therapists is the only way to prevent these further molestations.

Chapter 13

Sexually Assaultive
versus Seductive Offenders

In Chapter 12, I dealt with the seductive-pedophiles and hebophiles. Force or assault to that group was unheard of and even the thoughts of force or pain terrified them.

Now I deal with the sexually assaultive sex offenders who use force, coercion, and pain as a matter of course. This group includes children, adolescents, and adults. I do not consider a sex offender who kidnaps, beats, terrifies, and even kills his victims as belonging to the child-molester or seductive pedophile/hebophile group of offenders. Their personalities as well as their behaviors differ greatly from the inadequate group in Chapter 12 who accepted their inadequacy (refer to Chapter 2); the sexually assaultive personalities denied their inadequacy and developed a compulsive need to prove their superiority through total control. As this chapter develops, this difference will become clear.

CONTROL: THE MAIN DYNAMIC

If I had to choose a single factor that typifies and is common to all sexual assault, it would be *control.* Having been controlled in some manner (directly or indirectly) from as far back as he can remember, the sexually assaultive personality fears being controlled more than even the seductive pedophiles do. He deals with this fear by making sure that in all of his sexual acting out, he begins by taking control mentally (threats), physically (brute force), or with a weapon (knife, gun, etc.). His control begins the act, continues during the act, and even exists after the act through more threats of harm if the survivor tells anyone. He also protects himself with masks, disguises, or by controlling the environment (darkness, pillow over the victim's face, hoods over their heads, etc.). The element of control is more important than the sexual release he needs. The danger here is that the ultimate control is control over life and death. Many serial rapists often end up killing their victims.

My very first sex offender evaluation became my first contact with the sexually assaultive personality. In 1962, having just completed an internship at a state reformatory for boys, I transferred to the now-defunct New Jersey State Diagnostic Center as a first-level, wet-behind-the-ears psychologist. The inpatient department evaluated children and adolescents who had come into contact with law enforcement. I had dealt with several cases of sexual offenses, both offenders and victims, at the reformatory during my internship, and my interest was now fairly well established.

The very first case I was assigned to involved rape. That was all I was told. I would be a member of a three-person team (psychiatrist, psychologist, and psychiatric social worker) who would have ninety days to evaluate the case and send a recommendation to the courts as to how the offender should be handled. Our choices were

1. return the offender to his or her home on strict probation with outpatient treatment,
2. incarcerate him or her at a state reformatory, or
3. send him or her to a residential treatment center for a specified period of time.

The case involved a rapist who had brutally assaulted and beaten three young girls in their own grammar school. His folder contained the pictures of the postrape victims, and they made me both sick and angry. A knock on my office door began my real education into the world of sexual pathology.

In walked SKIPPY, a three-foot six-inch, forty- to forty-five-pound, skinny and openly aggressive seven-year-old boy. At this point, I was sure that this was my initiation by the staff. It was not. Skippy had been arrested for the rape of three of his female schoolmates. In addition, he smoked at least a full pack of cigarettes a day and could not sleep at night without drinking a six pack of beer. All of these facts were verified in his folder by the investigating juvenile detective.

From this first visit and for several more to come, a confrontational relationship developed between Skippy and me. He was not the least bit inhibited and had an adult sexual vocabulary (slang). Rather than being frightened or embarrassed by his situation, as most other children his age were at the center, Skippy took pride in his "macho" (his word) accomplishments. He intimidated the other children on his housing wing and even some of the staff. Whenever he got angry at me for pushing too hard in an area he did not want to discuss, he threatened to urinate on me.

How could this have happened? The literature available in 1962 was of little help, and it became quickly apparent that only Skippy knew the answers to the puzzle. Through many, many hours of establishing rapport and trust with Skippy—we eventually became good friends—the following facts emerged.

Skippy and his mother came to the United States from Puerto Rico looking for streets lined with gold. They had lived in abject poverty in Puerto Rico and felt their only hope was to come to the United States. They settled in a largely Hispanic city that was known in New Jersey as "Little Puerto Rico." Skippy's mother soon discovered that there was little work for her because she spoke practically no English and had no skills. Friends found a single room for her and her young son in a rooming house and, rather than starve or return to Puerto Rico, Skippy's mother made a living the only way she knew how: she prostituted.

At this time, Skippy was between two and three years old (as far as investigators could determine) and, since there was no money for a baby-sitter, he sat or lay on the bed while his mother serviced her customers. Eventually, Skippy admitted that some of the customers preferred him to his mother and, as a result, he was molested on a regular basis. After a period of time, he felt that this was normal behavior and admitted that, at times, *he enjoyed the sex* as well as the gifts and affection the male customers lavished on him. His poor mother told him how proud she was of her "real man," since Skippy's father deserted them when he found out that the mother was pregnant. They had never been married, so she had no legal recourse.

The real trauma occurred when Skippy was six years old and was sent to school. Innocently, he told his newly found friends (boys and girls alike) about his mother's "friends" and the "games" they all played. He was immediately ostracized by both the children and the teachers. Their comments were hurtful and insulting and, for the first time in his life, Skippy learned to hate. From that point on, Skippy became a serious behavioral problem: fighting, stealing, smoking, and drinking beer. Vandalism became an outlet, especially where female teachers were concerned.

At no time did Skippy tell his mother what was happening at school, and they both continued earning their subsistence through sex. By age seven he had heard about fags and queers, and his anger turned into uncontrollable rage. He began to daydream about showing everyone that he was "macho" and not a *chulo* (a male prostitute). Being too small to attempt an assault on an adult woman (the fantasies centered on one specific sadistic female teacher at school), he chose schoolmates who rejected him and made fun of his speech, clothing, and his difficulty in learning to read. The physical assaults and rapes resulted.

WHY RAPE?

Skippy's anger and rage, although consciously directed at the sadistic teacher and then projected onto his age-mates, was, on a deeper level, directed at his mother. After many, many therapy sessions that were always emotional, threatening, and quite stormy, Skippy was finally willing to explore the possibility that he was really angry at his mother. He was asked to *imagine* possible reasons that he might have for being angry with his mother and the following emerged:

- She was poor.
- She did not have a husband and, therefore, Skippy did not have a father.
- She earned a living through prostitution.
- She could not speak English well, and this embarrassed him.
- She was not getting him out of the center.

Finally, after many difficult sessions came the real key to the anger:

- She allowed the men to *use him* homosexually, and he was still fantasizing to those homosexual acts and even masturbating to them.

This last reason was paramount, since Skippy felt that it made him a "queer" or "fag," and he had to deny it. The only way to deny being a homosexual prostitute was by being the greatest heterosexual performer that his victims would ever meet. For most sexually assaultive offenders, intercourse becomes the method of regaining their lost manhood, even though it is forced. This group often makes the victims tell them how great the sex was and how they had been satisfied better than ever before. This delusional behavior actually works for many of them until they are confronted and put in prison. There, many of them become the "wives" or "punks" (female-role sex partners) of the stronger sexually assaultive or just plain assaultive inmates. This is one of the major reasons that in many prisons sex offenders are segregated from the general population.

In many of the rape cases I have seen and treated, regardless of the fact that a male was the molester during the rapist's youth, the *mother* was the one he deeply blamed. Developmentally, children see the mother as their *protector,* not the father or father figure. Therefore, regardless of who sexually traumatized the rapist as a child or adolescent, he sees it as the mother's fault for not protecting him by knowing what was happening and preventing it.

The rapist tends to develop an extreme dependence on his mother that prevents him from venting any rage he feels directly on her. Instead he "displaces" the rage onto a substitute female who in looks, behavior, or attitude reminds him of his mother. This triggers the rage, and it surfaces. The victim could also be someone that the mother appears (in the distorted mind of the rapist) to love more than him. Thus, the substitute victim could be *anyone:* a student, a neighbor, an employee, or even a total stranger. Note, however, that in child molesters, the anger would most likely be aimed at the mother's favorite: his brother or sister or even one of his friends.

REPRESSION

Joey, now an adult rapist, came from a family with marital conflicts. When Joey was around twelve years old, the following set of circumstances occurred.

JOEY's father began to take him out every Saturday, explaining to Joey's mother that he and his son needed more time alone to become friends and to get to know each other better since Joey was entering adolescence. Joey's mother believed the story. In reality, Joey's father was using him as an alibi to visit his secret paramour. Joey would be given a game or some comic books to read and instructed to sit on the porch of the paramour's home while the father visited upstairs.

Joey was quite streetwise by age twelve and knew or fantasized what was going on upstairs. However, as long as his father treated him well, bought him gifts, and later took him somewhere such as an amusement park, swimming pool, or bowling alley, he really didn't care. He also wanted and needed the individual attention he was getting from his father and was unwilling to upset the applecart.

These Saturday excursions continued for more than six months until a dramatic change occurred. One day, as he was reading a comic book on the front porch of the paramour's home, his father came downstairs in his underwear and took Joey by the hand, leading him upstairs. Upon entering the bedroom, the frightened Joey became aware of two things: (1) a naked woman, quite large, lying on a frilly bed and (2) a strong odor of cheap perfume. Joey's father ordered him to undress. When he hesitated, the father undressed him, stating, "It's about time you became a man, if you're good enough!" The boy was then ordered to lie on top of the woman and to "show me what kind of a man you are!"

Though he knew about sexual intercourse, Joey was a virgin and, under the circumstances, was so frightened and confused that he could not get an erection. The woman (he never was told her name) put her arms around him, held him tightly, and whispered in his ear, "Be a good boy, Joey, and don't cry."

Joey, more frightened and confused than ever, felt his father climbing on top of him. The next thing he felt was terrible anal pain as his father penetrated him. Joey now was in shock, and the woman kept trying to calm and comfort him. When the father was finally finished, he said, "Boy, you've got the best and tightest 'pussy' I've ever had!"

Joey was never to forget this phrase, which to him meant that his father had used him as a woman. When they left the house, not a word was spoken between them. Upon arriving home, Joey was obviously in pain and wet since he was bleeding quite a bit. His mother treated his bleeding by packing cotton up his rectum (a second rape). She never asked a single question as to what happened, and Joey assumed that she knew what his father had done to him and really didn't care.

From this point on, Joey became a real behavior problem both at home and in school. He was constantly disrespectful to his teachers and to his mother, and was always getting into fights and doing all sorts of daring feats to prove his strength and masculinity. In less than a full year after that episode, Joey committed his first rape on a high school girl whom he so terrified and threatened that she never reported it. Joey was on his way to becoming a compulsive rapist. By the time he was finally apprehended, some eight years later, he had raped more than twenty-five women.

During his first year or more of therapy, there was no conscious memory of his own rape. Joey had *repressed* the entire incident. He had rationalized his rapes with his difficulties in all female relationships and the resulting anger and rage he felt at being ridiculed, rejected, or put down by females, regardless of age.

Before I continue, an explanation of repression may be necessary. Repression can be best understood in the following definition (Wolman, 1989, p. 292): "Repression is an unconscious exclusion from the consciousness of objectionable impulses, memories, and ideas. The ego, as it were, pushes the objectionable material down into the unconscious and acts as if the objectionable material were nonexistent."

Thus, one of the most difficult problems faced in treating these individuals, as well as their victims (survivors), is to discover whether there are any repressions. If repressions are suspected, it is important to bring them to the conscious level. The following rule or guideline may be helpful in determining whether a repression exists in a particular case: *Whenever a compulsive behavior is discovered that has no logical explanation or etiology, look for a repressed trauma.* This is especially true where *compulsive ritual* is concerned. Several examples of such rituals may shed some light on the concept.

Choosing a Particular Setting

- Except for his first rapes that occurred in the girls' rest room at school, Skippy *always* lured his potential victims to his room and assaulted them in his mother's bed. (By this time, his mother had found employment and was no longer prostituting.)
- Joey *always* broke into apartments or homes and assaulted women in their own bedrooms. If this was not possible, then he would take them to a "cheap and crummy hotel since that was all that whores deserved."
- Kevin *always* used the backyards of homes where he had been stalking his victims.

Finding Victims in a Particular Place

- Skippy's victims were *always* classmates from school.
- Joey *always* chose women in diners or bars, nowhere else.
- Kevin *always* cruised middle-class neighborhoods and chose women who were out late at night, walking home alone.

Looking for Victims Exhibiting a Specific Behavior Pattern

- Skippy's victims *always* had to be female classmates who directly or indirectly put him down or made him feel below them.
- Joey *always* chose women who were seductive and came on to him.
- Kevin *always* chose women who appeared weak and defenseless and who also appeared pious and proper.

Following Certain Set(s) of Behaviors During the Assault

- Skippy *always* made the girls undress and lie naked on the bed (as he remembered his mother doing) and then smile and act astonished at his erect penis size.

- Joey *always* made his victims kneel, beg, ask permission to fellate him, take his pants down, and after he was aroused beg him to rape them. They also had to tell him that his performance was *great* after he climaxed. (All of this was accomplished by threat and a knife.)
- Kevin *always* forced his victims to choose between fellating him or being raped. He preferred the fellatio but would do whatever they chose.

RAPE AS OVERCOMPENSATION FOR PERCEIVED MALE SEXUAL INADEQUACY

One of the most frequent underlying dynamics of rape is *an overwhelming (compulsive) need to prove masculinity.* These individuals, for reasons that must be discovered in their treatment, lack feelings of masculinity in their sexual performances as well as in many or all other aspects of their lives. Reality has little to do with these feelings, as often the significant others in their lives feel the opposite is true. Their daily appearance and behavior also often contradict the perceived deficiency.

TED, from his earliest memories, was raised in a totally female environment. He never knew his father and, to this day, has no idea of who his father was or why the man abandoned him. The women in his home included his mother, his grandmother, and two spinster aunts, who all hated men with a passion. As a consequence of this misanthropic situation, each time Ted arrived home from anywhere (going to the store, playing in the yard alone, visiting a friend, returning from school), he was made to undress completely in the foyer of the house and then to dress from the skin outward in female clothing. In the house, he was called Teddy but in a manner which intimated that he was a girl, not a boy. His chores were traditionally female tasks; he was taught skills and crafts such as needlepoint, cooking, and housekeeping tasks and was never allowed to play typical boys' games. Even his toilet behavior was feminine, as he was made to sit down to urinate and to be sure his penis was never seen or touched. Through this conditioning, his mannerisms became totally feminine, and he was labeled a sissy by the neighbors as well as by his teachers and peers when he began school. The fact that he was good looking, in a soft way, added to the problem.

At adolescence, Ted did not develop physically, and at age sixteen he still had the body and genitals of an eleven-year-old prepubescent boy. The teasing in high school was intense, and Ted began acting out in passive-aggressive ways, such as stealing other pupil's belongings (especially those who taunted him) or hiding to avoid gym classes. Eventually, his anger and rage burst into vandalism. Once he came to the attention of the juvenile justice system, he was removed from his home environment and placed in a foster home. He was physically examined and given hormone shots to induce adolescence. (Interestingly, the physician could never find a physical cause for the lack of pubertal development and concluded that somehow it was all psychologically based.) He began to grow physically and to develop sexually and quickly learned all the myths about sex from other boys in the home.

Ted's first dating attempt at his high school prom was a disaster. He was awkward, could not dance, and stammered badly when he tried to communicate. He felt an anger in the company of his date that he did not understand. He tolerated the situation for as long as he could and then disappeared from the prom, abandoning his date. The ridicule and censure he received at school the next Monday was too much, and he ran away. While hitchhiking, he was picked up by an older woman who attempted to seduce him by rubbing his leg and crotch. Again, he felt the rage and panicked, jumping out of the moving car and hiding in the woods where he eventually fell asleep. He awoke to the singing of a sixteen-year-old girl walking home from church. Without even thinking, he jumped from the woods, grabbed her, and dragged her into the shrubbery where he raped her under threat of her life.

Ted was arrested walking down the same road within an hour of the rape and was sent to the treatment unit. Prison terrified him, and living in a large open dormitory with open bathrooms and showers was even more terrifying. However, contrary to his expectations, the men in the unit adopted him as a sort of *mascot* or younger brother whom they protected and advised. In therapy, Ted was totally open (again due to his immaturity and naïveté) and painfully verbalized what had been done to him in childhood and the lingering effects of feeling feminine. He also stated that he felt that he should have been born a girl.

While psychotherapy dealt with his conditioning, his anger, and his self-image problems on one level, the group members took on the task of "masculinizing" Ted. They taught him sports on a basic level and how to play pool, work out in the gym (after a year of therapy), and lower his voice to sound more manly. As his therapist, I encouraged him to *release his anger as it occurred if it were appropriate* (certainly not with the prison officers). He did so in therapy situations or with his peers in the dormitory.

In three years, although the feminine traits were still visible from time to time (especially when he was embarrassed and blushed from ear to ear), Ted appeared to be a new person who acted masculine for the most part and was much more openly assertive than ever before.

Six months after his release he met a hometown girl and married her. They have three children and, at his last check-in, were doing

quite well. What was done to Ted was not an active sexual molestation but was definitely a passive sexual trauma for him. Other forms
of *identity conflicts* that may also result in sexually deviant behavior
are described in the sections that follow.

The *"You Are a Failure!"* Cases

DENNIS, who was first discussed in Chapter 6 and then again in Chapter
12, comes from an old-world family with a passive, compliant mother and a
dominant, tyrannical father whose word is law. Dennis's older brother was
the favorite of both parents, and Dennis was told by his parents early in his
childhood that he was an "unexpected gift from God that made life difficult for
the whole family."

From this point onward, his life was full of misery and rejection. No matter
what he did, it was never good enough, and the father's persistent prediction
was that Dennis would never amount to anything. Desperate for acceptance,
Dennis tried even harder, and the harder he tried the more often he failed in
his father's eyes. Looking to his mother or his older brother for support was a
waste of time, and Dennis soon learned to stop trying. This became the pattern for his whole life: at home, in school, and playing with other children (a
rare occurrence since most of the time he was an observer).

Somehow, he squeaked into college and eventually graduated with a C
average. His parents were unimpressed and did not even have a party or cel-
ebration for his graduation. Dennis found a menial job in his chosen field
(television broadcasting), but here again he was isolated, never socialized
with other employees after work, and never really tried for promotion. When,
at age twenty-nine, he began to take an inordinate interest in six- to seven-
year-old boys, he requested therapy.

Throughout his therapeutic involvement of over five full years, he has
made only minimal progress in any area. He begins each session by enu-
merating the failures of the previous week, looking for the rebuke and punishment he would receive from his father (this factor is now conscious and
accepted). Both Dennis and the therapist remain frustrated at his lack of real
growth. Recently, Dennis finally stated, "I guess I'm so used to being a failure
that I'm comfortable this way and know how to act. If I change, I'll have to try
new things and that is too frightening. I guess I'll stay this way."

Although this certainly is his right, the problem is that his attraction for
young boys has become overtly sexual, and he is masturbating to fantasies
of fondling them and, at times, of forcing them to have sex with him. I have
maintained contact with Dennis primarily to prevent another victim of child
sexual abuse. His passivity and fears are so intense that they have remained
a control mechanism for at least fifteen years.

Update: Dennis recently became involved with an adult homosexual and
although he does whatever his "special friend" wants for sexual pleasure, he
will not permit him or anyone else to pleasure him to orgasm. To uncover the
reason for this "block" is the next goal in therapy.

The "Who Am I?" Cases

The following case exemplifies the "Who Am I?" problem quite clearly.

LARRY was a handsome, well-built, athletic instructor at a local health club. He was in college and hoped to become either a teacher of physical education or possibly a lawyer. Although his father had deserted the family when Larry was only nine or ten, he seemed to have found sufficient male figure substitutes to develop along normal lines. He was the most popular male in his senior high school class, was elected class president, and was voted most likely to succeed. Larry's mother was a hardworking domestic for a wealthy family, wanted only the best for her son, and tried to be both mother and father. One day, Larry was searching for his high school diploma and went through his mother's private papers. To his total shock, he found his birth certificate and learned that he was illegitimate and that his father was a well-known millionaire, living in the same town but in a very different neighborhood.

Feelings of anger, rage, hatred, confusion, and depression all fused, and he went out and got sickeningly drunk. When he came home, he confronted his mother, and she told him the whole story. She had worked for the father's family and became pregnant. However, she did not fit in the family's plans for their son, so they gave her a small amount of hush money and paid her medical bills for the pregnancy. She had had no contact with his father since and to her knowledge he had never seen or known his own son, nor did he want to.

Larry attempted to see his father but was refused admittance to the mansion and told that it was impossible for him to be related to this *great man*. While consciously feeling anger and hatred for his father, Larry began mistreating women at the health club where he worked and was terse and defiant toward his mother. Within five months, he was picking up prostitutes and having violent sex with them, attempting to make it as painful as possible and then literally throwing them out of his car without paying for their services. On the third or fourth such incident, the prostitute charged him with rape, and Larry was given a thirty-year sentence to the treatment unit. Therapy was quite rapid, since he was open and quickly revealed the real problem, his illegitimacy, and the meaning he put on it: "I'm inferior, dirty, useless, unwanted," and "I don't deserve having clean and good girls, only prostitutes who are as bad as . . ." Eventually the ending became "My mother!"

Update: In eighteen months, Larry was released and returned to both his job as a health club supervisor with the hotel chain and to college. Today he is a successful attorney (this required special exemption from the morals code of the bar which a state senator helped him to gain). Larry is married and has two boys of his own who are helping him to regain the missing father-son childhood connection of which he was deprived.

The terribly sad thing about both of these cases is that had they been discovered early enough and treated appropriately, the sexually deviant behavior (in both cases, rape) could have been avoided. This is where communication between parents and children, as well as sex education in the home and in the school, with peer discussion included, could make all of the difference in these children's lives.

THE CHILD/ADOLESCENT SEX OFFENDER

There is a myth that aggravated sexual assault (rape included) is an adult behavior exclusively. To the contrary, both children and adolescents are more than capable of this behavior. Skippy, introduced earlier in this chapter, is a classical example. His acts were violent, sexual, and controlling, the three main elements in an aggravated sexual assault. He not only terrified his smaller female classmates but also controlled them, humiliated them, and raped them. Skippy was quite capable of having an erection and was also capable of penetration, which he had learned in his mother's bed.

I have treated many other children and adolescents who were also capable of sexual assault. There were ten- to twelve-year-olds as well as many thirteen- to sixteen-year-olds. These children and adolescents, as with pedophiles and hebophiles, had also themselves been sexually molested, and many had been forcibly and extremely painfully sodomized.

One of the dynamics common to all of these cases was a need to "undo" what had been done to them in order to regain their feelings of lost masculinity. Another common dynamic was the intense degree of anger and rage they all possessed: some exhibiting the rage on an almost daily basis; the rest repressed it and were like ticking time-bombs. Skippy fell into both categories: before he raped, the rage was internalized and repressed, then he "exploded" on the day of the rapes, and three innocent victims resulted. From that day on the rage was always present.

In my experience over the years, there were many coconspirators involved in all of these violent offenses: parents who did nothing to get help for their child(ren), relatives and neighbors who witnessed the rage and destructive behavior and did nothing, and teachers, religious personnel, and others who had contact with these children/adolescents and who also did nothing. I seriously doubt that any of the cases I have treated could not have been stopped before their rage erupted sexually and injured someone else.

In today's world, everyone connected in the least way to acting-out, angry, and out-of-control children and adolescents must take a role, even if is simply alerting the parents or authorities regarding what is going on. I carefully inquired in each case whether there was anyone that could have reached them, that they trusted and/or admired, and each individual was able to name one or more adults in their lives who could have helped.

The warning signs in child/adolescent aggravated sexual assault are many and include

- any abrupt change in behavior or performance,
- an increase in acting-out behaviors,
- a sudden drop in scholastic performance,
- an increase in social interaction problems, especially with peers,
- a tendency to associate with older youths and avoid contact with their peers,
- secrecy at home and everywhere else, responding to questions with silence or an angry outburst,
- new complaints of their privacy being invaded and increased paranoidal-type complaints,
- and many others.

The common factors in all of these warning signs are their suddenness and their obvious increase and frequency of occurrence. More on these changes appears in succeeding chapters.

Chapter 14

The Sex Offender's Motivation
May Not Be Sexual

In all my years of dealing with sex offenders, both in a correctional setting (convicted and sentenced) and in private practice (referred, self-referred, or on probation), I have never encountered a case in which *sex* was the primary motivation. In all of the cases I have treated or examined, one or a combination of the following primary motivations could easily be identified:

- *Power/domination* needs (in all sexual assaults and incest)
- *Seductive/acceptance* needs (in all child molestation)
- *Ritual/undoing* needs (in both sexual assault and child molestation)

POWER/DOMINATION NEEDS

Two major groups of offenders are found with power and/or domination needs: the sexually assaultive personalities (rapists, assaultive child molesters, etc.) and the incestous fathers group. Where sexual assault is concerned, the power/domination elements are clearly visible and understood: the use of a weapon, threat of death to the victim and/or her or his family, physical force usually in the form of a beating, cutting with a knife, or burning with a cigarette, and many other forms of violent damage to the victim in order to get her or him to submit and cooperate. These individuals come under the deny-ers category (see Chapter 2). They are grossly overcompensating for their perceived inadequacies and have an insistent need to prove their manhood.

Sexual assault ranges from minimal to sadistic and is a "progressive" pathology in that these individuals tend to increase the force, anger, and injuries to the victim until the ultimate sexual assault is reached—*murder*. Having control over the life of the victim gives the offender *power,* a desperate need, since for the majority of their lives they have felt powerless.

The sexual component is not uniform in this group. Not all sexually assaultive persons commit rape (vaginal penetration) or sodomy (anal penetration). For some, depending on their own original sexual trauma, oral sex (one sided or mutual) is the act of choice; for others, a variety of deviant acts may be forced upon the victim including analingus, urophilia, and even coprophilia.

At this point, I will consider the distinguishing characteristics of three ascending degrees of sexual assault.

Stage 1 Sexual Assaults

- Minimal physical force is used in the offense. The sexually assaultive person primarily uses threat, coercion, physical overpowering, and may show but not use a weapon to achieve his end.
- Abusive and degrading language is used and may include cursing, demeaning insults, accusations, and obscene put-downs.
- The victim is often forced to say that she or he enjoyed the act or that she or he loves the offender. The purpose here is to assuage the resulting guilt of the offender, which occurs as soon as he reaches orgasm, and also to justify his behavior.
- Once the sexual act is completed, members of this group tend to become guilt ridden and even remorseful. They have been known to attempt to comfort their victims and even to drive them to their homes or to a hospital. (Many have been captured doing just this.)
- The assaults tend to occur following a sudden *trigger* and are not premeditated. Any occurrence that triggers the sexually assaultive person's feelings of being controlled, being put down, or being rejected can trigger an attack.
- Rather than following a ritual, the assaults can take place anywhere, anytime, and in any manner.

Stage 2 Sexual Assaults

- The sexually assaultive person uses as much force as he feels is necessary to subjugate the victim and to accomplish his goals of both complete control and sexual submission to his most deviant fantasies.
- Control and threat are the main themes of his language. He repeatedly verbalizes his control to the victim and poses the possible dangers that she or he faces unless there is a total conformity to his will.
- The sexually assaultive person usually demands *silence* on the part of the victim and often orders the victim to either close her or his eyes or not to look at him or what he is doing. A blindfold is frequently used.
- Physical harm to the victim is frequent and includes bloody noses, sprained arms, facial battering, and even minor cutting with a knife "just to prove who is in control and what can happen if you don't do exactly what I want!" The physical harm and injury are primarily a result of his seething rage (over which he has lost control) and secondarily due to his need to punish the victim for what someone else has done to him. This rage usually results from his own sexual molestation and/or trauma.
- The assaults are more premeditated and planned than those in Stage 1. The offender becomes obsessed with thoughts of revenge and anger (to the point of uncontrolled rage) and masturbates compulsively to rape and assault fantasies. The assault is usually the outcome of his fantasies being perpetrated on a victim in reality, when he no longer can maintain control and his fantasies no longer satisfy his needs.
- When the assault is over, the offender cares little for the victim and often leaves her or him where the attack occurred, giving strict orders for her or him not to move or call for help for a period of time. There is also the extended threat that if she or he goes to the authorities or tries to identify him that he knows who the victim is and where she or he lives, and he will come back and get her or him.

Stage 3 Sexual Assaults

- Force is *sadistically* employed to ventilate anger and rage, not because the victim is unwilling to cooperate. The sadism includes cutting, burning, and various other forms of torture. Bondage is employed as a control method and to ensure that the victim does not fight back. It is not uncommon for the offender to bludgeon the victim into unconsciousness and then undress and tie the victim up, often in her or his own bed.
- The sex acts are made painful, degrading, and humiliating. In intercourse, the offender uses his penis like a *battering ram,* deliberately causing pain for the victim even if he experiences pain himself. He may make the victim lick his penis clean (see Harry, Chapter 5) or perform analingus just to add to the humiliation and degradation.
- If the offender suspects the victim is enjoying the sex, he will become furious and change the act or make sure that he inflicts pain to the point of bleeding or physical damage.
- Power and anger needs dominate the entire experience, and the offender will do anything necessary to prove to the victim that he is in complete control of the victim's life.
- The assaults may take place over an extended period of time. Often the victim has been kidnapped and taken to a safe and isolated area where the sexually assaultive person can keep the victim for his own use as long as he wants, even for weeks at a time.
- The sexually assaultive person tends to *panic* and fear capture and punishment after he finishes and empties his vast need for revenge and retaliation (displaced from his own life experiences onto the victim). This is the most dangerous part of the assault for the victim and often results in the victim's death.

These three degrees of sexual assault are not intended to be all encompassing. There are as many varieties of sexual assault as there are individuals perpetrating these assaults. Each sexually assaultive person is an individual with unique needs and his own deviant practices. Each time I felt that I had seen the final type of assault, I met a new offender with a new set of needs and methods of satisfying them.

SEDUCTION/ACCEPTANCE NEEDS

Three groups of offenders are found with seduction and acceptance needs: the seductive pedophiles, the seductive hebophiles, and the seductive incestuous fathers. The term *seductive* is a necessary prefix to each of these groups since there are also parallel *assaultive* types of pedophiles, hebophiles, and incestuous fathers.

These groups are composed of the *most inadequate* of all of the sex offenders. They are frightened of and repulsed by any form of violence, no matter how minimal. Some of their traits include the following:

- Their overall desperate need is for *acceptance* from their victims.
- They are gentle, friendly, kind, and persuasive.
- They use money, gifts, special privileges, friendship, and other seductions to accomplish their goals.
- Their patience is incredible, and rather than surrender to their sexual needs, they take care to first form a trusting and caring relationship with the intended victim.
- The goal of the initial sexual exploration with the victim is to *please and satisfy* him or her so that the victim will not only like him but also will *return for more*.
- Their choice of sex act is totally dependent on their own early sexual molestation and/or sexual trauma.
- They are manipulative, cunning, seductive, and prefer to *manipulate* their victims rather than use force of any kind. The one exception is their tendency to use photographs as a form of *blackmail*.

The pedophile and hebophile groups have large numbers of different victims. Some offenders I have treated had as many as 600 verified cases. These large numbers of victims are due to the fact that even *successful* molestations *do not meet the offender's needs*. They are never satisfied with the acceptance and love they feel they are receiving from their present victim, *but they cannot explain why*. They continue to look for one victim after another. Each time they fantasize that "this will be the one I've been looking for!"—but it never works.

The issue, of course, is simple to state but very difficult to treat: *The real need is for love and acceptance from the parent(s) of their childhood, at the time when the trauma occurred and the need was generated.* Even admitting this insight to themselves can take years of therapy and confrontation. Communicating this insight to their parents (if they are still alive) is an even more formidable task. However, without this admission, the problem will never be fully resolved.

RITUAL UNDOING NEEDS

"Ritual undoing" is a defense reaction of many sexually abused children who never reported or resolved their trauma through some form of therapy. In these cases, the offenders, often as adolescents or young adults, find a victim who is of the same age, general appearance, and personality type that they were at the time they were abused *and repeat the sexual abuse in the exact same manner* that occurred during their own abuse. This often includes the same setting, the same seduction or threat, and the same acts. In this way, they hope to "undo" or "normalize" what happened to them.

LEON was raped at age twelve in a state reformatory where he had been sent for school truancy. At the time, he was small of build, shy, timid, and unable to defend himself. In addition, he was quite a good-looking young boy and friendly to all (a mistake in a reformatory). He trusted an older youth who was the "duke" (leader and strongest boy of the cottage who is trusted by the cottage parents to be left in charge while they are away).

After an initial period of friendliness and protection, the duke decided it was time for Leon to *pay for his friendship.* One night, he assigned Leon to mop the downstairs shower room after lights out. While Leon was mopping, the duke came in and forcibly raped him. From that day on, Leon trusted no one, and his self-worth (what little he had) was destroyed. When released from the reformatory, Leon could not readjust to society. He was always in trouble, hated and resented anyone in authority over him, and began flashing. At age twenty-two, he was caught and sent to the sex offender treatment unit, where I met him. He worked as a clerk in the office, was a well-behaved and well-liked inmate, and never received a disciplinary report. One morning he declared an emergency, and I interviewed him in my office. He painfully and tearfully confessed to raping one of the new, younger, shy, and frightened inmates, whom he perceived as being similar to himself at age twelve in the reformatory. When I asked him why he had committed the rape, he stated, "Now I'm not the only one!"

However, within a week, Leon returned to say that his *undoing* did not last and that the old negative feelings of being dirty, used, and unworthy had all returned. He was feeling intense *guilt* for what he had done to the younger inmate who had trusted him. I suggested that he bring the problem to his primary group, and he did. The group, although shocked and angry, did not reject Leon or ask for his removal from the group. Instead, they asked how they could help and all rallied around him. They also suggested that he now help the young inmate he raped to deal with his feelings and reactions to the sexual assault. To aid this process, I transferred the new victim from another group to Leon's primary group. (In a group treatment facility, a move such as this can be made with minimal risk due to the many safeguards [e.g., officers, group members, etc.]).From that day on, Leon's progress in therapy accelerated; he became a group leader and worked hard and diligently with the young male he raped. In helping his victim to realize that it was not his fault, that it did not make him a bad person or dirty, etc., he began to accept the same messages for himself. Within a month, Leon's demeanor began to change, and he became more assertive, was more open with criticism and positive feedback in group, and earned the respect of everyone in the treatment unit. In a year or so, he was released. Nine months later, he married and has been doing well without a recurrence for the past ten or more years.

If it were possible for all sex offenders to work in the same group with their victims, therapy could be accelerated and be much more positive in its outcome. However, this is not always a practical or workable solution, and other means must be found to alter the negative self-image.

THE DANGER OF SYMPTOM SUBSTITUTION

One of the most serious mistakes that was made during my first year of dealing with sex offenders was overlooking the dangers of "symptom substitution." One of our therapists was an expert in behavior modification techniques. At that time, none of us really knew how to treat offenders, and so we each tried our own expertise first and then discussed results.

KEN, a thirty-one-year-old rapist discussed in Chapter 6, admitted readily to at least three other rapes, although this was his first arrest and conviction. Ken was an extremely bright (WAIS IQ 140+), well-educated young man with a smooth social approach to everyone. He came from a fairly wealthy family that was totally supportive (especially his mother and sister) throughout his treatment and institutionalization. From day one, Ken was open and revealing in group and soon became his group's leader and spokesperson. He utilized very few recognizable defense mechanisms and made very rapid progress. Ken's behavior was exemplary, and he soon earned a high position of trust in the prison (captain's clerk) and was respected by inmates and staff alike.

After eighteen months in the treatment unit, he was paroled. Although initial readjustment appeared excellent, he was never perceived as being *happy.*

As discussed in Chapter 6, after visiting me in the hospital to ask for a recommendation to graduate school, Ken committed another rape.

As was our practice, Ken should have been reassigned to his old therapist—me. It was apparent that I had been fooled the first time and that it would be wise to assign Ken to another therapist. His new therapist was a specialist in behavior modification techniques, and Ken again was treated basically in this modality. After four years, he was released for the second time on parole. Within a year of release, Ken was rearrested on a charge of conspiracy to murder a relative and is serving a life sentence for that offense. Fortunately, I was able to interview him for a lengthy time, and the gist of what he told me was that the sexual aspects of the therapy worked well. He never wanted to rape again, and his sex life with his fiancée was excellent. As will be seen however, we had been conned again.

Ken never let go of or resolved the rage he felt for the relative who he felt was abusing his mother. His displaced anger toward women still existed, but now the outlet was physical, not sexual. Working exclusively on the *symptom* simply converted the symptom into another outlet, and the plans to kill the offending relative resulted.

Update: Ken was released a third time after three years. Initially he adjusted and then, again, committed a serious rape. This time he was not sent to the treatment unit but to a maximum-security prison where he received no therapy. After an initial period of adjustment (as he had done on his previous incarcerations) the rage at his relative reemerged. He tried to hire a young, highly assaultive person to kill this relative. The plot was uncovered and he is now serving a life sentence. He will most likely die in prison.

In my experience, behavior modification *alone,* as with any other single treatment technique used with offenders, does not seem to work. This was especially true where anger and rage were concerned. *A confrontational approach, aimed at the release of any and all emotion, remains, in my experience, an effective treatment choice when utilized with ancillary programs to deal with other aspects of the offender's personality makeup.*

MASTURBATORY RECONDITIONING

There is a particular type of sex offender who, no matter how hard he works in therapy and no matter how much intellectual insight he develops, is unable to eradicate his obsessions with his own form of sexual deviation. These obsessive fantasies and daydreams are especially persistent when he is alone with nothing to do. They result in masturbation to the deviant fantasy, *no matter how hard he tries to avoid it and no matter what promises he makes to himself each time it occurs.* The consistent result is guilt that prevents self-esteem from improving and a resistant judgment that he will never be able to change or get better.

Dennis (discussed in Chapters 6, 12, and 13) has had such a masturbatory problem for over ten years and uses it to destroy any progress he makes, due to a still undiscovered trauma that fuels the guilt. Regardless of how well he does at work or in a social situation, at night, after fighting and resisting for hours and hours, he always ends up with the same deviant masturbation fantasy. He has convinced himself that he will never be able to achieve orgasm without his deviant fantasy of young boys.

One of the techniques that I have found successful in dealing with this type of unwanted, undesirable, deviant masturbatory fantasy problem is a modified form of masturbatory reconditioning. There are several types of reconditioning found in the literature, including a form called "satiation," (the offender is asked to masturbate to his deviant fantasy over and over, until he theoretically can no longer reach orgasm to the fantasy) which I found over the years does not work well in my practice with compulsive sex offenders. As early as 1969, I modified the then-known techniques and developed my own form.

Masturbatory Reconditioning Technique

For compulsive masturbation to deviant fantasies followed by guilt, I instruct the client to follow these eight steps *exactly:*

1. When you find yourself masturbating to a deviant fantasy, allow it to continue up to the PEI (preejaculatory inevitability) phase.
2. Never allow orgasm to be reached using the deviant fantasy.
3. Have a positive fantasy prepared (in writing) to use when the PEI phase is reached. This fantasy should be preapproved by a therapist.
4. When PEI is reached, switch the deviant fantasy to the positive fantasy and reach orgasm and ejaculation.

5. Do the exercise no fewer than three times a week for at least two weeks to one month, and always when the deviant fantasy occurs.
6. Following orgasm, *evaluate* why the masturbation to the deviant fantasy occurred; in particular, focus on identifying the *trigger.*
7. Plan an alternate *positive response* to the same trigger before the next occurrence.
8. Continue until it is impossible to reach orgasm to the deviant fantasy.

It is prudent to test the process at the end of one month.

Some Caveats

The therapist must carefully supervise the masturbatory reconditioning technique since it is totally dependent on self-report, the least valid form of information. During the first month, the excitement at success that comes with the technique is clearly visible in the client's attitude, behavior, and demeanor, especially when he is unaware of being observed. Here again, the need for *confirmation* from outside sources is essential.

A major danger with the technique occurs at the *first failure,* which is inevitable. Due to the perfectionism of the offender, this failure often becomes devastating and total, especially if an intervening month or more of success has occurred. Reassurance that this may happen and that, if it does, it is normal and important to the therapy process, helps the offender or private client through this perceived *disaster.*

Analysis of the reason for the failure will usually result in some new therapeutic knowledge and insight into the client and his personality, sensitivities, and potential pitfalls. Here again, turning all *failures into positives* is a means of altering the negative perceptions and outlook of the client. All in all, the effort is worth the time and the problems associated with it. When done correctly, this form of masturbatory reconditioning rarely fails and will provide hope to the client that change really is possible.

THE CHILD/ADOLESCENT SEX OFFENDER

In this instance, although all of these insights apply, in one way or another, to child/adolescent sex offenders, there is a major difference.

Of all the sex offenders, this group has the most *sexual motivation.* However, even here the sexual motivation has an underlying psychological origin—in most cases the need to lose their virginity, as they hear their peers bragging about their sexual exploits. They are too naive and immature to realize that the majority of this bragging is fantasy and that many of their peers are as virginal as they are. Thus, becoming *equal* to their peers becomes a primary motivation in their sexual misbehaviors. A second factor is their insatiable curiosity and the need to experience things for themselves. This is true for oral, anal, or vaginal sex. Dom in Chapter 1 is a perfect example of these needs resulting in his becoming involved in a problem with his sister.

There is another group of child/adolescent sex offenders who are imitating sexual behavior that they have directly observed. Ernie in Chapter 7, Tony and Jill in Chapter 9, and Skippy in Chapter 13 all belong to this group, as does a sizeable percentage of these offenders.

A final group is involved in ritual sexual offending. Many of this group are involved in satanic cults where sex is not only openly practiced but also is a required behavior for membership. The majority of this group were initiated into a cult by submitting to sexual victimization, mostly with the high priest, the leader of the cult who makes the rules to fit his own deviant needs.

It should be mentioned that this is another form of spiritual molestation and results in the identical triple trauma described fully in Chapter 19. Therapy for this group is a long and difficult process. Deprogramming is a necessary element of their treatment.

As I have mentioned over and over again in this work, the earlier these children/adolescents are discovered and sent for specialized treatment, the better the prognosis. Dom in Chapter 1 is a perfect example of this early exposure. Dom has never actually molested anyone, but in therapy it became clear that the first possible molestation was quite close. Jeffy in Chapter 1 is another example. Although the beginning of a molestation occurred, it was minimal and nontraumatizing to the child.

Parents, school personnel, religious personnel, and others involved with children often excuse these initial behaviors by saying "he's just going through a stage" or "all boys do these things" (especially exposing themselves). The truth is that they do not want to be perceived as enemies of the child or to admit their own roles (especially parents) in the problem.

PREVENTION

Prevention begins in early childhood for all sex offenders. I can honestly say that in all my experiences, the highest majority of convicted sex offenders could have been discovered and their offenses prevented. That would have meant far fewer survivors of sexual molestation or assault.

The most important element for this entire group is *total, open communication between parents and children.* This is defined as the child's ability to talk about *anything,* especially sex, with at least one of his or her parents without fear of punishment, fear of exposure to other family members, ridicule, or being turned-off ("You're too young to talk about sex," "Ask your father/mother, etc.").

When this communication is not possible at home, then other members of the family (aunts, uncles, cousins, etc.) must be available. When this is not possible, then the community must provide someone for the child to turn to rather than his or her peers where he or she is sure to be given misinformation. This should be the role of teachers, coaches, priests, ministers, and rabbis.

School counselors, from the youth I have had contact with, are rarely available for counseling or are grossly unprepared to perform this function. Over the years, my child and adolescent patients have complained bitterly about this group not even helping them with applications for higher education. None of them in answering the question "Who might you have spoken with at school?" has ever answered "the school counselor."

The last resort for this group is their peers. When all else fails, they turn to a peer, usually an older, more aggressive one who boasts constantly of his prowess in sex and other areas. They end up confused and/or misinformed and eventually come into contact with the law.

Prevention must be everyone's responsibility. Our children are that important.

Chapter 15

A "Whole-Man" Approach to Treatment

INTRODUCTION

As stated in the preface and in other sections of this work, one of the first things that I quickly learned about the treatment of the compulsive sex offender is that, in my experience, *conventional techniques usually failed.*

In 1976 the first sex offender treatment unit in New Jersey was opened (Rahway Treatment Unit). In over a year or more of trying all the traditional therapy modalities, including psychoanalytic, behavioral, cognitive, Rogerian, nondirective, and supportive techniques, therapists from all different backgrounds and professional trainings ended up deeply frustrated. Nothing at the time seemed to work. Even when we realized that "confrontational techniques" were necessary, they also failed to produce the positive overall effects that were necessary to treat the compulsive sex offender.

I quickly realized that psychotherapy alone would not work to produce a safe, healthy, and, above all, happy individual. I finally found a positive and workable treatment for sex offenders, which I term a "whole-person" or "holistic approach." Basically, this means treatment not only for the *psyche* of the offender but also for his body, mind, and social being. Since, as can be seen from the list in Chapter 1, every facet of his being has in one way or another been negatively affected from an early age, so every facet of his life must somehow be involved in the treatment process. Over the years, the following elements of a holistic approach were formulated.

GROUP PSYCHOTHERAPY

Individual therapy did not work and was dangerous in that the therapist could too easily be fooled by the manipulative and clever sex offenders. Group became the therapy of choice. The types of groups run were largely confrontive but proceeded from therapeutic philosophies ranging from cognitive to behavioral to a combination of both. For a more complete discussion of the specific techniques used in this group psychotherapy process, see Chapter 9.

SEX EDUCATION

A *basic course* in sex education starts at approximately the sixth grade level. I found that sex offenders knew relatively little of the true facts about sexuality and could not pass a sex education test at this level. An admission that they do not know everything there is about sex is a requirement for entry into this course. Course members are encouraged to use their own terms rather than to try to use precise, medical terminology. This makes everyone in the course more comfortable. The therapist may use the correct terminology, explaining that this is done not to show the individuals how dumb they are but to give them the choice of using more precise vocabulary at the doctor's office or in the hospital. The basic course primarily covers:

- anatomy and physiology, both male and female;
- relational values and responsibilities;
- sexually transmitted diseases, again emphasizing responsibility and positive prevention factors;
- body-image technique introduction, including penis-size concerns (positive suggestions for change are included and mainly come from peer group members);
- birth and its attendant facts and issues (birth control, male responsibility, decision making regarding children, etc.); and
- films where appropriate, with homework assignments, at times based on the individual's reactions to the films.

The *advanced course* continues from where each class in the basic course ended (the speed and learning ability of each group was quite different). At this point, the course remains at grammar school vocabulary level and high school content level. Again, the members may choose to use their own words and descriptions without appearing ignorant. This encourages the more timid members to participate. The advanced course includes

- body-image work (utilizing the Hartman-Fithian [1987] model);
- value formation and value change discussion and techniques (see Chapter 17 for specific content);
- film exposure and reaction homework;
- general discussion sessions on any sexual topic that the class suggests;
- encouragement to share sexual developmental histories; and
- an evaluative report by each class member on a book of choice from a large sex education library.

At this point, the offender is ready to enter the *sexual dysfunction level course*. The requirement for this level of the sex education program is that both prior levels (basic and advanced) were passed by the offender and that he secures his primary therapist's recommendation. The sexual dysfunction course continues work in the area of distorted or deviant sexual values and how to change them. The focal topics include

- sexual guilt and how to deal with and overcome it;
- the skill of identifying one's own sexual dysfunction(s), becoming able to discuss it with others and to ask for help;
- methods of preparing a treatment plan for dealing with and overcoming the identified problems; and
- expansion of body-image work from the purely physical aspects to the psychological aspects. This technique is called "self-confrontation" and will be discussed and explained fully in Chapter 18.

The basic and advanced levels of the sex education courses run the length of a normal U.S. college semester at the rate of three hours per week, while the advanced level course lasts at least a year and could go on for more than that, depending on the needs of the individual.

SOCIAL SKILLS TRAINING (SST)

As I previously concluded, one of the many failings in the sex offender is his low level of social skills and his inability to function socially with other individuals of his peer level. A terminal course that
lasts about twelve weeks, the social skills training (SST) class is designed to help remedy this problem; it includes basic instruction in all
aspects of social functioning. Role-play that is videotaped and then
played back immediately for the group and the therapist's critique is
crucial to the course. This group is usually conducted by two therapists: a female and a male. Areas covered include

- how to meet someone and initiate a social conversation;
- how to successfully ask for a date;
- meaningful small talk;
- how to say "No" in an acceptable and appropriate manner;
- how to be *laughed at* and not take it personally (this includes being the center of attention in a group, making an error, or acting
  silly and laughing at yourself with the group); and
- all other aspects of a normal adult social life that may be suggested by the class.

The "learning to be laughed at and not falling apart" segment of the
class is extremely important due to the sensitivity and fear of failure
or rejection that the sex offender brings into the class. Exercises are
designed to promote laughter (sometimes to a hysterical level) and to
prove to the individual that he will not die or collapse if this happens
to him. A frequently used skit is for one of the group to stand in front
of each of the other group members pounding his chest and saying in
a loud and affirmative voice "Me Tarzan, you Jane!" The reactions
from each member are spontaneous and include not only laughter but
also many other catcalls and taunts such as "Oh, yeah! Well, prove
it!" If the actor in the skit freezes or reacts with fear when this occurs,
this becomes the subject of that group's discussion. He receives feedback and suggestions as to how to handle the situation.

Periodically, the therapists request any changes or the lack of
changes seen in each group member by requesting feedback from the
primary therapists as well as any other staff or family members who
have contact with the offender. As their clients progress in this

course, the behavioral changes are visible in any situation where he interacts socially.

ANGER MANAGEMENT

Anger management is another terminal course of approximately twelve weeks. The title of this course is misleading since participants are not taught to *control* their anger but rather learn how to *express* their anger appropriately.

As previously discussed, where emotions are concerned, sex offenders are either impulsively explosive or suppress any emotional reaction whatsoever due to an immobilizing fear of punishment or rejection. Intellectual responses using emotional terms (love, anger, sorrow, hate, fear, sadness, sympathy, empathy, etc.) are meaningless in therapy since there is no expression/ventilation of the original emotional reaction to an event, abuse, etc. There is also the phenomena of "short circuiting," that is, when hurt by someone, immediately converting the hurt to anger since anger is "manly" and hurt is "feminine" and "wimpy," the sign of a coward. Also, they feel that showing hurt will make them vulnerable and lead to more victimization.

Sex offenders do not have to be taught emotions; they need to find a way to permit themselves to *feel emotion spontaneously* and to react emotionally toward individuals who precipitate the emotional response *as it occurs but in an appropriate manner*. In this way, projection and displacement of emotions onto an innocent victim will hopefully be avoided.

This course permits and encourages emotional reactions to real events in the offender's life, either past or current. Each class member is asked to take the floor and to retell an emotionally laden event, either in his past or in the present, and instead of repressing the emotions due to fear, allow them to spontaneously occur to whatever degree they are felt. Videotaping is utilized so that the offender can see himself emoting and so that the group and the therapist can offer feedback on the appropriateness of the emotional reaction and/or its degree.

As the offender becomes more comfortable with being an emotional human being and sees that his emotional response is appropriate and accepted by both peers and authority (the therapist), he is encouraged to begin taking risks in his daily life and to react emotionally when he chooses and/or when it is appropriate. Here again, the primary therapists can see the effects of this course in their groups. Others in the offender's life (family members, instructors, wing officers in a prison, etc.) also report the change from a nonreactive "wimp" (pedophiles) to a more assertive and emotionally spontaneous person or from an explosively angry person (sexually assaultive person) to someone who can control his emotions and state or show them in an appropriate way.

RELAPSE PREVENTION

Somewhere during the offender's treatment, the extremely important factor of relapse prevention must be dealt with. In institutional and correctional settings, a group setting for this course may be more appropriate and practical (due to numbers). However, in a community private practice it must still be dealt with on an individual basis.

The main thrust of this course/discussion is to face reality about returning to society at termination of treatment. The most important reality to present to the offender is that progress will not always remain upward and positive. In other words, *setbacks can and do occur.* These setbacks begin at the thought or fantasy level and should be reported immediately to the former therapist or a close friend or relative who knows the individual's past problems. Failures occur when this rule is not followed either due to an inflated idea of his own self-control or due to fear of being perceived as a failure.

Offenders tend to think in extremes: everything is all or nothing, black or white. Too often, without proper prerelease/termination preparation, the offender can encounter the following feelings when first confronted with a setback:

- Therapy didn't work.
- I'm still the same old person.
- What's the use? I may as well do it rather than go crazy thinking about it.
- I can't tell anyone I'm failing and disappoint them after they put their faith and trust in me.
- I can't let my therapist know I let him or her and my group down.

Being *forewarned* that this type of situation may occur, especially under pressure, stress, rejection, or similar circumstances that triggered the original deviate reaction, is *essential*.

This course also aids the offender in preparing emergency and contingency plans for all sorts of unpredictable problems including

- deciding whether to tell about his past in an employment interview;
- being fired when the employer finds out he is an ex-offender;
- rejection or distrust from a family member or loved one;
- discovering he can still be *turned on* by his victim type (especially problematic in pedophiles and hebophiles);
- having problems with loneliness and not knowing where to meet new friends;
- needing support groups for a particular problem and not knowing where to find them (especially for AA and NA);
- discovering his wife/fiancée/lover has been unfaithful while he was institutionalized;
- having his wife divorce him and take his children away upon his release; and
- not being accepted as husband/father after a long institutionalization where the family learned to live without him.

This course, through consciousness raising about these problems and role-playing situations that might occur, helps the individual to prepare for almost any eventuality.

VOCATIONAL REEDUCATION

For many sex offenders, it is impossible to return to their original profession/employment. This is especially true of teachers, priests, ministers, gym instructors, institutional personnel, police and correction officers, and many other types of professionals who are exposed/convicted as sex offenders. This applies automatically to those involved with children or adolescents under their care.

For this very large group of offenders, a new life and vocation must be considered before release/termination and possibly new skills and requirements developed. Considering the *indecisiveness* of these individuals, it is dangerous to leave this task up to them alone. Vocational reeducation provides a forum for group discussion and presentations of the possibilities that exist, especially for the specific geographical area in which the ex-offender intends to live upon release from either an institution or correctional facility. Requirements, costs, training opportunities, and vocational testing are all part of the knowledge that the course affords the prerelease offender. The final decision of a new vocation *remains solely his own.* If done in a group setting, the course may also afford previously unknown contacts and job opportunities.

For sex offenders in private and individual therapy, it is incumbent upon the therapist to handle this task and to provide resources where the patient can go for help in finding new employment or developing new skills.

SUBSTANCE ABUSE TREATMENT

For offenders with either a drug or alcohol abuse history, this type of group is a *must,* either in the community or in an institutional setting. Upon release from an institution, these affiliations must continue if successful reentry into the community is the goal.

Although *alcohol and drugs never cause the sexual deviation,* they quite often are contributing factors, usually affording the offender both the rationalization and the extra courage to perform the act.

Substance abuse groups help to dispel the *myth* that the abusing agent caused the sexual problem and place full responsibility on the offender where it belongs. Since these are ongoing groups, senior group members can correct these distorted perceptions in new members. The fact that to be a member one had to be a substance abuser eliminates the denial mechanism that therapists simply cannot crumble.

The *support* and *networking* elements of substance abuse groups, such as AA (Alcoholics Anonymous) and NA (Narcotics Anonymous), are their most important elements.

Feelings such as "I'm the only one this has ever happened to" disappear almost immediately, and phone numbers are exchanged for those serious moments of temptation to dispel the "nobody cares!" cop-out (alibi, excuse, rationalization).

The difference in this group from the groups discussed previously in this chapter is that rather than being terminal, it is a lifelong affiliation, although for many the frequency of attendance may decrease in time.

In private practice and individual therapy, this requirement should be the same, but here it is critical that the therapist establish and maintain contact with a leader/supervisor of the community-based program to be sure that the patient is attending and participating.

AFTERCARE

Although the aftercare group has been mentioned before (see Chapter 10), it cannot be stressed enough. Abrupt release or termination from therapy, regardless of the amount of preparation, can be disastrous without providing some form of aftercare modality. In my opinion, this should preferably be a group format but can also be accomplished in individual therapy contact. Emergency telephone numbers to call on an around-the-clock basis are also a necessary part of the aftercare modality.

In my experience, there is always some unfinished business and quite often a *secret* that was never divulged during formal therapy that is now causing problems for the released/terminated offender. In my years of conducting aftercare sessions for released sex offenders, I have asked the same question of each new member of the group: "Can you look me in the eye and honestly tell me that you never hid anything or kept any secret while you were in therapy?" I have *never*, in all those years, had an affirmative response.

An open, accepting format for these types of "confessions," when they eventually occur (and they will!) must be provided if a new victimization and another failure are to be prevented.

Where terminating therapy on an individual basis is concerned, I make it a practice never to use the terms *finished, terminated,* and most especially *cured.* My preference, when a patient is ready, is to promote him to PRN status, explaining that this status means that it is okay and desirable for the individual to maintain contact by telephone on a regular basis (I suggest monthly to begin) and to stop in for a visit at least annually.

THE CHILD/ADOLESCENT SEX OFFENDER

Every element of this chapter also pertains to children and adolescents. The difference is in the *speed* of each program. Where groups are being run, this becomes an easy task based on the "readiness principles" (refer to Chapter 9). In individual therapy cases, readiness is even more critical. Many of the elements of the different treatment modalities covered in this chapter may be incorporated in the weekly sessions of these individuals to provide a break in intensity in a difficult case. This break benefits both the patient and the therapist.

Another major difference in these cases is that the parent(s) must be involved in many of the different modalities, especially where future planning is concerned. Precautions and restrictions must be discussed and agreed upon with not only the parent(s) but also the patient. If these agreements are not made, the prognosis for future adjustment falls to very guarded.

Some families have to be taught open discussion, equal time, compromise, and other skills. At times, these become the most difficult sessions for the therapist. Care must be taken not to breach confidentiality issues at these times. I often find that holding a session or two with only the parent(s) and me (without the child/adolescent present) can do a world of good. Setting basic rules and procedures for future combined sessions is done at these times, and prohibitions are given as well, including no yelling, threats, demands, bringing up old matters, and so forth. Therapists must remember that there is *always* a solution to seemingly impossible situations *if* the therapist and clients work hard enough to discover it and *if* all parties really want to find one.

Chapter 16

Why Sex As the "Chosen" Deviation?

After a thorough analysis of the underlying dynamics of sexual offenses and the sexual offender, the question "Why sex?" remains one of the most important treatment issues that may take many years to resolve. It also is the question that the offender must answer fully before any progress can be made or any recommendations for treatment promotion to PRN status can be given.

For example, the sex offenders' main dynamic, the *need to control* (either through force or seduction), can also be expressed in many nonsexual ways and behaviors. Money, position, power, and fame are just a few of the means frequently used to control other people by individuals with a need to control but who do *not* become sexual offenders. Certainly one's boss, a policeman in uniform, a judge in a courtroom, a Broadway or Hollywood star, a teacher, a father or mother in a family, an investor behind the scenes, and many, many other individuals in similar roles control people's lives daily *without* resorting to sex or sexually motivated behavior. Although control and all of the other sex offender traits can be clearly seen in other individuals who do not resort to sexual behaviors, the sex offender may find only *temporary* satisfaction in his deviant sexual behavior leading to his repetition and compulsion to continue in his deviant lifestyle and produce a staggering number of victims. Why this is his exclusive predetermined choice is still to be seen.

CHILDHOOD SEXUAL TRAUMA: CONSCIOUS/REPRESSED, ACTIVE/PASSIVE

In the discussion of the inadequate personality (in Chapter 2), the development of the repetitive compulsive sex offender was clearly seen and illustrated.

The essential and *differentiating factor* that separates the deny-ers and accept-ers from the adjust-ers, who did not become compulsive sex offenders, is the *sexual trauma,* conscious or repressed, that occurred to most, if not all, sex offenders and that was never discovered, never reported, or never properly treated. In Chapter 2, I presented the relationship between childhood personality, sexual crisis in adolescence, and normal or pathological sexual adjustment in adulthood.

This trauma can occur at any age level but usually does not become traumatic until the child reaches puberty, when there is a major psychological change in the developing personality. This change consists of a *shift* from needing to please adults (parental figures) for acceptance, nurturance, and love to needing to please and be accepted by *peers.*

Thus, the adolescent "Sturm und Drang" (storm and stress) period for parents occurs during this time. The concern over what their peers think, feel, and judge them by becomes a paramount issue for adolescents and determines their self-acceptance or rejection, their feelings of being normal or not normal, their ego strength, and their self-esteem. Thus, whether they consider themselves to be normal and acceptable is not solely an internal judgment or decision but is externally dependent on what others, especially peers, say. Locker-room talk (predominantly about sex and sexual exploits) shapes their guilts and derogatory self-perceptions and the overall feelings of *inequality* that characterize the adolescent sex offender.

This psychological change also helps explain the *delay,* especially for boys, in reporting sexual abuse by adults that may have been going on for several years prior to adolescence. Were their involvement exposed (especially where boys are concerned), how could they remain in school with their peers? Permission from a higher authority is needed for the reporting to occur with some assurance that they will not pay the additional price of peer rejection.

In Monmouth County, New Jersey, a program called "It Happens to Boys, Too!" was able to overcome this barrier in a simple and direct manner. First, posters were put up on school bulletin boards with the catch phrase and a hotline number. Concurrently, the posters were made into highway billboards. *Nothing else was done to promote the idea.* Calls from abused boys began coming in almost immediately and were then referred to proper agencies and therapists who had volunteered for the program. (The therapists, by the way, were *both screened and trained*). When I interviewed one of the boys who responded and asked why it had taken him so long to report the abuse, his simple but profound answer was "I didn't know I was allowed to report a teacher. He told me I couldn't and then I saw the poster, so I called."

Pedophiles are well aware of this developmental characteristic (need for adult approval/acceptance) and take advantage of it on a regular basis. They find preadolescent children whom they perceive as lonely, rejected, and in need of acceptance and a relationship with a nurturing parental figure, which is usually missing from their lives.

The child victim, in turn, is so needy for this love and nurturing that he or she is willing to pay *any price* to keep it, once it has been experienced. No noticeable behavioral change may occur until adolescence and junior high school, when the need for adult (parental) acceptance diminishes and is replaced by a need for acceptance from peers.

Hebophiles are also aware of their chosen victim's needs (fear of peer rejection) and instill the concept of the sexual behavior remaining "their secret." Polaroid pictures and the threat that, if the hebophile is apprehended, these pictures will be seen by parents, friends, and teachers also cleverly exploits this developmental knowledge.

NEGATIVE EFFECTS OF UNREPORTED SEXUAL ABUSE

Although it is obvious to state that unreported or unresolved sexual abuse will have negative effects, it is necessary to discuss the degree of this damage and the types of problems that connect to possible early sexual abuse.

The *trauma* occurs as the child enters adolescence and learns that sexual involvement with an adult, especially a same-sex adult, is neither accepted nor tolerated by their judgmental and unforgiving peers. The adolescent may then either succumb to the trauma (and become depressed, sometimes to suicidal proportions, turn to drugs and/or alcohol, and in general ruin his or her life) or use every defense mechanism possible (denial, rationalization, even repression) to cope with the new dilemma. *Anger* at the adult offender, and also at the parents who should have protected them from the offender, now replaces *love,* and all blame is projected onto the adult (and all adults like the offender). A perception of victimization replaces the acceptance and love previously felt.

A catch-22 situation also exists for these victims: Should the relationship continue and become known during this developmental period, the trauma will be even more severe and the guilt will be more deeply ingrained. Should the relationship end but remain undetected/unreported, the negative effects will remain and affect adjustment on all levels (self-worth, negative motivation, poor social interaction, isolation, and either intellectual or physical overcompensation), especially the sexual level, and may also lead to becoming a sex offender in role-reversal behavior.

Sexual dysfunctions abound in these survivor groups, beginning at the onset of the trauma stage and continuing into adulthood. These sexual dysfunctions range from impotence to deviant arousal patterns, either pedophilic/hebophilic or sexually assaultive. The degree of the deviant fantasies or behaviors is usually directly proportional to the extent and depth of the original trauma and its duration.

If however, the child or adolescent gets into treatment with a *qualified therapist* trained to deal with sexual abuse and its effects, and is able to put the experience into a proper and healthy perspective, the effects will be minimal and adjustment positive. However, the adolescent's *trust levels* will never return to preabuse levels. Box 16.1 presents some reactions of both male and female survivors of sexual abuse.

It is logical to conclude that some form of *dysfunctional sexual behavior* results from sexual abuse, as other dysfunctions result from any other trauma. For example

- A *power trauma* begets a power need and abnormal behavior in a related function of power. An example is the power-hungry politician or supervisor who goes beyond usual boundaries to obtain the so badly needed power.
- *Physical abuse* begets physically abusive behavior toward others, especially those who remind the abuser of himself at the time of his own abuse.
- *Money trauma* begets an obsession with wealth, and no matter how much the individual accumulates, it is never enough. Individuals born in poverty or during a period of war or depression commonly show this symptomatic behavior.

16.1

Negative Reactions of Survivors of Sexual Abuse

I. *Deny-ers:* Tend to repress the event. Their behavior abruptly changes, but the true results of the trauma do not surface until later in life, usually due to some triggering event (marriage, loss of employment, sexual dysfunction, death of a loved one, etc.).

Boys	Girls
• Often become satyrs to prove their manhood.	• Develop problems in their adult sex lives, especially frigidity.
• If the behavior becomes pathological, they become sexually assaultive persons, especially if they were forcibly sodomized and interpreted this as being seen as a girl.	• See sex as dirty or disgusting; may become physically abusive parents without knowing why. Nudity is embarrassing and any arousal produces shame/guilt.

II. *Adjust-ers:* Usually have no negative effects because they
  • put all blame and responsibility on the abuser,
  • vent appropriate anger onto the abuser who molested them,
  • discuss what happened with their parents and friends,
  • want the abuse reported to the authorities, and
  • ask for counseling or therapy if they feel they need it.

III. *Accept-ers:* Accept the abuse as deserved and their fault. As a result, self-image is damaged and the effects are long lasting and sometimes permanent.

Boys	Girls
• Repeat their own abuse on a same-age child, almost ritualistically in order to reverse roles with the abuser.	• Tend to prostitute, become promiscuous, or develop other self-punishing behaviors. This is an attempt to undo the abuse.
• They feel that they are the adult aggressor in control rather than the victim being controlled.	• If they marry, they tend to marry an aggressive, battering type (dominant) husband.
• They may show no other visible signs or problems in their employment or in their social lives.	• They tend to lose all goal motivation and isolate socially.

In *incest,* there are more specific effects, as displayed in Box 16.2.

WHEN TO SUSPECT SEXUAL ABUSE

As discussed in Chapter 10, when the presenting problem of a new client includes *unwanted sexual thoughts or fantasies, deviant masturbation fantasies, or overtly deviant behaviors* that make no sense to the client and that he or she cannot connect to any specific event in his or her life, it is logical and appropriate to consider sexual trauma in childhood or adolescence as a major causative factor.

It is quite rare during the intake session for a client to identify childhood sexual trauma as the reason for his or her presenting problem (although a percentage do). In these cases, the trauma is possibly still being repressed.

What these clients do report is impotence, desire-phase dysfunction, frigidity, compulsive and unwanted masturbation with disturbing fantasies, premature or retarded ejaculation problems, and all other forms of sexual dysfunctions. When queried as to their thoughts about the cause of their problem, they simply have "no idea whatsoever; it just started."

At this juncture of the intake process, careful attention to the interviewing considerations in Chapter 9 will be helpful. The most important considerations are *readiness* and eliciting all of the *nitty-gritty details* of the trigger-incident that began the dysfunction.

ROBIN is a twenty-two-year-old, attractive and intelligent graduate student who was recently married. The marriage lasted six hours, and she presently is separated and miserable. Robin was referred by her family physician with complaints of *sexual anxiety resulting in frigidity, depression, and fears that she was insane.* Although quite anxious and emotional, she insisted on discussing the precipitating cause of her marital woes and related the following story.

Robin met Jess in college, and they were almost immediately attracted to each other. They dated for a full year and were then engaged. During the year and a half before their marriage they were affectionate and petted, but that was all that Robin would allow. Jess accepted her terms, based on her rigid Catholic upbringing, and patiently waited until they were married for sex. Following a large and extravagant wedding, they drove to Niagara Falls for their honeymoon. They arrived around 11 p.m. and went straight to their suite.

16.2

Negative Effects of Incestuous Abuse

Boys	Girls
• Repeat the offense in a ritualistic manner on younger siblings or other children as sibling substitutes.	• Attempt to look and act more adult than their age. This change occurs as a sudden onset occurrence and includes clothing, makeup, language, and other adult behaviors.
• If forced, painful sodomy was involved, they often choose rape to deny their femininity feelings and also to project their rage against their perceived nonprotecting mother.	• They overuse makeup and dress to be seductive, to satisfy their need for attention, and sometimes to gain their fathers' continued approval.
• Display generalized rage at females throughout their lives that they cannot justify or explain.	• Start using their bodies and their looks for gain (learned from their fathers).
• Tend to be aggressive, pain-producing, and humiliating in their sexual encounters.	• Become teases to boys and often to older men.
• Often have unresolved bisexual feelings and tendencies that frighten them and that they feel the need to deny.	• Become outrageous flirts—partially to confirm their attractiveness, partially out of anger.
• Lose interest in grades and often exhibit behavioral problems in school.	• Lose interest in school; want money, gifts, jobs, travel.
• Feel ambivalent toward their fathers: love and hate them at the same time.	• Consider the incestuous fathers their boyfriends or lovers. This is usually the fathers' idea.
• As parents, fear having children since they might pass on their deviation or, even worse, become sexually abusive toward them.	• Become physically and emotionally abusive parents but not sexually abusive. At times, this abuse ends in the death of a child.
• The worst of all results is the potential for suicide to escape the emotional pain or, if the abuse is ongoing, to escape the abuse.	• The suicide potential is quite high to escape the emotional pain or as a result of feeling "there is no way out" of this lifestyle.

Robin was the first to get ready for bed and went into the bathroom to change, closing and locking the door. She emerged in a new and proper nightgown, sat at the dresser, and combed her hair. Jess went next and emerged from the bathroom nude and walked over to Robin. When she saw that he was nude, she screamed "Cover yourself up!" and went to the bed. She lay there, staring at the ceiling, and said, "Do what you have to, but don't expect me to enjoy it!" Jess was hurt, confused, and angry all at the same time and yelled for her to get dressed since he was taking her home. They arrived back at their family homes around 4 a.m. without speaking a word during the entire trip. That was the last time Robin had seen Jess, more than three weeks ago.

There was little doubt that Robin had been sexually traumatized, although when asked directly about child sexual abuse, she denied it. In our second session, I felt she was more stable and less frightened or emotional, and I opened by stating that she had done well in the first session and looked much better today. She smiled, and I then said, "Let's not worry about what happened at Niagara Falls right now. Instead, why don't you tell me about what happened to you as a child?" Robin immediately panicked and yelled, "I promised him I would never tell! He threatened to kill me if I did!" She then cried for some time, as the memories flooded in, and for the next several sessions she related her sexual abuse at the hands of her father from ages nine to fourteen. Her father was still alive, and that made it more difficult for her to tell anyone what he had done. Therapy progressed quite rapidly after that, and fewer than three months later, we were into couple therapy with Jess. Therapy focused on desensitization to the male nude body, especially the male genitals. Sex therapy homework assignments were given when appropriate therapy progress had been made, and at the six month level, Robin and Jess consummated their marriage.

Months of time could have been wasted on what happened during the couple's honeymoon, and we still would not have touched the real problem. Once the indicators of childhood sexual abuse are evident, that is where the therapy should focus, rather than on the presenting symptoms.

MASTURBATION AS AN ESSENTIAL RULER

Estimating progress levels in treating sex offenders, whether in an institutional setting or in private practice in the community, is a very difficult task. The credibility of their self-report is even lower than that of other client groups, and the therapist must be careful not to be fooled. This is especially true where the therapist holds the keys to release from either an institution or from private therapy as a probation condition.

I have found careful analysis of the fantasies that the client uses for masturbation to be one of the best and most accurate rulers or measures of progress. Having the client *write out* these fantasies as homework assignments provides more details and exposes more deviant elements than if the client had to verbally describe the fantasy face to face with the therapist. It is also important not to read the client's homework in his or her presence, but to do so later and use the material gleaned for the next therapy session. I have also required a tape recording made during the masturbation as a ruler. There are times that the fantasies change several times during the act. The most important of these fantasies is the one that results in orgasm. The fact that several fantasies were used often indicates the need to appear normal and a feeling of shame of the orgasm-producing fantasy. This technique works extremely well where incarcerated sex offenders are concerned.

Clients often try to "analyze" their therapist, and this is especially true of incarcerated sex offenders whose freedom relies on the therapist's evaluations (which would not be the situation were it the therapists' choice). Once the clients realize that the homework will be read in their presence, a form of "censoring" occurs, and the homework has less validity and meaning. The therapist, specifically trained in this field, will be able to find clues in the client's fantasies and writings that may never emerge in the formal therapy situation.

WRITING THERAPY

This form of adjunctive therapy is extremely useful with sex offenders in institutional or outpatient settings. Having them keep a journal (in bound notebooks rather than spiral, since they could easily remove pages from the latter) in which they record feelings, behaviors, interpersonal incidents, and anything else that occurs between sessions, provides another valuable therapy resource. I even ask them to make an entry following each of our sessions, evaluating both of us and how they felt the session progressed. Sharing this journal with the therapist is strictly the offender's choice. Were it forced or conditional to the treatment process, it would lose much of its value and could become a means for the client to manipulate the situation, which is always a major danger. After an explosive therapy session during which Richie (Chapter 10) tried to kill me by trying to smash my head with a camera and tripod (he missed by less than a sixteenth of an inch), none of the therapists would allow him into their groups. He was segregated in his room and had to be escorted anywhere he went. I used writing therapy with Richie to continue his therapy and through it was able to get him off his restrictions and after several months took him back into my group with no additional problems.

THE CHILD/ADOLESCENT SEX OFFENDER

Where the child or adolescent sex offender is concerned, there is a different motivation for the sexual behavior than for adults. These patients are just beginning to feel their hormones rising. Sex is on their minds continually, especially when they "hang out" with other boys their age. Curiosity and the desire to be normal play a large role in their first incident. If one of these individuals was molested earlier, the chances are that he or she is conscious of the event and is trying to hide it from others, especially his or her peer group.

Therapists and counselors cannot plunge into this area like a bull in a china shop. Caution and patience are essential in treating this group, and the *readiness principles* are more important here than anywhere else. Direct questioning regarding their own sexual abuse will usually result in denial and the patient not continuing treatment since this area is terrifying for them. In order to relate the nitty-gritty details to the therapist, they have to relive the molestation and all of the shame, guilt, pain, and fear that accompanied it.

Trust and confidence are essential in working with this group. They cannot be expected to believe in and trust another adult if they have been molested by one. I find that discussing confidentiality with them and asking them to test me with a made-up story works best. The client tells an illegal untruth and waits to see if I will tell the parents on the police. One seven-year-old came in, and his test involved having brutally killed his mother, who was sitting in the waiting room. His choice of this material for his test was highly significant since up to this time he had not disclosed his anger toward his mother or the degree that it had reached.

The adjunctive modalities are critical in this group, especially sex education, assertiveness training, and anger management. In groups (my preference for all offenders), these adjunctive treatment techniques are extremely effective since following any exercise, they receive group reactions and usually group approval for sharing their own experiences. (I do not begin treatment of child/adolescent sex offenders with group therapy. I begin with individual sessions and bring up joining the group when I feel they are ready. I also permit them to not reveal certain elements of their cases that may be too shocking or too much to expect their peers to accept.) The following case will help clarify this issue.

CHARLIE, age fifteen, was his school's captain of the wrestling team. He was rejected and physically abused by his father, and he quickly adopted his coach as the father he always dreamed of. Partway through the school year, the coach noticed his need and began fostering a personal relationship with Charlie. One day he asked Charlie to stay late and come to his office after the other team members had left the locker room. He told Charlie how special he was and that he felt very close to him. He gave Charlie a hug and groped Charlie's crotch. Charlie did not object and in fact became erect. The coach asked to see the erection, and Charlie took his shorts off.

The sex progressed with speed over the next few weeks and finally resulted in the coach sodomizing Charlie. He was gentle, and Charlie reached an orgasm without touching himself. This became their regular sex act from then on, and the relationship continued until the end of the school year when the coach left the school, without saying anything to Charlie. (He had been molesting other boys in the school and was permitted to resign. He should have been reported to the authorities but never was.)

Charlie became a truant, his grades dropped, and in general had become a serious behavior case when he was referred to me for treatment.

I taught Charlie the self-confrontation technique (see Chapter 18) and, in less than a month, Charlie was back to his old self. He once again was the captain of the wrestling team, and both the team and Charlie won state championship status that semester.

Charlie was put on PRN status in five weeks and checks in regularly with visits about every three to four months. His bad behavior has not recurred, and he is presently dating a girl his age.

Charlie was allowed to tell his group that he had been molested by a stranger at a mall men's room and not expose his relationship with the coach.

Adult offenders in my groups were also allowed to change a detail of their behavior when I felt that the group would be unable to handle it. An equivalent behavior was substituted.

As stated over and over again, the sooner these child/adolescent offenders receive treatment with a specially trained therapist, using a "whole-man" therapy approach, the shorter and more successful the treatment. Charlie is one successful example of this approach.

Chapter 17

An Overview of Value Formation

Before any discussion of value change can be considered, it is necessary to first understand how values develop. Dealing with both offenders and victims of all ages made it necessary to formulate a descriptive, easily understood value formation progression. I have developed a five-stage value development schematic that has worked successfully for me for the past forty years.

FIVE STAGES OF VALUE FORMATION

Stage 1: The Prisoner Stage
(from Birth to Two Years)

- All values are learned from parents and other adults in the child's home.
- Body language cues contribute a great deal to the child's knowledge of right and wrong (e.g., a parent's smile when child does something means good, versus finger wagging and a frown when child does something wrong or unacceptable to the parent).
- Absolute obedience is necessary for acceptance and love.
- No comparisons are made at this stage.

Stage 2: The Neighborhood Stage
(from Two to Five Years)

- Friends, neighbors, relatives, and others outside the home introduce new values.
- Comparisons by the developing child begin, and result in confusion and the first negative perceptions of parents and self.

- The first blame and guilt for failures also occur during this stage.
- *Inadequacy* as a characteristic most likely begins in this stage.

Stage 3: The Societal Stage
(from Five Years to Puberty)

- School, religion, society, and the law introduce additional values.
- Teachers, ministers, priests, scoutmasters, police officers, and other authority figures become new parent symbols, and comparison intensifies.
- Value confusion is strong, especially when a behavior is acceptable at home and is not acceptable in school or vice versa.
- The need to please adults appears strongest in this stage, and the child is therefore more vulnerable to seduction by the child molester, especially when the home is not fulfilling his or her needs.
- Parent-substitute interaction during this stage is critical to the mature and stable development of the child. Each needs to know what values the other is teaching and which values they are in disagreement with.

A child, like Bobby (see Chapters 4, 6, 7, and 9), who cannot speak his mind at home due to a tyrannical father, becomes confused in school when he is encouraged to be assertive and to speak his mind. Having opinions is acceptable and positive in school but forbidden and results in punishment at home. Which should he choose? On the one hand he still wants to *please* his father to earn acceptance and love, but on the other hand he wants to be his own person and the teacher and other authority figures in the community support and encourage this. Should he be disloyal to his father? The first time Bobby tried this new assertive behavior at home, it resulted in one of the worst beatings of his life. His feelings of being *different* are confirmed and magnified by this incident, since everywhere else he is expected to be someone that his father cannot accept. *Confusion* becomes the characteristic of this phase.

For others, like Mark (see Chapters 5, 7, 8, and 18), the confusion results from his school and community experience of observing other children receiving physical and emotional attention and comfort that was totally foreign to his home. His initial reaction is a feeling of being *undeserving*. However, when teachers and other authority figures offer him the same physical and emotional support outside of his home, he experiences the same confusion and feelings of being *different* that Bobby experienced.

The fact that this is the *prepubertal stage*, when physical and emotional changes begin, makes the reactions of the inadequate child even more exaggerated and affects the outcome of the next stage in a detrimental way.

With the completion of Stage 3, the child's need to please adults also ends. An *abrupt change* now occurs in the child's life.

Stage 4: The Peer Stage
(from the Onset of Puberty)

An abrupt psychological change occurs from the beginning of this stage until its completion, with the needs for acceptance and approval *shifting from adults to peers*. The initial result of this shift depends on the first three stages and how smoothly they were experienced.

Parents are most upset and disturbed with their children during this stage since they do not understand what is happening. Their formerly wonderful, obedient, and loving child may now turn into a monster who is defiant, disobedient, argumentative, and a constant source of irritation or even embarrassment.

In his or her quest for independence and personal identity, the child must now *break away* from the parents' protection and direction and develop his or her own values, behaviors, decisions, and even his or her own appearance (dress, hairstyles, etc.). The delusion that the awakening adolescent experiences is that these new decisions are his or her own, when in reality they are strongly influenced and dictated by peer standards and pressures. The fear of *being different* is magnified in this stage to its greatest proportons. Parents who, for status's sake, force their adolescent to attend high school in shirt, tie, and jacket when his peers are in casual clothing, even shorts, can expect problems of all sorts as a result, including defiance, torn or damaged clothing, and hostility (bordering on rage). For the sex offender and his or her victims, *this stage is the most upsetting and leaves a lasting set of effects that must be dealt with in therapy.*

The following problems may occur:

- Fears, self-doubts, confusion, and shifts of loyalty emerge.
- Body-image problems and constant *testing* of both themselves and others occurs.
- Communication abruptly stops and needs to be fostered regularly.
- Definitions of "adult" are fluid. Subtle help in deciding on a mature definition is needed but feared and/or rejected.
- Sexuality explodes and becomes a major focus. Indecisiveness and confusion about all aspects of sex dominate this stage.
- A war between old values (Stages 1, 2, and 3) and peer pressure occurs and adds to the confusion.
- Guilt of all types flourishes and imprints.
- AIDS- and STD-phobias makes sexuality even more disturbing and confusing.
- Boy/girl expectations and demands separate more widely here than in any other stage.

Should sexual molestation occur during this stage, the effects will be *magnified* and become more *long lasting* than in any other stage. In addition, there is a major difference in peer reaction to an exposed molestation. These effects are displayed in Box 17.1.

Two different types of examples of why boys *cannot* seek support from male authority figures follow.

While speaking to a high school senior class assembly on the effects of sexual molestation and the serious need for treatment when it occurs, I invited anyone who wanted to speak to me personally to remain after the assembly. (This had been prearranged with the school principal.) Six girls and five boys remained, forming two small groups on opposite sides of the auditorium.

In speaking to the girls first, I discovered that all but one were being incestuously molested at home. The sixth girl was molested by a male baby-sitter and never forgot the experience. All six were affected by the presentation and were now sobbing and allowing emotional reactions to pour out. There was little trouble in getting them all referred to therapists (this was prearranged with specialists in this area). The girls were willing to discuss their feelings with one another as a group, and I *networked* them, since they all lived in the same general neighborhood.

The five boys were a totally different story. Although seen individually and confidentially, I learned that they were all involved with the same male

17.1

The Magnified Effects of Sexual Abuse
When The Molestation Occurs in Adolescence

Boys	Girls
• If molested during Stage 4, they have a totally different reaction and experience. The need to be strong, macho, and heterosexual dominates the male adolescent value system. If their peers find out about their molestation, they are rejected, physically and emotionally abused, and often either leave school or attempt suicide.	• If they are molested during Stage 4, they receive support, empathy, and protection from both male and female peers as well as authority figures that they are involved with daily (e.g., their teachers).
• A strong homophobic aura exists in male peer groups during this stage. In fact, it is my personal belief that this is the stage where true and intractable homophobia develops and remains with many males throughout their lives.	• Although the molestation is still traumatic, they do not suffer rejection by their peers nor are they labeled or blamed for the occurrence, as boys frequently are.
• Boys molested by older men during this stage cannot seek support and comfort from their peers or from the majority of their male authority figure contacts, such as teachers, coaches, gym instructors, or, most important, their own fathers.	• They tend to report more readily and are much more motivated to become involved in therapy and then to get on with their lives. Naturally, there are exceptions to these reactions, especially when a girl is chronologically an adolescent but emotionally still a much younger child.
• Therapy, if mandated by parents or the courts, will not work. Even those who willingly agree to therapy are highly resistant to revealing the "whole story" of their molestation or their true emotional feelings about the molester. It could take many sessions to develop rapport sufficient to overcome this resistance.	• Therapy, while still difficult and still full of resistances, is more successful, and most teenage girls do not need to be forced into treatment. Pregnancy, if it results, causes a great deal of ambivalence toward the molester. Moral decisions, although they may be discussed if initiated by the survivor, must remain her decision with no undue influence by the therapist.

teacher. The time span of the molestations ranged from a minimum of one year to three years. *None* of the boys would consider reporting the problem or becoming involved in therapy. Their unanimous opinion was that if the story was ever revealed, they would have to leave school, leave home, and run away to a different state. They anticipated total rejection, put-downs and labeling as "fags" or "queers" should their friends (peers) or other teachers find out.

The problem of the teacher was resolved with the school authorities without my revealing the facts or the identities of the boys. However, none of the boys (to the best of my knowledge) was ever treated for the molestations. Coincidentally, I was conducting a training seminar for all of the teachers, administrators, and school board members of a different school district where a similar teacher-student sex scandal of several years' duration had recently erupted. A male teacher had been arrested for his molestation of more than ten boys over a three-year period. My function was to clarify and desensitize the situation. Still bothered and affected by the five boys in the first school, I decided to use a dramatic opening. I asked for a gym instructor or coach in the audience to stand up and help me with the presentation. A burly, muscle-bound football coach stood and said, "Glad to be of service, Doc."

I knew I had the right person. I then instructed my "assistant" to be prepared to answer a question as quickly as possible without thinking or hesitation. He agreed. The question was "What would you do if you discovered that one of the boys on your basketball team has been sexually involved with one of the other male teachers in the school?" I then snapped my fingers, and the coach instantly replied, "Kick the fuckin' fag off of the team and make sure that all of the rest of my boys knew about these two perverts!"

Needless to say, the five boys' predictions had been correct. A silence fell on the entire auditorium, and I then thanked the coach for *explaining why the molestations in his school had been going on unreported* for several years.

Until we change these destructive values and reactions in adults, including parents and anyone entrusted with molding the minds and values of our children, sex offenders will have little trouble finding as many victims as their perverse desires require/demand. As mentioned in Chapter 16, Monmouth County, New Jersey's program "It Happens to Boys, Too" is a simple and effective method of attempting to correct this inequity between the way male and female victims (survivors) are treated by both peers and adults in authority that they deal with. Boys need to be told that it is *acceptable and proper* to report their molestations without being labeled, rejected, and ostracized. Without programs of this type or new ones modeled on the same principles, the *merry-go-round of sexual abuse will continue perpetually.* Group therapy limited to boys who have been molested can achieve similar results since the survivors will be supported by one another and will network both at school and in the community. I have found these groups shorten therapy time without losing effectiveness.

Stage 5: The "I" Stage

All other stages and values are reexamined and decisions for adult life are made in this stage. Most adults either never reach this stage or continue throughout life to fluctuate between Stage 4 and Stage 5, depending on their emotional maturity, reaction(s) to trauma, need for approval, and degree of ego strength.

Adolescents need to be made aware of this goal early in their development and must be encouraged to make decisions that will result in happiness. They must be urged not to settle for mere acceptance by peers but to aim for self-acceptance.

SEX EQUALS LOVE

Another insidious value learned early in the life of both the sex offender who was molested as a child/adolescent and the child victim is that "sex equals love." How often has the challenge "If you loved me, you'd . . ." been used by teenagers as well as adults to get a sex partner to do their will? Equally damaging is the molester's (both pedophile and hebophile) explanation of his sexual behavior as "showing love" to the victim.

As mentioned previously, in the United States more than in any other country, the damaging and destructive phrase "making love" has been used—due to embarrassment or puritanical needs—to justify or explain sexual behavior. Parents caught in the act of sex teach children from the earliest age that what they are doing is "making love," not having sex (see Ernie, Chapter 7).

"Love" then becomes "sex" and vice versa, and physical disability, old age, and so forth—in other words, conditions in which sex is no longer possible—must mean that love no longer exists. Learned in the home, this becomes an easy tool for the molester to teach his victims all about adult lovemaking and to avoid the use of the dirty word "sex" at all costs. Even upon involvement in therapy, whether in a correctional setting or private practice, this euphemism acts as a defense mechanism against accepting the responsibility for the damage done to the victim. Hardened, repetitive-compulsive rapists have stated in the beginning of therapy that they were only trying to show love to their victim (whether he or she wanted it from them or not!) or that they were hoping that if they satisfied her or him, she or he would then "love me."

VALUE CHANGE TECHNIQUES

No discussion of value change can be undertaken without first giving consideration to the important works of Professors Jane Loevinger (1996) and Lawrence Kohlberg (1981). The reader is encouraged to take the time to research their all-important theories.

For the sex offenders and their victims that I have worked with, *changing a distorted, damaging, or guilt-provoking value has been a seemingly impossible task.* As stated several times before, traditional or behavioral modification methods have not worked for me in this area and have produced levels of frustration that resulted in many clients quitting therapy. One of the most common guilt-provoking values found in these individuals is "masturbation guilt." Regardless of the intellectual exercises that the patient goes through, when he next masturbates the guilt returns and is perceived as even stronger. For years we struggled with this dilemma with no success until we developed the following explanation and homework assignment.

The client was given a worksheet containing five columns titled "the unwanted behavior," "the associated value," "the source of that value and any other associated values," "the chosen new value," and the change/confirm column.

In the old behavior modification techniques (that were used for many years and failed), the client was instructed to first identify his unwanted behavior (e.g., masturbation guilt). Next, he was told to identify the value attached to the behavior (masturbation is dirty, bad, or sinful) and then to choose a new behavior and a new value (it is okay to masturbate; it's perfectly normal), next to confirm that new behavior and value (masturbate that night), and finally to confirm the new value (How do I feel? Do I still feel guilty?). Failure results most of the time, and the masturbation guilt either remains or even increases.

Adding the "source of the value" column and carefully analyzing this area before attempting to change the value produces a positive result. When tested (for example by masturbating that evening) the guilt is gone, the frustration does not occur, and the individual feels encouraged to attempt to change other, more difficult and entrenched values. An example of this process is seen in Box 17.2.

One phenomenon we have observed in this process is that in the "source of the value" column there are "embedded attached values" in addition to the obvious one that is being worked on. An example, at this point, will help.

NATE, when eleven years old, was caught masturbating in the bathtub by his mother. With a stern and shocked look, mother admonished Nate, telling him that "he will run out of sperm and never have babies if he continues this dirty and disgusting practice." Although guilt ridden and embarrassed for a short time, Nate continued with his masturbation but now experienced terrible guilt following each orgasm. Of course, he was careful to never again get caught by his mother. In working in therapy to change this value, Nate intellectually realized that he would not run out of sperm and that what he was doing was natural and not dirty. However, try as he might to change or eliminate the value, he suffered severe guilt after each masturbatory event. When Nate first used the value change method, there was still no change in the guilt reaction. He was encouraged to search for an *embedded attached value* that might also have been learned from his mother (the source). When he came to the realization that his mother's love was dependent on his conforming to her values (total obedience) and that *rejecting one of her values would result in his being rejected by her,* he was able to see the total picture of conditioning that had occurred from his earliest memory. That evening, his masturbation was the best and most pleasurable he had experienced, and he fell asleep content with no guilt reaction.

Nate was able to apply this same *source* method to rid himself of many other negative, limiting, and guilt-producing values, and his progress in therapy accelerated.

It appears quite clear that beneath each surface-value that cannot be changed through normal therapeutic methods there is an important person in the child's life who taught him that "love equals obedience."

Bringing memories that contain this value to consciousness must be an essential part of the value change process and must be initiated early in the overall treatment process with both the offender and the survivor. These insidious values are imprinted at an early age and will remain there, affecting behavior and self-image to the point of sexual dysfunctions, if not resolved. The damage is multiplied in cases

17.2

Value Change Worksheet Using Masturbatory Guilt As a Working Example

- *The unwanted behavior:* Guilt following each masturbatory episode.
- *The associated value:* Masturbation is dirty, sinful, abnormal, unhealthy.
- *The source of that value and any other associated values:* I was caught masturbating by mother and punished; Mother also stated that masturbation would lead to insanity and sterility. An associated mother-taught value was that "obedience equals love."
- *The chosen new value:* Masturbation is normal, and I don't have to give blind obedience to all of my mother's values to receive her love or to prove that I love her. The new value that I choose may also confirm the old value as my own.
- *The change/confirm value:* I masturbated tonight and there was no guilt. Also, the sensations and pleasures were greater than before.

where *pleasure results in guilt* and the persistent tug-of-war produces a level of mental anguish that easily leads to use of alcohol, drugs, and other forms of escape from the pain.

There are many other distorted and destructive values that need to be identified when working with sex offenders or their victims.

"Sex equals love" and "obedience equals love" are two defective values that most frequently affect the adult behavior of this group. The remaining list of destructive values includes

- love equals slavery,
- acceptance equals conformity,
- sex equals pain,
- pleasure equals evil,
- love equals punishment,
- free will equals delusion,
- deviancy equals heredity,
- silence equals loyalty, and
- love equals loyalty.

The list is endless. However, the value change technique is the same for any distorted, justifying, or deviant value that is identified.

Caveat: Values tend to change as society changes, especially in individuals lacking the confidence to choose values using their own beliefs, experiences, and observations. This scenario certainly fits the sex offenders. Most are locked into Stage 3 (needing adult approval) or Stage 4 (needing peer approval). Some vacillate between the two stages. It is rare, if even possible, to meet a sex offender in Stage 5, at least at the beginning of his therapy.

Finding the offender's complete set of values, especially those involving sex and social interactions, is an essential treatment task. Often the offender exhibits his values in these areas in his word choices and emotional attachments to statements he makes. The therapist must remain highly observant throughout each session for these cues and note them after the patient leaves the office.

THE CHILD/ADOLESCENT SEX OFFENDER

Again, everything described in this chapter applies directly to the child/adolescent sex offender group. This is where values are learned and, as with everything else about child/adolescent sex offenders, the sooner we identify distorted and dangerous values in these individuals, the sooner we can begin the work of helping them to change them. The particular problem of substance abuse is depicted in Box 17.3.

Where sex is concerned, in the majority, if not all, of the child/adolescent sex offenders, the distortions are unbelievable. The distortions may include issues regarding

- physical size and development,
- penis size and development,
- quantities of seminal fluid ejected at orgasm,
- how long they can last when stimulated before reaching orgasm,
- how old they should be when they lose their virginity,
- definitions of what a "real man" is or should be,
- values concerning girls and women and how they should be treated,
- the use of violence: when and how much,
- obeying society's laws,
- relationship to parents and lying to them to get what they want, and
- theft and cheating values.

17.3

Substance Abuse in Adolescent Sex Offenders, Including Food, Alcohol, and Drugs

1. Ninety to 95 percent of all adolescent sex offenders have a substance abuse problem to some degree.
2. This abuse should be treated separately in a group setting, preferably a self-help drug group.
3. The relevance/importance of the substance abuse may be and, at times, should be also part of the sex therapy.
4. Counselors/therapists should not allow the client to use the substance abuse as an excuse/alibi for his deviant behavior.
5. Self-image issues are usually involved in substance abuse in adolescents.
6. Group-conformity issues are also usually involved where alcohol and drugs are concerned.

The list is endless and is quite specific to each individual that comes into the therapist's office. Finding these distorted values and their sources (very important as discussed previously) requires time and trust, commonly termed "rapport."

Values that have internalized in both the adult and the child/adolescent groups will be the hardest to deal with, especially where there is an emotional connection to the value or a trauma that resulted in the adoption of the value.

Although the child/adolescent group is usually more challenging than the adult group, the changes occur more rapidly and are more gratifying for the therapist and more beneficial for the patient. These group members have their whole lives to look forward to, and giving them *hope* through treatment is a rewarding profession.

Chapter 18

Self-Confrontation and Resistance in the Compulsive Sex Offender

In most compulsive sex offenders, regardless of the therapeutic setting, "resistance" is most often the primary barrier to therapeutic insight or change.

This has certainly been true in my experience with hospital, correctional, and private settings. The need to develop a method of eliminating this barrier is paramount to any successful treatment. Part of the reason for this resistance is the compulsive sex offender's major use of *denial* as a primary defense mechanism. The more intense the guilt he is experiencing, the stronger the denial, and consequently the greater the resistance.

Since therapist-confrontation methods did not work with these most resistant cases, we had to develop a "pre-therapist confrontation method" that the clients could be taught to do by themselves in the privacy of their rooms or at home. The result was called "Now Therapy: A Method of Self-Confrontation for More Frightened and Resistant Cases."

After many, many frustrating hours of trying to break down the resistance and minimize the denial, the task appeared hopeless, until one patient made the following casual remark in the heat of an emotional outburst: "How can I admit something to you I haven't even admitted to myself!" Following this session, I did a quick survey of other highly resistant clients and found they all described the same problem, situation, or quandary.

THE FIRST "NOW" THERAPY SESSION

While pondering how to tackle this perplexing dilemma, a fortuitous incident occurred. In the sex education courses I conducted, an important module in the advanced section was the Body-Image exercises of Hartman and Fithian (1987). For many reasons, I had to modify the original technique to the following format:

- The exercise is conducted in a group setting, utilizing a three-paneled mirror.
- The client stands before the mirror in the nude and touches each part of his body, from the top of his head to the soles of his feet.
- As he touches each part, he describes how the part *feels* to him, whether he *likes* the part or not and why, e.g., "I don't like my body because it's too short and fat; it makes me look like a slob!"

When this exercise is completed, the client is told to do the following three tasks:

1. "Rate the body you are looking at on a 0 to 100 percent basis, comparing it to your peer group and considering your age." Once he makes a determination, he is told to now explain the reasons for his rating.
2. "Choose just one part of the body you are looking at that you would like to change." Once the part is chosen, he is asked to explain the reason for his choice.
3. "Choose just one part of the body you are looking at that you would like to take with you to a totally new body." Once the part is chosen, he is asked to explain the reason for his choice.

The answers to these three follow-up questions alone are significantly diagnostic. The therapist must pay close attention, especially to the *reasons* for the choices.

When this part of the exercise is completed, the client turns around and faces the group. Each group member is then asked by the therapist to answer the same three questions about the body they are looking at and to give his own reasons for his choices. When this is completed, the client is asked if his rating percentage is still the same or if it has now changed. In more than 75 percent of the cases, the group's evaluation and rating alters the body-image perception of the client. Most frequently, the rating increases, but there are cases (especially in narcissistic personality types) when the reevaluation results in a lower rating.

The day after MARK took his turn doing the body-image exercise, he asked to see me in my office. He appeared quite anxious and stated, "That sex ed thing last night really affected me. I didn't want to leave the mirror. It just wasn't enough. I would have liked to talk to the guy in the mirror about himself, his behavior, and other things, not just about his body." Since the therapy room was available at that hour, I asked Mark if he would like to go and continue the session. He readily and happily agreed. Back in front of the mirror he began, "Well, I guess you are a nice guy . . . and people tend to like you and want to be your friend"—then a silence of over twenty minutes, followed by "But you're not worth shit!"

I then asked him to tell the man in the mirror why he felt that way about him *today,* without using anything from his past. Another lengthy silence followed, after which he stated, "I can't." I then asked him to reappraise the man in the mirror, and he said, "Well, maybe you're not so bad after all." Smiling, he left the mirror and said that he felt as if a thousand-pound weight had been lifted from his shoulders.

Excitedly, he told his group what had occurred during their next session; they all wanted to try the technique. Instead, a small committee was formed to develop the format and procedures for such a group. Concurrently, I presented the technique to the treatment staff of the institution for their appraisal and asked them to refer clients who fit the same resistant-to-change category.

The final technique that emerged pivoted on self-confrontation in a private and safe setting where no one could hear or observe. The reason for this condition was to prevent "censoring" if others were present and to eliminate any need to be defensive. Since "admitting it to myself" appeared to be the key, it also became the key element in the technique.

Expecting the client, no matter how motivated, to bare all in the first session was senseless, and so a slow, gradual approach to complete openness had to be built into the system. Since *identity* was also an issue, this became another critical element of the technique approach to the problem. The question to begin the first mirror session then became "Who are you?"

The client's first assignment was to stand in front of a full-length mirror (in his bedroom or alone in a therapy room prepared for the technique) and to "distance" himself from the person in the mirror by using the second person "you" rather than "I" in all of his statements, e.g., "I have something important to talk to you about."

After several months of experimenting, two other elements were incorporated: the technique worked best when (1) the client was in the nude and (2) the client spoke aloud. Upon first presentation of the technique to a small group of professionals with whom I was associated at the time, there was some immediate concern and criticism about using nudity with sex offenders. In order to deal with these concerns, several other methods were tried. Shorts, underwear, and bathing suits were all tried, and the technique failed. Defenses remained stronger than ever, and blocking occurred. The offenders themselves felt the discomfort and returned to the original method. I have hypothesized that being nude greatly helps the individual to be as defenseless as possible and also to be totally vulnerable to the feedback of his "best friend in the mirror." Other therapists who have seen videotape demonstrations of the technique agreed.

Where the second condition is concerned, thinking or mental confrontation (as opposed to speaking aloud) also failed. Apparently, all of the lies, fantasy materials, and distortions that the sex offender uses daily kept intruding. However, if the client looked himself in the eye and spoke out loud, *it became impossible to lie.* He would actually interrupt himself and confront any attempted lie or distortion, such as minimizing.

An unexpected bonus also occurred in all clients using the technique: there was a noticeable increase in self-confidence, although no direct work had been done in this area. Others in the sex offender's life (therapists, parents, wives, children, work supervisors, etc.) reported the change, as did the client himself.

What appears to happen is as follows. For most of his life, the compulsive sex offender has been out of control or at least *perceived* that others controlled his life and decisions, whether parents, teachers, friends, employers, wives, lovers, or even his children. In this technique it is *impossible* not to accept credit (that could never be tolerated before) for any change, insight, or faced experience or responsibility and guilt for past behaviors that were illegal, immoral, or that ended in his being in trouble. Once motivated to attempt the technique, the technique and the individual take over, and most of what occurs is unplanned, regardless of the amount of rehearsing that precedes the actual session.

The greatest fear, in a majority of cases, is facing the fact that he is a sex offender. Standing there telling his "friend" in the mirror that he is a sex offender has a permanent shock value that does not disappear.

In an institutional setting, the group mirror technique may not work for all members of the group. Some simply will be unable to bare all in front of their peers. For this group, a special arrangement must be made.

In my experience with incarcerated sex offenders, I arranged with security personnel to allow individuals to have a private session in the studio in the evenings. This is where the most resistant individuals completed their homework assignments. All of the sessions were videotaped, but control of the tape was given to the individual. After the session, the tape was sealed until he felt ready to share it with his therapist or his group. This method removed the last alibi for not doing mirrors. The majority of these individuals shared their tapes within a week and mostly with their primary group. The quality of these sessions was excellent and shortened therapy time to a large extent.

THE COMMUNITY OR PRIVATE PRACTICE "NOW" TECHNIQUE

Converting the "Now" technique for use in private practice in the community was a simple task. The client is instructed to perform the technique at home in the privacy of his bathroom or bedroom in front of a full-length mirror. It is essential that *no one else be present during the exercise.* This is a means of eliminating any possible defensive reaction based on what others would think or feel. It is also strongly suggested that an inexpensive cassette tape recorder be placed on the floor by the mirror to record the session, since it has been our experience that clients will defensively "forget" parts of the session that were highly sensitive or traumatizing. The client is told to listen to the tape within twenty-four hours and to note, for himself, what he hears on the tape that he had forgotten (re-repressed). Although the tape is strictly for the client's use, it has been my experience that many clients will bring his or her tape(s) to the following session to share with the therapist.

To my surprise, many of my private clients owned video cameras and videotaped their sessions. The majority brought these tapes to their next therapy session for playback with me. As in the institutional videotapes, a great deal of sensitive material appeared on the tape that the client was unable to share in person during a session. This made the "Now" technique even more valuable.

Many of my clients, both in institutional settings and in private practice, also felt that this technique allowed them to share in the therapeutic responsibility with the therapist; it made them cotherapists instead of passive clients being treated.

When used in an institutional situation, the "Now" technique should either be continued after release and discussed in follow-up contacts, such as an aftercare program, or be initiated when the need arises if the released individual had never used the technique before.

CAVEATS

Several caveats must be discussed.

- The session should always be at least audiotaped when video-taping (the ideal method) is not available. The most traumatic and shocking revelations and/or accusations can be re-repressed following a session, thus the need for a permanent and objective record. Instructions should carefully explain that this taping is for the client, not for the therapist, in order to prevent *performance-oriented* sessions.
- The therapist must ensure that these sessions do not become *self-punishment* sessions, a real danger with the compulsive, guilt-ridden offender. His negative self-image is bad enough when he starts therapy, and care must be taken that this negative image does not become intensified. Weekly reports from the client on the self-confrotation sessions are used for this purpose, and the client himself will often volunteer a tape of a session that he was either pleased with or that disturbed him. Listening to the tapes in his presence becomes highly therapeutic (and revealing as well) since they all run a *commentary* on their performance as the tape plays. This playback session also affords the therapist an opportunity to provide guidance for future sessions through the use of subtle suggestion or highly directive suggestion, depending on the circumstances.
- *Mirrors* then become a major homework assignment with the content left entirely up to the individual. The reason for this is that the current issues in his therapy may be overshadowed by an immediate and pressing problem in his life. Should he feel the

obligation to do what the therapist told him, he may use his directed homework as a means of avoiding his daily life problems.

- As the client becomes more comfortable with self-confrontation, the therapist, either in an individual or group setting, can begin to become more directly confrontive with him.

The overall major benefit is a new self-confidence and a lessening of the almost complete dependence these clients have on the therapist. More risks will be taken and more new behaviors attempted. Here, as in all therapy modalities, *nothing succeeds like success.*

The following example concerns a man who had been in therapy first with a well-known therapist in the community and then in an institutional setting. After his release the following occurred.

JUAN was a thirty-five-year-old rapist who was well liked at the treatment center. From his entry into treatment he appeared open, cooperative, and willing to tell all. Progress in therapy was rapid, and the insights developed in his case appeared to logically and firmly explain his behavior. Juan had begun his sexual problem history with flashing (exposing himself) to younger girls in his neighborhood and school. This behavior began at age eleven and continued through early adulthood, when he was first arrested. Juan was sentenced to one year of probation with the condition of weekly psychotherapy and was promoted quickly to biweekly, monthly, and finally terminated (all in six months). The flashing continued both during his treatment and afterward, but he was not arrested again until his first rape of a young adult female.

Juan was married with three children at the time and had a steady job where he was subjected to long hours, nasty comments, constant criticisms, etc. Rarely did he express a negative emotion, and he appeared frightened of anger. The reasons he allowed himself to be used and taken advantage of were never discussed in his probation therapy sessions. Once institutionalized, his progress was rapid and convincing. In a relatively short period of four years, he earned his parole and was enrolled in the aftercare program that I conducted. From the start, I had a gut reaction that something was wrong but could not identify the problem. He smiled at anything and everything, and appeared to be adjusting well to his return to society. He reported some minor problems with reestablishing his role as father and head of the household, but since his children were adolescents, this did not appear to be unusual. One year after his release, almost to the day, Juan was arrested for flashing two young girls at a crowded shopping center in midday. He was immediately apprehended and released on his own recognizance with a court date in one month. He arrived at his next aftercare session depressed and needing to take the floor. After telling the group what happened, he insisted that he had no idea why it occurred and it made as little sense to him as it did to anyone else.

After having him begin the "now" self-confrontation exercises, the following individual session took place.

JUAN reported that standing in front of the mirror and talking to himself produced an unexpected anger outburst. He told the man in the mirror that he was *"no good, rotten, and deserved to go back to jail!"* I immediately sensed that he was hiding something and kept asking for more until he finally told me that while confronting himself in the mirror, he suddenly remembered being sexually abused when he was a small child.

Juan's father deserted the family when he was only seven years old, and his mother, who spoke very little English, could not find work. The rent was due, and they were evicted. His mother's only recourse was to ask friends to take them in. After two or three of these short-term visits, she found a woman who said she would let them live there as long as they liked as long as Juan's mother would do some housework, cook, and look after her two teenage boys so she could go to work. Juan's mother happily agreed, and they moved in. Juan had to sleep with the two boys while his mother shared the only other bedroom with their benefactor.

During the second night, the boys undressed themselves and then Juan and introduced him to his first sexual experience. Their penises looked gigantic to him, and the boys made fun of the "little finger" he had between his legs. They then made him masturbate each of them and threatened to kill him and his mother if he told anyone. After a week of abuse, Juan went to his mother and told her the whole story in Spanish. She answered "Juan, we have nowhere to go! Please, be a good boy and do what the two brothers ask you to do or we'll be out on the street." Disappointed, confused, and angry, Juan submitted to the abuse which eventually escalated to painful sodomy. After the first sodomy experience, Juan considered himself a *puta* (female prostitute) and his self-image totally changed. He reasoned that since he was sexually attractive to the two boys, he must have appeared or acted feminine and that was why they "used him as a girl."

In all of his therapy, both individual in the community and group in prison, he never related this story and its connection to his flashing (his need to be accepted as a male, even with his small penis) or the anger at his mother that led to the rape behavior. Juan continued doing the "Now" technique at home and even taught it to his wife and to his children. Today they are a happy family, travel together, and have long, meaningful discussions. Juan could never relate to his wife or children in this way prior to the self-confrontation. At work, he is no longer the *whipping boy* and asserts his rights with everyone, including his employer. The result has been a raise in pay and better working hours.

"Now" or self-confrontation must become a way of life and a daily exercise for Juan and others. In the morning, it should be used to set realistic goals for the day. In the evening, it should be used to evaluate the day on both a positive and critical level. The *balance* is the important factor, as is the fact that the client now becomes his own therapist and takes charge of his life.

In formal therapy, the results of these self-confrontations are discussed to be sure that they are balanced and that the defective goal-setting pattern has not returned.

THE CHILD/ADOLESCENT SEX OFFENDER

The "Now" technique works exceptionally well with both young children and adolescents. The children love looking at themselves in the mirror and enjoy the nakedness as well. Parents must first have the technique explained and agree to first, installing a full-length mirror in the child's room, usually on the back of his door or on a closet door; second, they must agree to allowing the child the privacy to do his "mirrors" without intruding or questioning him in any way about what he was doing or what was said; and third, they must provide the child with a tape recorder to tape his mirror sessions. I can honestly say that in forty years I have never had parents of a child in emotional distress or suffering from child sexual abuse refuse to help in this unusual venture.

Young children love to discuss their mirrors and continuously bring me tapes of these sessions. As with the adults, these private sessions always contain material that was not forthcoming in the weekly sessions in my office.

Where adolescents are concerned, there are more problems due to their stage of development. Beginning with prepubertal ages through adolescence, body-image problems are prevalent that make facing themselves in the mirror a more difficult task. When adolescents do mirror sessions at home, the major problems reported in regular sessions are body development and penis size. One session has to be devoted to these issues as soon as they are reported.

I also use two excellent books to aid adolescents through this stage: *The What's Happening to My Body? Book for Boys* and *The What's Happening to My Body? Book for Girls* both by Lynda Madaras (1988). The book is given to patients to read at home. They are asked to keep a pen and paper next to the books as they read and to jot down questions that confuse them and the page it was on.

All of my teens to date have enjoyed the books and stated that they learned a great deal from them. Most important, the books uncovered and corrected myths and so-called facts that they had gleaned from their peers. Several wanted more of Madaras's books, and they were given sources for them.

Adolescents take much longer than preadolescents to reach the sensitive areas of their problems in the mirror. However, from direct questioning at the end of their treatment, I am convinced that these areas would never have come out in regular therapy sessions. The "Now" technique has been invaluable to me in dealing with these two groups, whether they were the sex offenders or the survivors of sexual abuse.

I have also discovered over the years that the personalities of the child/adolescent sex offenders and the personalities of the child/adolescent survivors of sexual abuse are amazingly similar. In some cases they are exactly the same: the inadequate personality discussed in Chapter 2.

Caveats: All the caveats mentioned previously apply to these two groups as well. The only additional caveat for the adolescent group is that there must be a concurrent sex education course undertaken that deals with specific questions and problems that a particular patient is experiencing.

Some of the mirrors will become sexually stimulating and end in masturbation, especially for the boys. A significant number of male adolescents use masturbation as a reward following a difficult and/or painful mirror, and this became the subject of the next therapy session. This subject must be handled with care and sensitivity to assure that no additional guilt occurs. To date, this occurrence has not become a problem for the patients I have treated.

On the whole, my experiences with this technique have been highly positive, and many of my "graduates" return even years later to tell me that they are still using the "Now" technique on a regular basis. From these retellings, I continue to learn more and more about the uses for the technique and share these stories (with the ex-patient's permission and with anonymity) with current patients. Also, when the dynamics of a past case and a current case are closely similar, I have the ex-patient join me for a session with the current patient (with both of them agreeing). The results are always positive and motivating for the current adolescent. Just knowing someone else who has gone through the same abuse and other problems that they have recently experienced helps a great deal.

As with all techniques, if a particular therapist is not comfortable using the technique it is understandable. All therapists are different and have their own methods of reaching and helping patients.

Chapter 19

Religious Personnel Who Molest Children and Adolescents

INTRODUCTION

Due to the worldwide "witch-hunt" going on at the time of this writing, I feel it necessary to include a chapter on the subject of sexual abuse by religious personnel. There is an incredible amount of disinformation being disseminated in the media on this topic. Considering its importance, it is my hope that the following will help clarify the issues.

The scope of the problem is not as the media would lead one to believe. The actual figures as of this writing are that 2 percent of the Catholic priests have been accused of child molestation, and the majority of these occurred fifteen to twenty years ago. In my own state of New Jersey, the total number of priests linked to sexual abuse is 146. All of these cases have been turned over to local prosecutors even though the majority of them have surpassed the limitations in time for these offenses. Many of them are also the subject of civil law suits. In addition, since the Dallas Conference of Bishops, all of the dioceses have formed a civilian diocesan response team to review these cases and to interview both the victims and the clerics where the committee feels there is a need. This is a new and encouraging change in the Catholic Church.

Disturbing to this writer and many others is the fact that there is little, if any, mention of the molesters exposed in other religions nor is there any credit given to the sincere and healthy priests who do a tremendous amount of positive work with their parishioners, including children and adolescents.

ERRORS CONCERNING CLERICAL ABUSE

There are several blatant errors being disseminated by a variety of so-called "professionals":

- *The majority of child sex abuse is perpetrated by Catholic priests.* This is not true! In my forty years of dealing with this problem, I have personally treated five ministers from Protestant denominations, three Catholic priests, one rabbi, and an assortment of church-connected employees such as choir directors, scout-leaders, counselors, and even janitors and school security personnel. I personally know of several more in each of these groups, but the Catholic priests have never been the largest group.

- *Homosexuality in the seminaries and the priesthood is a major cause of the present problem. Eliminating these individuals will solve the problem.* This is not true! Most homosexuals, both gays and lesbians, are more appalled at pedophilia/hebophilia than are most heterosexuals. The main reason is that there are always individuals who will connect the molesting of boys to homosexuality. Mature homosexuals, like mature heterosexuals, want relationships with adults, not with children. Pedophiles and hebophiles are not necessarily looking for long-term relationships. They go to children and adolescents since they can control them and cannot deal with their peer group out of fears of rejection and of being controlled. They mostly are "replaying" what happened to them as children in a role-reversal way. All three priests I have treated, as well as the ministers and rabbi, also were molested as children but never reported it nor were they ever treated. Amanda Ripley in *Time,* May 20, 2002, has an excellent article titled "Inside the Church's Closet" on this subject that I strongly recommend to the reader.

- *Only the Catholic Church covered up these crimes and transferred priests to other parishes in order to protect the reputation of the church.* This is not true! All of the cases I have had contact with including the ministers, the rabbi, and several choir directors, were either transferred or were allowed to resign "for the good of the church or synagogue." None was ever reported to the authorities, and I was never given any names or locations that would permit me to report these molestations nor was I permitted to interview the victims. My requests were all denied with the reasons of confidentiality or church eyes only. In fact, the five ministers traveled from another state to my office for their treatment so that no one in their locality would know they were in treatment. During their treatment, many were pastors of different parishes from the one where the problem occurred. *Dateline* on NBC on May 28, 2002, presented an exposure of child/teen sex abuse in the Jehovah's Witnesses in which the victims were forbidden to report these crimes under pain of being excommunicated by the religion. They defended the abuser using the Bible, which they quote as saying "there must be a witness to the crime before it is given credence." Therefore, because of the one-on-one situation that child/teen abuse almost always is, they refuse to even hold a hearing.

• *Celibacy in the Catholic Church is a cause of these abuses.* This is not true! All of the non-Catholic religious abusers were married, and this did not prevent them from becoming abusers. Celibacy is integral to priests of the Roman rite. It is a special gift that God bestows on these men and also on Catholic nuns, who are also celibate. Changing this discipline will not diminish the number of child and adolescent victims.

REASONS FOR CLERICAL ABUSE

Why did these molestations occur? This is a question that no one appears to want to discuss in any depth except to blame homosexuality as described in the previous section.

As covered in Chapter 12 of this work, more than 90 percent of the sex offenders that I have dealt with over the years were themselves molested as children or adolescents. The majority of these cases were being seen for pedophilia or hebophilia, and the details, circumstances, choice of place, and act were all *identical* to what was done to them.

A troublesome and sad fact is that the majority, if not all, of these cases could have been prevented with proper screening of seminarians by experienced professionals trained in the area of sexual deviations. Also, had the churches, schools, and parents properly educated their children about this problem, especially using the "Good Touch, Bad Touch" model, most of the cases would have been prevented and the rest reported after the first attempt. "Bad touch" always precedes actual sexual behavior in these deviant and psychotic individuals. Back rubs, spankings on bare buttocks, nude swimming (skinny-dipping), changing clothes together with the children in locker rooms for gym, making comments about their development (especially in hebophiles looking for teen boy victims), sleeping together in the same bed or same sleeping bag on camping trips, and many other ploys that should have been prevented or reported are indicators of serious problems on the part of the cleric.

Also, children and adolescents should be better schooled in their religion so that ridiculous statements such as "God gave me permission to do this to you," or "God will punish you if you tell anyone about this," or "Nobody will believe you—it's my word against yours," will not be believed and will be reported to someone that the child trusts. Likewise, children and adolescents have a greater chance of becoming youthful sex offenders if they do not have a solid base of moral values, social values, and religious values. Box 19.1 depicts the relationship between religious and moral issues and youthful sex offenders.

19.1

Religious/Moral Issues in Adolescent Sex Offenders

1. In a majority of adolescent sex offenders, religion is either nonexistent or rarely practiced.
2. Even when religious attendance is forced on the adolescent by parents or other authority figures, the adolescent rarely believes in or accepts the dogmas/tenets of the religion involved.
3. As a result, moral emptiness exists and most behaviors are selfishly motivated or for self-preservation.
4. Even in sociopathic adolescents, morally acceptable behaviors can be taught with special techniques:
   a. victim-identification role-playing
   b. "what if" techniques
   c. the "empty chair" technique

Note: Without instilling moral and social values, positive, long-term treatment effects will never exist.

Parents have an even greater responsibility and are often extremely naive where religious authority is concerned. Permission slips for camping trips, overnight stays following tutoring, special tutoring after everyone else has left the church (a favorite of choir directors), and teachers tutoring at their homes should all raise a red flag. Before giving permission, parents need to know

- who this person really is,
- why there will be only one adult present with one child or adolescent, and
- why a specific child or adolescent is chosen over and over again for some special time with an adult minister, priest, rabbi, choir director, or other connected church employees.

Two concerns regarding the parents' behavior and their responsibility if abuse occurs are

- why parents did not fully question the child/adolescent about the visit, trip, etc., and
- why, when the child does not want to talk about it, is evasive, is moody and not his or her normal self the parents do not see this as a red flag and do some serious checking while showing serious concern and not being dictatorial in questioning.

This does not mean that we need a witch-hunt or that no religious personnel can ever be trusted. In reality, the majority can be trusted and will not constantly plan scenarios that assure him of a one-on-one opportunity to molest.

Pedophiles and hebophiles all have similar traits that can be used as identifiers:

- They are loners and timid individuals who prefer to avoid social gatherings or activities but can *act* charming, friendly, and sociable in situations to *mask* their true feelings. They develop a Jekyll-and-Hyde personality as an effective defense tactic.
- They are obviously more comfortable with children or adolescents than they are with adults.
- If they do attend social functions, their behavior and interactions are short and impersonal. They are performing a mandatory function and obviously are not enjoying themselves.

- They are secretive. They know all about everyone else's behaviors and life, but no one knows anything personal about them.
- They are either underachievers or overachievers, depending on whether they are accept-ers or deny-ers (see Chapter 2 on the inadequate personality).
- They appear perfectly normal to almost everyone since they are "on stage" and performing in order to prevent others from seeing them as they really are.
- They will have an unusual interest in all sex-related events, occurrences, etc. Their interests in these things go beyond the normal: they need to know every personal detail, even the smallest. (I have had adults complain to me about this fact when they go for religious counseling or confession. The overly detailed questioning makes them really uncomfortable, although they do not know why.) An example will clarify.

JEFFY who was introduced in Chapter 1, was brought up a Catholic. He was a "Sunday-go-to-church" type who was never too interested in religion. When he reached adolescence, his mother made him attend Catholic Youth Organization (CYO). During the Easter season, all of his CYO group went to confession. Jeffy was a compulsive masturbator and confessed this to Father Bob, who was the chaplain for the CYO in his parish.

In addition to the usual questions, Father Bob asked the following questions: "Are you circumcised or not?" "How big an erection do you get when you masturbate?" "What fantasies give you the greatest orgasm?" "How much do you ejaculate?" "Do you masturbate in the nude or with just your penis exposed?" and on and on and on. After this interrogation, Jeffy was told that Father Bob could not give him absolution (forgiveness) unless he came to the priest's office in the rectory.

Jeffy, upset and angry, left the confessional and the CYO, never to return. Years later, his girlfriend convinced him to try her religion, Methodism, and his first question was, "Do you have to go to confession?"

As of today, Jeffy continues in the Methodist faith but will never forget or forgive Father Bob.

These religious personnel volunteer continuously for activities that will give them power, authority, and contact with either children or adolescents. Rarely do they volunteer for activities where only adults will be involved.

Of course there are exceptions to all of these, as each pedophile or hebophile is an individual with his own personality traits. There are others that are specific to individual molesters and not to the entire

group. Each of these individuals is different with only their inadequacy and choice of victims the common element.

THE DAMAGE

Sexual abuse by religious personnel results in *triple trauma*. Stranger
or peer sexual abuse results in a single trauma: the abuse; parental
abuse results in a double trauma: the abuse itself and then the betrayal
of trust and concern by a parent or loved one; and abuse by religious
personnel results in a triple trauma: the abuse, the betrayal of trust in
an authority figure, and, most damaging, the trauma of spiritual betrayal and threats regarding God and damnation.

Due to this third abuse factor, fewer of these cases are reported until one of the victims in this group finds the courage to expose his or
her religious abuser. In all of these cases, the fear of retribution from
God, whom the abusers related "gave me permission to do this to
you," and "if you tell anyone, God will punish you in hell for eter-
nity," produces an intense fear as well as a feeling of confusion. The
confusion results from the fact that their religion teaches them that
what they are doing is wrong and sinful, but the religious abusers
teach them that the God of their religion gave him permission to sexually abuse them. Too often, suicide, many years later, is the result. At
minimum there will be sexual dysfunction and trust issues in the survivor for the rest of his or her life unless he or she is identified as soon
as possible after the molestation and treated by specially trained therapists.

The pedophilic-personality of all of these cleric-abusers *existed
long before they entered their religious training.* Thus, fuller and
more accurate psychological screening administered when an individual applies for religious training would go a long way to prevent
the extent of the current pedophilia/hebophilia being reported daily.
This screening must be done by qualified and experienced psychologists or psychiatrists with training in sexual offending and abuse.
Most of these professionals have had little or no training in this field
and still are chosen to perform these screenings. This is a terrible and
inexcusable error.

Several of the religious clerics that I have treated were (and I assume are) in an adult heterosexual or adult homosexual relationship

and have no interest or predilection for becoming involved with children or adolescents.

Treatment for the religious-abuser is the same as for all other pedophiles and hebophiles. Where the victims are concerned, treatment is more complex and takes much longer since the spiritual elements have to be discussed and resolved. Often, when I reach this point in therapy with the victim (which can be from the very beginning or when the victim is ready to deal with it), I often ask another religious member of the same denomination to sit in on the session and discuss this element with the victim. Of course, prior permission from the patient must be obtained to do this.

Last and most important, the churches, themselves, must change their attitudes toward this problem, especially about *protecting* these molesters with rationalizations, allowing what the molester told the child/adolescent ("You won't be believed" or "God will protect me and punish you") to come true in the eyes of the victim.

The attitudes toward this problem in Europe, especially the Vatican, are not changing. As late as March 23, 2002, the following appeared in an editorial in the *Star Ledger.* They quoted the Reverend Gianfranco Ghirlanda, dean of the canon law faculty at the Gregorian University in Rome, and Archbishop Julian Herranz, president of the Pontifical Council for the Interpretation of Legislative Texts. Ghirlanda says

> an accused priest should not be required to undergo psychological testing and that parishioners have no right to know that a newly assigned priest has a history of sex abuse. (*Star Ledger,* 2002, p. 22)

The Catholic News Service held an interview about Ghirlanda's quote and stated

> Most troubling is the idea that a bishop who is being a good pastor to a troubled priest should not have to notify civil authorities. Instead, the bishop would conduct his own investigation. Should he determine there is something to the allegations, he would reassign the priest. Instead of telling the prosecutor, even if the priest is guilty, the first thing a bishop should do is try to (spiritually) recover him . . . Herranz argued that reporting all sex

abuse cases was unnecessary and that in handing over files, U.S. bishops were responding to "an emotional wave of public clamor."

It appears that the Vatican is not ready to deal realistically with this incredibly serious problem. Catholic bishops in the United States, however, heeded the needs of their child/adolescent charges and did what is both necessary and just. The United States Conference of Catholic Bishops (USCCB) approved a Charter for the Protection of Children and Young People in Dallas, Texas, on June 14, 2002, and then revised and approved the charter on November 13, 2002, titled Essential Norms for Diocesan/Eparchial Policies Dealing with Allegations of Sexual Abuse of Minors by Priests or Deacons. For more information, please consult the USCCB Web site: <http://www.nccbuscc.org/bishops>. The actual norms are complex and integrated with canonical law. The following is an abstract of the essentials of the norms contained in the document.

1. The dioceses will have a written policy on the sexual abuse of minors by priests and deacons, as well as by other church personnel.
2. Each diocese will appoint a competent individual to assist individuals who claim to have been sexually abused when they were minors by priests or deacons.
3. Each diocese will have a review board which will act as consultants to the bishop in implementing the new policies. The board will be composed of at least five persons "of outstanding integrity and good judgment." The majority of the board members will be laypersons not employed by the dioceses, but at least one member should be a priest and one member should have expertise in the treatment of the sexual abuse of minors.
4. When an allegation of sexual abuse of a minor by a priest or deacon is received, a preliminary investigation will be conducted. All steps to protect the reputation of the accused shall be taken, and the accused will be encouraged to retain assistance of civil and canonical counsel. When sufficient evidence is uncovered that the abuse has occurred, the bishop

will remove the accused from the sacred ministry, impose or prohibit residence in a given place or territory, and prohibit public participation in the Most Holy Eucharist pending the outcome of the process.

5. The accused may be requested to comply with an appropriate medical and psychological evaluation.

6. When even a single act of sexual abuse by a priest or deacon is admitted or established, the offending priest or deacon will be removed permanently from ecclesiastical ministry. In every case, cannon law must be observed, and if the penalty of dismissal from the clerical state has not been applied, he will not be permitted to celebrate Mass publicly or to administer the sacraments and will be instructed not to wear clerical garb or to present himself publicly as a priest.

7. The priest or deacon may at any time request a dispensation from the obligations of the clerical state. In exceptional cases, the bishop may request of the holy father the dismissal of the priest or deacon from the clerical state ex officio, even without the consent of the priest or deacon.

8. The diocese will comply with all applicable civil laws with respect to the reporting of sexual abuse of minors to civil authorities and will cooperate in the investigation. In every instance, the diocese will advise and support a person's right to make a report to public authorities.

9. No priest or deacon who has committed an act of sexual abuse of a minor may be transferred for ministerial assignment to another diocese or religious province. Before a priest or deacon can be transferred for residence to another diocese or religious province, the bishop shall forward in a confidential manner to the local bishop and religious ordinary any and all information concerning any act of sexual abuse of a minor or any other information indicating that he has been or may be a danger to children or young people.

10. Care will always be taken to protect the rights of all parties involved, especially those of the persons claiming to have been sexually abused and of the person against whom charges have been made. When an accusation has proved to be unfounded, every step possible will be taken to restore the good name of the person falsely accused.

In addition to the ten norms listed here, other safeguards are proposed by the USCCB. Primary among these is the "Safe Environment for Minors" proposal which includes an evaluation of seminary applicants as well as all church personnel who have the responsibility for the care and supervision of children and young people. Although this is certainly a great start, other issues remain, especially the matter of applying these same norms to religious orders that are not covered by the bishop's norms at this time.

PREVENTION

Prevention is possible if not for all cases then at least for all cases after the first time it happens.

First, proper testing and interviewing by a specifically trained sex therapist who specializes in this field is needed. This should be a requirement for all potential prospects/applicants for any religious training. It can also be accomplished during the training of priests, ministers, rabbis, imams, and others. The identification of potential sex offenders then allows the specific organizations to decide on either removal or treatment during the training process. When treatment is terminated, the therapist can then make a recommendation of either removal as inappropriate for the position or approval for the ministry with specific limitations and guidelines, such as "not to work with children or adolescents."

Second, all religious denominations need to conduct training sessions or seminars for the children and adolescents in their flocks aimed at giving these groups not only permission but also a mandate to refuse any attempted sexual involvement with any religious personnel and a second suggestion/mandate to report it, at least to their parents if not to the authorities. Coming from the religious group itself, this will carry incredible weight with the children and adolescents and eliminate the religious-oriented threats and coercion by religious personnel in their attempts at molesting these groups.

None of the child/adolescent victims that I have treated were ever present at such a training nor had they been informed in any of their religious classes that they had these rights.

For more information on treating survivors of religious abuse, I offer my book *Sexual Abuse of Children and Adolescents* (Continuum Publishers), which contains a specific chapter on the subject, or many other good books on the subject.

Author's note: Since this manuscript was submitted in its final edit, the United States Conference of Catholic Bishops has finalized the Charter for the Protection of Children and Young People and published a booklet titled *Promise to Protect—Pledge to Heal.* It is numbered Publication No. 5-540 and is available from USCCB Publishing, Washington, DC. Their toll free number is 1-800-235-8722. This is the Charter that all Dioceses in the United States are following in the examination and review of cases of alleged sexual abuse by priests and other clergy in the Catholic Church.

Chapter 20

Conclusion

YOU, THE THERAPIST—CONSIDERATIONS

In all of our training sessions, a pretest is used to raise the consciousness levels of the participants (see Chapter 1). A primary question and concern during this test revolves around the qualifications of the individual wanting to treat or already treating sex offenders. Besides a degree or certification, there are personality requirements (see Box 20.1) that are of utmost importance, raising the question "Of all the many required traits and characteristics of the intended sex offender therapist, which is the most important and most frequently absent?"

Rarely is the correct answer obtained in the pretraining questionnaire. The most important trait or characteristic of the intended therapist for this group, in my opinion, has always been *comfort with sexuality—both his or her own and that of others.* An example will clarify the importance.

BRIAN, a twelve-year-old survivor, is being interviewed by a middle-aged female psychologist for the first time after his sexual molestation. They are in her office, with Brian sitting next to her desk and the therapist facing him. Her first comment to Brian is "Brian, tell me what happened." Brian then asks if it is all right to tell her what the teacher did to him, since she is a woman. She replies, "Of course it is. You can tell me anything you want. Use your own words." Brian then replies, "He [Brian's fifth grade teacher] took me into the cloak room and made me suck his dick!"

Immediately, the therapist swivels in her seat to face the desk, lowers her head, and begins furiously writing. Brian glares at her with obvious anger and says, as he gets up and leaves the office, "You lied to me!" When questioned later about the incident, Brian states that he does not want any of that therapy stuff. He never returns to therapy.

20.1

Qualifications *Necessary* for a Therapist to Work with Either Adolescent or Adult Sex Offenders

1. Knowledge of "who" they are treating
2. Specialized training with a qualified, experienced trainer
3. Personal comfort with all types of and aspects of human sexuality
4. Comfort with the offender's *language*
5. Comfort with listening to the nitty-gritty details
6. An overall nonjudgmental attitude and approach
7. Comfort with being a directive, confronting therapist
8. The ability to remain objective and not become an offender advocate
9. The ability to leave the work at work
10. The ability to work with or have contact with survivors of sexual abuse

Since this was a supervised session and was videotaped, the supervisee was asked what she felt had happened, and she replied that she was "shocked at the boy's filthy language!"

Unfortunately, this was Brian's first contact or experience with therapy and *also his last.* He refused to return to the clinic or to see anyone else about his molestation and became a consistent behavior problem in school, ending up involved with the juvenile authorities.

Not only *language* but also the *content* of the sexual behaviors themselves may shock the naive or untrained therapist. Remember the incident of the young boy who masturbated the elephant? (See Harry, Chapter 5.) This was definitely not everyday sexual behavior.

In addition to specialized training (which is a *must*), it is my opinion that attendance at an SAR (sex attitude restructuring) seminar or course is a necessary prerequisite to becoming a therapist for either sex offenders or survivors. Supervision with an experienced and qualified sex therapist becomes the next necessary experience. For some trainees, therapy with a certified and trained sex therapist may also be necessary to deal with their own personal issues, especially those that could adversely affect their treatment of clients. Many individuals who choose sex therapy as a major focus of their psychological training have either been victimized themselves or find themselves sexually attracted to children and/or teens. They hide these secrets deeply, afraid that if they reveal them to anyone they will lose the chance to become a sex therapist. The dangers are obvious in both cases. Careful training that involves individual work and focus on the part of the therapist in training may prevent this from happening.

Need to Separate from Your Personal Moral Code

The ability to separate your own personal moral and religious values from the therapeutic experience is an absolute necessity in working not only with offenders but also with survivors.

If the sex offender can *shock* the therapist with graphic descriptions of his sexually perverse behaviors, he will use this as a *control mechanism* (his primary need) to change subjects or to end sessions that are becoming uncomfortable or anxiety provoking. Similarly, the survivor constantly *tests* the therapist before revealing his or her most horrible experience (subjectively perceived). If, as in Brian's case, the therapist reacts with shock, revulsion, or disgust, that can become the survivor's justification to quit therapy and never have to face his or her most dreaded memories.

In cases of *homosexual molestation* of males of long duration, the survivor is often confused as to his present sexual identity. A major concern in exposing himself to the therapist may be revealing that he enjoyed many of the sexual encounters and still is fantasizing and/or masturbating to memories of these past experiences. In addition, he may be feeling attracted to other boys his own age or to men who remind him of his abuser. The therapist must take great care not to reveal his or her own feelings on this subject, especially if he or she is opposed to a homosexual lifestyle. Training, in this instance, will aid the therapist in helping the survivor to make *his or her own decision* as to a sexual preference or lifestyle, including the possibility of a *bisexual option* rather than either extreme. Females molested over long periods of time may choose not to marry but rather to live with someone or to turn to another woman since she cannot trust men. Here, again, the therapist's own moral preferences and/or convictions should not enter the therapeutic situation.

No Job Is Worth Harming Yourself
or Your Family

This is an appropriate juncture at which to consider whether an individual choosing to work in this field (which I refer to as the "cesspool of sex offenses") can afford the price. Consider several areas:

- Listening to the sordid and often horrifying details of the sex offender's own life and his deviant behavior can be too much for some individuals.
- Having to remain neutral on subjects of moral values and decisions can affect the personal life of the therapist.
- The depressive quality of daily encounters with human suffering at levels never before experienced or even imagined can affect the emotional life of the therapist.
- Coming home daily from the emotionally charged atmosphere of working with offenders can alter the therapist's reactions to his or her partner and family.
- Some individuals are unable to distance themselves from their work sufficiently to prevent problems being brought home and dumped on family members, including spouses and children.
- There is a constant danger of becoming overprotective and restrictive with one's own children after working daily with the child molester group.
- The effects of keeping secret other sex crimes, including sex murders, which are covered by confidentiality, can and does affect the therapist without a prepared support system of his or her own.

The bottom line is that not all therapists are emotionally equipped to work in this field, but it is not a reflection on their professional ability or competence.

The Program Must Change with Each New Group
of Offenders Encountered and Must Fit
Their Individual Needs

Anyone wanting to be successful in this endeavor of treating the compulsive sex offender must throw away traditional concepts and techniques and become a "pragmatist." What succeeds in this field is whatever works, and that changes from one offender to another. Even with the basic similarities in personality traits that I listed in Chapter 1, the *individual differences* of the sex offender dominate the overall picture.

"Flexibility" is a major requirement for any treatment program that is to succeed. The techniques and principles I used and followed in 1967 with the first treatment program no longer worked in 1976. Similarly, techniques devised in 1976 no longer worked in 2000, and so on.

Redefining Professionalism: Too-Close-To-Home Cases and Personality Conflicts

Individuals choosing to work in this or related fields must first re-define traditional concepts of professionalism. The old precepts of the conservatively dressed therapist with multiple degrees, diplomas, and certificates hanging on the wall does not, by itself, qualify any-one for this field, nor does it bode success.

When facing each new group of offenders, the therapist must make adjustments, such as dropping all professional jargon and college-level vocabulary that puts distance between the offender and the ther-apist. In addition to these exterior changes, the therapist must also alter his or her way of thinking. Constant *self-monitoring* and *peer supervision* must be an integral part of the program. Cases that come *too close to home* or that pose a serious *personality conflict* from the first meeting must be transferred to another therapist to avoid disas-trous results for everyone.

If, for example, the school, neighborhood, and age of the victim that the offender molested is identical or nearly identical to the therapist's own child, it is unrealistic to expect "objectivity" from that therapist.

Similarly, if a sexual assault was experienced by someone in the therapist's own family or by a close relative, cases that are similar to that assault should not become part of his or her caseload. Certainly, a therapist should not treat a rapist who raped the therapist's own wife (although I know of a case where that was attempted, with disastrous results for both the client and the therapist) or who molested one of the therapist's own children.

Where personality conflicts are concerned, there will always be cases that from the first meeting (especially if the details in the indi-vidual's record have been read beforehand) result in immediate dislike and anger or rage toward the client. The therapist must be professional enough in such cases to decline the assignment. Two specific examples from my own experience will clarify.

When young and new to the field, I was assigned to do an evaluation that would result in a recommendation to the court on a particularly violent and sadistic sex offender. I made the error of reading the police investigation from cover to cover, prior to seeing the offender. The report included color photographs of the autopsies of three young children that the offender had raped and then mutilated, cutting their bodies into multiple parts and disfiguring the faces. The pictures and autopsy description made me ill.

Fewer than fifteen minutes after finishing the report, the offender was escorted into my office, and my immediate urge was to attack and harm the man. I excused myself, went to my supervisor, and told him I was unable to do a fair and objective evaluation. He threatened me with suspension for "acting unprofessionally" and insisted that "a good professional can handle anything and anyone." Young and arrogant, I stood my ground and went over his head to his supervisor, who agreed with my position and assigned the case to my supervisor.

I learned two things from that case:

1. A good professional knows when he or she is in over his or her head and when to say no.
2. One should never read an investigative report on a case *until* an evaluation is completed and impressions recorded. I still advise new individuals to the field to do this.

Knowing When to Ask for Help

A second opinion is also of vital importance in working with sex offenders. "Gut reactions" can be important clues that something is not right with a case. When any doubt arises, consultation with another individual in the field is the professional course of action.

"False professionalism" may dictate total independence and autonomy in all cases. The results can be disastrous for the offender, the therapist, or for potential new victims. Where possible, the consultation or second opinion should be with a therapist of the opposite sex. Why? For many reasons, *sex offenders behave and react differently with men and women depending on their proclivities and needs.*

Rapists, for example, tend to be less aggressive or challenging with men than with women. It is much easier for a female therapist to trigger their anger and rage. I would never make a final decision as to readiness for release of a SAP (sexually assaultive person) from treatment without first exposing him to several months of contact with a female therapist, trained to *trigger* male anger and rage reactions.

Sex offenders tend to identify with male therapists who satisfy their needs for paternal acceptance, affection, and love. If such an offender is with a supportive, gentle, and highly positive therapist for a long time, he should concurrently be working with a confronting, strong, and more challenging female therapist. This is true for both rapists and child molesters.

Child molesters who have been working exclusively with a warm, supportive, female therapist (substitute mother figure) should be exposed to a male therapist as well to provide a role model and because the child molester generally fears men more than women. Being accepted as his old passive and frightened self will not ensure success in the child molester's treatment.

In general, where feasible, co-therapy works much better with sex offenders than being in long-term treatment with one person.

Transference and Countertransference

In no other form of treatment are the concepts of transference and countertransference as important and as frequent an occurrence. Due to the sex offender's desperate need for acceptance and love, transference occurs almost in every case.

A simple definition will suffice for our purpose here: "Transference is the phenomenon of projection of feelings, thoughts, and wishes, on the part of the client, onto the therapist, who has come to represent an object (person) from the patient's past" (Wolman, 1989, p. 352).

Transference can be both positive and negative, can refer to identification, libido, love, sibling, group, or affect. The main concern for the therapist or anyone else working with the offender is to be able to *recognize* the transference when it occurs and not to interpret it as the offender's real feelings for the therapist.

"Countertransference is the phenomenon of projection of feelings, thoughts, and wishes, on the part of the therapist, onto the patient who has come to represent an object (person) from the therapist's past" (Wolman, 1989, p. 78).

The danger here is obvious. If the therapist is not aware of the countertransference occurring, he or she can become omnipotent, retaliatory, or controlling and *use* the patient to satisfy his or her own unresolved needs.

Both of these phenomena are complicated and should be studied separately from this work. They are mentioned here only to indicate the need for constant peer review and supervision.

Any Failure Is His, Not Yours

Too often, therapists working with sex offenders accept responsibility for the failures of the offender, especially if he is released from treatment and recommits his deviant behavior. This reaction on the part of untrained therapists reflects the old and constant misperception that *therapists treat patients.*

The longer one is in the field, the more obvious it becomes that *patients treat themselves* and that the therapist, counselor, parent, or friend is only a coach or guide during the therapy. A football or basketball coach does not go out onto the field and win or lose the game—the players do. The same applies to therapy. The most important concept to learn from the beginning is that *all change comes from an inside motivation and need, not from outside pressure, pleading, or cajoling.*

No change will occur until the client wants it to. This is more true for the sex offender than for any other group I have worked with. As long as the offender feels unworthy or undeserving, nothing will occur that is perceived as positive. If a positive occurs, he will destroy it. Too often, that is exactly why a failure occurs: *the offender does not feel that he deserves to be happy or successful and deliberately (although on an unconscious level) sets himself up to fail.*

Years ago in the original treatment unit at the then Rahway State Prison, I used the phrase "can't stand prosperity" as the major diagnosis in most returnees or failures. Usually, everything was going *too well* for the offender, and past unresolved guilts tortured him to the point of such discomfort that he had to find a way to return to prison *where he belonged and felt comfortable.*

Regardless of how well trained and intentioned the therapist may be, the content of what the client exposes is always in his control. No matter how sure the therapist may feel that everything has been exposed and resolved, it is too often the case that a secret remains that is simply too terrible to tell anyone. Placing all responsibility on the offender, where it belongs, is a major therapeutic element and applies to returning to deviant fantasies and behaviors as well. The offender's failure is his and not the therapist's.

FINAL THOUGHTS

Forty years of "swimming in the cesspool of sex offenses" has taught me conclusively that *sex offenders can be successfully treated.* All the same, it would have been much easier had specialized training been available in 1967, or even earlier in 1961, when I began working with children and adolescents who had either committed sex offenses or were the victims of them.

The major purpose of this work has been to help prevent other individuals new to this field from making the same mistakes that I and other therapists working with me have made. My experience has convinced me beyond doubt that there are techniques that work with offenders and others that definitely do not.

This book has not pretended to be all inclusive. Supervision is still paramount, regardless of the amount of knowledge that one accumulates. What one knows is much less important than what one does not know. Therefore, *questions* play a major role in all training and learning. Trainees sitting passively in training sessions, afraid to ask questions due to image problems, remains the most difficult barrier for a trainer to overcome. I encourage my trainees to write their questions in disguised handwriting and leave them unsigned where the trainer can find them and include them in the training. This is especially true when line personnel are placed in the same training session with their supervisors. However, those who really want to learn will overcome this problem.

Besides the constant push for specialized training that I have included in the book, the caveats come next in importance. Although treating sex offenders is necessary and urgent, it is not worth trying to help one offender at the cost of damaging another individual (the therapist, counselor, etc.). Although the successful conclusion to a treatment case can be both rewarding and professionally satisfying, the cases that we do not reach and who carry on unhappily in their deviant lives can be depressing and discouraging. There must be a balance in the life of the helper for it to make sense. A strong family life, support at home and from professional colleagues, friends to talk to and ventilate with, and tons of love to replace the pain are all essential to maintaining a healthy helper.

If I have been able to help just one offender from recommitting, I have succeeded in my goal, and it has been worth all the grief and pain. Just consider the numbers: if I help one rapist from recommitting, then at least twelve to twenty-five potential victims have been spared. If I help just one child molester, then as many as 100 child victimizations may have been prevented, as well as *their* future victims if their molestation is not successfully resolved. *Successfully treating sex offenders is a major sexual abuse prevention task and more necessary than ever with today's rising victim rates.*

Appendix A

Answers to True-False Test
(Box 1.1)

1. All adult sex offenders, regardless of offense, have major personality traits in common. *True*
2. All adult sex offenders were themselves sexually victimized as children and this explains their behavior. *False*
3. Sex offender pathology can be genetically linked. *False*
4. Pedophiles and hebophiles have the same characteristics and prognosis for treatment success. *False*
5. Fixated pedophiles may appear normal in their social, work, and interpersonal functions. *True*
6. Hebophiles and incestuous fathers have many traits in common and a similar (and more positive) prognosis for treatment success. *True*
7. The King-of-the-Castle syndrome is a major distinguishing characteristic of incestuous fathers. *True*
8. Supportive and nonconfrontational treatment techniques work better with adult sex offenders than other treatment modalities. *False*
9. Psychotherapy itself will produce positive results with both the adult and the adolescent sex offenders. *False*
10. Following their victimization, victims of sexual abuse have many traits in common with sex offenders. *True*
11. Adolescent sex offenders have the same traits as adult sex offenders. *False*
12. Adolescent sex offenders have no visible (i.e., detectable) signs of their problems. *False*
13. Peer relationship problems are a major factor in the development of adolescent sex offenders. *True*
14. Adolescent sex offenders always come from a home where there are problems. *True*
15. Of all the problems in the adolescent sex offender's life, lack of or poor communication is a major one. *True*
16. Treatment issues and techniques for the adolescent sex offender are identical to those for the adult sex offender. *False*

17. Parent(s) or guardian(s) must be an integral part of the adolescent sex offender's treatment. *True*
18. Supportive and nonconfrontational treatment techniques work better with adolescent sex offenders. *False*
19. A combination of individual and group therapy plus ancillary treatment modalities is the best complete treatment program for the adolescent sex offender. *True*
20. Both the adult and the adolescent sex offender can be cured with an intensive treatment program. *False*

Appendix B

Confidential Questionnaire

Instructions: This is a personal and confidential questionnaire that is necessary for me to help you in your therapy. Please answer all questions truthfully. *Do not lie!* If a particular questions is too embarrassing or upsetting to you at this time, answer with the codeword *"Later."* Then when you are able to fill in this answer, just let me know and I will return the questionnaire to you.

There are some special instructions that I want you to follow:

1. Be sure your answers give all the details needed for me to understand your answer. Do not worry about language or spelling. Use words that you are comfortable with.
2. If there any words in the questions that you do not understand, please ask me (without disturbing anyone else).
3. Be sure to include your age in all questions that ask for it. If you are not sure, guess at the closest age you remember.
4. Remembering confidentiality laws, decide if you want to include names of other individuals you have been involved with.
5. Take all of the time you need. If you cannot finish in this session, you can continue in our next meeting. You may not take the questionnaire with you when you leave.
6. Finally, read my confidentiality agreement at the bottom of this page and, if you agree, sign and date it.

This questionnaire is for your therapist's personal and professional use only. It may not be read by anyone else without your specific written consent. This is my agreement and promise to you. If you agree, sign on the line:

NAME: _____ DATE: _____

If you need more space than a question allows, continue your answer on the back of the page. Be sure to start with the number of the question you are continuing.

DEMOGRAPHICS

1. Name: _____

2. Home address: _____

3. City, state, zip code: _____

4. Present age and date of birth: _____

5. Highest grade in school you completed: _____

6. Who are you (or have you) been living with? _____

REFERRAL HISTORY

7. What brought you to therapy? _____
   _____

8. Is being in therapy your idea or someone else's idea? _____
   If someone else, who? _____

9. What do you want to gain from therapy? _____
   _____

10. List specific changes you want to make in your life. _____
    _____

PHYSICAL AND MEDICAL HISTORY

11. What is your present physical/medical condition? _____
    _____

12. Are you taking any prescription medications at this time?   Yes/No
    If yes, which ones? _____

13. List serious illnesses you have had: _____
    _____

14. Did your physical problems contribute to your present problems?
    Yes/No
    If yes, how? _____
    _____

PSYCHOLOGICAL/PSYCHIATRIC HISTORY

15. Have you been treated for any psychological problems?   Yes/No

    If yes, list and explain. _____

    _____

16. Do you have any psychological problems now for which you were never treated?   Yes/No

    If yes, list and explain. _____

    _____

17. Will any of these problems affect your therapy?   Yes/No

    If yes, how? _____

SEX HISTORY

18. At what age did you learn anything about sex? _____

19. What did you learn? _____

    _____

20. How did you learn it and from whom? _____

    _____

21. At what age did you first masturbate? _____

22. How did it happen? _____

    Did you discover it yourself or did you learn how to from someone else? _____

23. If from someone else, who? _____

24. Did you enjoy your first orgasm?   Yes/No

    If no, why not? _____

25. At what age did you first see a female naked? _____

26. How did it happen and whose idea was it? _____

    _____

27. Have you experienced intercourse?   Yes/No

    If yes, at what age and whose idea? _____

    _____

28. Have you experienced a homosexual act?   Yes/No

    If yes, at what age, with whom, and whose idea? _____

    _____

29. At what age did you first fantasize your sexual problem area? _____
_____

30. Were you ever sexually abused?   Yes/No

If yes, at what age and by whom? _____
_____

31. When it was over, how did you feel about yourself? _____
_____

32. Who did you blame for the abuse, then and now? _____
_____

33. How many times did it happen or for how long? _____
_____

34. Did you ever tell anyone about the abuse?   Yes/No

If yes, how did he or she react? _____
_____

35. Were you believed?   Yes/No

If not, how did that make you feel? _____
_____

36. Do you still think about or dream about the abuse today?   Yes/No

If yes, explain: _____

37. Does the abuse affect your life in ways other than sexual? Yes/No

If yes, explain: _____

38. Do you believe that this abuse is in any way connected with your pres-
     ent sexual problems?   Yes/No

If yes, explain: _____

39. At the time of your sexual acts were you using either alcohol or recre-
     ational drugs (marijuana, cocaine, heroin, or hallucinogenics such as
     LSD)?   Yes/No

If yes, what? _____

40. If your answer in # 39 was *Yes*, what effect did the substance have on
     your sexual behavior? _____
_____

SOCIAL LIFE

41. Would you describe yourself as a social person (many friends, easy to make friends) or a loner? _____

_____

42. Did you hang out with a few friends, a large group of friends, or were you in a "gang" type group? _____

_____

43. In the group or gang you were in, were you more of a leader or a follower?   Yes/No

Explain._____

44. Did the group you were in influence your behavior?   Yes/No

If yes, how? _____

_____

45. If you were a loner, how did you spend your spare time? _____

_____

46. As you grew older, did this choice of social behavior change? Yes/No

If yes, how? _____

47. During this time, what was your attitude about the opposite sex? _____

_____

48. What is your attitude today about the opposite sex? _____

_____

_____

ADDITIONAL INFORMATION

Please add any other facts, behaviors, values, or beliefs that you feel will be important for your therapist to know in order to help you in your treatment.

_____
_____
_____
_____
_____
_____

Bibliography

Abel, Gene G. and Osborn, C.A. 1992. Stopping sexual violence. *Psychiatric Annals* 22(6), 301-306.

American Heritage Dictionary, Second College Edition. 1985. Boston: Houghton Mifflin Company.

American Psychiatric Association. 1994. *DSM-IV.* Washington, DC: Author.

Araoz, Daniel L. 1982. *Hypnosis and Sex Therapy.* New York: Brunner/Mazel Inc.

Ashford, Jose, Sales, Bruce, and Reid, William, Eds. 2001. *Treating Adult and Juvenile Offenders with Special Needs.* Washington, DC: American Psychological Assocation.

Bach, Marcus. 1961. *Strange Sects and Curious Cults.* New York: Dorset Press.

The Beacon Foundation. 1991. *The Beacon Foundation Information Pack.* Wales: Beacon Foundation.

Berry, Jason. 1992. *Lead Us Not into Temptation: Catholic Priests and the Sexual Abuse of Children.* New York: Doubleday.

Brancale, Ralph and Ellis, Albert. 1956. *The Psychology of Sex Offenders.* Springfield, IL: Charles C. Thomas.

Briere, John. 1996. *Therapy for Adults Molested as Children: Beyond Survival.* Second Edition. New York: Springer Publishing Company.

Burgess, Ann, Groth, A. Nicholas, Holmstrom, Lynda, and Sgroi, Suzanne. 1987. *Sexual Assault of Children and Adolescents.* Lexington, MA: D.C. Heath & Company.

Coleman, Eli, Dwyer, S. Margretta, and Pallone, Nathaniel J., Eds. 1996. *Sex Offender Treatment: Biological Dysfunction, Intrapsychic Conflict, Interpersonal Violence.* Binghamton, NY: The Haworth Press, Inc.

Davies, Maureen. 1991. *Helping Individuals and Agencies to Deal with Problems of Ritual Abuse.* Rhyl, Clwyd North Wales: The Beacon Foundation.

Diamond, Vera. 1992. Satanic Ritual Abuse Syndrome. Unpublished Paper.

Dorais, Michel. 2002. *Don't Tell.* Montreal, Canada: McGill Queen's University Press.

FBI Behavioral Science Unit, Quantico, Virginia. 1991. A Statistical Report on Child Sexual Abuse. March 11.

Finkelhor, David. 1984. *Child Sexual Abuse: New Theory and Research.* New York: The Free Press.

Finkelhor, David. 1992. *Parent to Parent: Talking to Your Children about Preventing Child Sexual Abuse.* VHS. Hubbard Scientific Teaching Aids, p. 57.

Groth, A. Nicholas. *Men Who Rape.* 1979. New York: Plenum Press.

Harris, Michael. 1990. *Unholy Orders: Tragedy at Mount Cashel.* Hammondsworth, Middlesex, England: Penguin Books, Ltd.

Hartman, William E. and Fithian, Marilyn A. 1987. *Body/Self Image.* Los Angeles, CA: Sensate Media Service.

Kahaner, Larry. 1988. *Cults That Kill.* New York: Warner Books, Inc.

Kohlberg, Lawrence. 1981. *The Meaning and Measurement of Moral Development,* Volume 13. Worcester, MA: Clark University Heinz Werner Institute.

Lavey, Anton Szandor. 1969. *The Satanic Bible.* New York: Avon Books.

Lavey, Anton Szandor. 1989. *The Satanic Witch.* California: Feral House.

Laws, D. Richard and O'Donohue, William, Eds. 1997. *Sexual Deviance.* New York: The Guilford Press.

Loevinger, Jane. 1996. *Ego Development, Conceptions and Theories.* New York: Rossey and Bass.

Madaras, Lynda. 1988a. *The What's Happening to My Body? Book for Boys.* New York: Newmarket Press.

Madaras, Lynda. 1988b. *The What's Happening to My Body? Book for Girls.* New York: Newmarket Press.

National Center on Child Sexual Abuse Prevention.1992. *Statistical Report.* Washington, DC.

Oke, Isaiah. 1992. *Blood Secrets: The True Story of Demon Worship and Ceremonial Murder.* New York: Prometheus Books.

Pallone, Nathaniel J. 1990. *Rehabilitating Criminal Sexual Psychopaths: Legislative Mandates, Clinical Quandries.* New Brunswick, NJ: Transaction Books.

Pallone, Nathaniel J. and Chaneles, Sol, Eds. 1990. *The Clinical Treatment of the Criminal Offender in Outpatient Mental Health Settings: New and Emerging Perspectives.* Binghamton, NY: The Haworth Press, Inc.

Pazder, Lawrence. 1980. How Widespread Is Satanic Ritual Abuse? Presentation at the American Psychiatric Association Meeting in New Orleans, March 31-April 3.

Prendergast, William. 1993. *The Merry-Go-Round of Sexual Abuse.* Binghamton, NY: The Haworth Press, Inc.

Prendergast, William. 1996. *Sexual Abuse of Children and Adolescents: A Preventive Guide for Parents, Teachers, and Counselors.* New York: The Continuum Publishing Company.

Ross, Colin and Gahan, Pam. 1988. Cognitive Analysis of Multiple Personality Disorder. *American Journal of Psychotherapy* 42(2)(April), 229-239.

Ryan, Gail and Lane, Sandy, Eds. 1997. *Juvenile Sexual Offending: Causes, Consequences, and Correction.* San Francisco: Jossey-Bass Publishers.

Sipe, A.W. Richard. 1995. *Sex, Priests, and Power: Anatomy of a Crisis.* New York: Brunner/Mazel, Inc.

Turkus, Joan A. 1991. Psychotherapy and case management for multiple personality disorder: Synthesis for continuity of care. *Psychiatric Clinics of North America,* 14(3), 649-660.

Wolman, Benjamin B. 1989. *Dictionary of Behavioral Science,* Second Edition. New York: Academic Press.

Zeig, Jeffrey K., Ed. 1982. *Eriksonian Approaches to Hypnosis and Psychotherapy.* New York: Brunner/Mazel, Inc.

Zell, Otter G., Ed. 1989. *Witchcraft, Satanism and Occult Crime: Who's Who and What's What,* Fourth Edition. California: Green Egg.

Index

Page numbers followed by the letter "i" indicate boxed illustrations.